A Functional Curriculum for Teaching Students with Disabilities

A Functional Curriculum for Teaching Students with Disabilities

SECOND EDITION

Volume III
Functional Academics

by
Peter J. Valletutti
Michael Bender
Bernita Sims-Tucker

pro·ed
An International Publisher

8700 Shoal Creek Boulevard
Austin, Texas 78757-6897

© 1996, 1976 by PRO-ED, Inc.
8700 Shoal Creek Boulevard
Austin, Texas 78757-6897

This book is designed in Bookman Light and Serif Gothic.

Production Manager: Alan Grimes
Production Coordinator: Karen Swain
Managing Editor: Tracy Sergo
Art Director: Thomas Barkley
Reprints Buyer: Alicia Woods
Editor: Teri C. Sperry
Editorial Assistant: Claudette Landry
Editorial Assistant: Martin Wilson

Printed in the United States of America

2 3 4 5 6 7 8 9 10   00 99 98

Contents

 UNIT 1
Functional Reading
13

 UNIT 2
Functional Writing
177

Preface

This volume of *A Functional Curriculum for Teaching Students with Disabilities* is the second edition of *Teaching the Moderately and Severely Handicapped* and is a major revision of the first edition. The major alterations made in the present edition have been impelled by several recent phenomena: (a) the changing perceptions of the nature of special education (e.g., inclusion, emphasis on a holistic approach, and the movement toward the development of independent living skills); (b) the identification of new and underserved populations (e.g., infants and toddlers, youth with attention-deficit/hyperactivity disorder); (c) modifications in service delivery (e.g., interagency cooperation and increased parental involvement); (d) recent federal legislation regarding education (e.g., P.L. 99-457, P.L. 101-476, and P.L. 102-119) and the civil and legal rights of persons with disabilities (e.g., Americans with Disabilities Act); and (e) reductions in targeted federal dollars.

The central problem, however, continues to be the nonproductive and, at times, destructive magical thinking engaged in by educators who believe that structural changes alone will automatically result in improvements in education. Unfortunately, many special students continue to receive an education that is not "special" whether they are placed in segregated or inclusive settings. Structural change that does not address the individual and special needs of students with disabilities or attend to the quality of instruction is merely cosmetic, not substantive. We consider this functionally oriented curriculum—if it is implemented by special education teachers, parents, and other trained personnel—to be a critical way of making the education of students with special needs an education that is truly special, regardless of the setting.

The first edition of this text, introduced in the 1970s, coincided with the movement for the educational rights of individuals with disabilities, as mandated by the landmark federal legislation P.L. 94-142. This was also the time when parent and advocacy groups, along with many other professionals, consolidated their efforts based on a collective mission not only to provide special education and related services to all children and youth with handicapping conditions but also to integrate them, whenever appropriate and feasible, in the public schools and the mainstream of society.

Instructional areas and emphases addressed by the first edition, such as functional academics, interpersonal and social skills, and leisure education, represented a significant departure from the curriculum traditionally being taught in many special education programs. Of equal importance was the attempt to comprehensively and clearly identify appropriate instructional objectives, strategies, and resources that would promote independence, be age appropriate, be suitable for teaching in a natural environment, and be of lifelong functional value.

Much change has occurred since then. Evolving ideological currents have had a significant impact on guiding and determining the content of this new edition of the curriculum series. Several recent developments—the need for interagency cooperation, reduction in targeted federal dollars, emphasis on a holistic approach, the need for a competent core of human service professionals, and the movement toward independent living—have all resulted in major changes in this profession. For example, special education terminology has been modified. The word *handicapped* is no longer used to describe a person who is challenged by a disability. The rejection of the word *handicapped* has come about because the problems experienced by persons with disabilities are viewed as not being within the person him- or herself but rather as arising from social attitudes and perceptions and by society's failure to provide needed programs, services, and resources that will compensate for or minimize the effects of the individual's disability.

This change in terminology has been incorporated in the recent amendments to P.L. 94-142 (the Education for All Handicapped Children Act). These amendments—P.L. 101-476, the Individuals with Disabilities Education Act (IDEA)—reflect the changing concept of disabilities and the role of society in meeting the needs of individuals who have special needs. Of particular importance is the addition of the requirements for transition services, which focus on the successful movement of students from school to community, thus emphasizing the functional skills of independent living and community participation.

Moreover, the preferred descriptor, *disability,* should not be used as a label, as in "He or she is a 'learning disabled' or 'mentally retarded' child." Rather, as a way of accentuating the personhood of the individual, expressions should be used such as "the individual with learning disabilities." In this way, the disability is seen as merely one aspect or part of a total individual, thus minimizing the placement of undue emphasis on the disability by others and by the person him- or herself, while at the same time emphasizing the person in all his or her myriad dimensions.

The concept of the least restrictive environment (LRE) shapes the placement provisions of P.L. 94-142 and its subsequent amendments (P.L. 99-457) as well as P.L. 101-476 and its various state legislative counterparts. LRE led to the implementation of a continuum of educational placements and services—from placement in a regular or mainstreamed class as the least restrictive of possible environments to the most restrictive environment in a nonpublic residential setting. Central to individual placement decisions, however, was the fundamental premise that placement within this continuum should be shaped by the concept central to special education, namely, that the primary determinants are the individualized needs of the students, based on the idiosyncratic nature of their disability.

Although mainstreaming was, at its inception, identified as the least restrictive or the most normalized school environment, it has not always been successfully realized in practice. Too often, needed support services have not been provided to mainstreamed students and their teachers, and inordinate emphasis has been placed on location of service rather than on effective and efficient instructional practices. Teachers assigned to mainstreamed classes, more often than not, were ill-prepared pedagogically and psychologically to teach their students with special educational needs on either an individual or a group basis. Invariably, the curriculum was not modified to reflect the needs of those integrated special students who required instruction in practical knowledge and skills taught from a functional perspective and with a functional purpose. Functional curricular modifications, if they had been assiduously pursued, might have benefited the students without disabilities as well. Typically, the curriculum of the mainstreamed class is test driven and tradition bound, resulting in too much time wasted on the teaching of atomized and irrelevant knowledge.

Recently, however, the concept of mainstreaming has been redefined as part of the inclusion movement or the Regular Education Initiative (REI). The REI maintains that a dual system of regular and special education is unnecessary, inappropriate, and ineffective, and that students with disabilities, regardless of the severity of their disability, can and should be educated in the mainstreamed (regular) setting. This service delivery approach rejects the continuum-of-services concept and views all other alternate placements, except the regular or mainstreamed class, as too restrictive. The collaborative teaching movement emanates from the REI and attempts to respond to some of the problems that resulted from more restrictive placements and misguided mainstreaming. The collaborative approach requires regular and special teachers to work as a team as they plan instruction for and teach all the students (both those with disabilities and those who are not so challenged) in their assigned classes. As the collaborative approach is increasingly being employed, it will be necessary for all teachers, regular and special, to modify the existing regular class curriculum so that it addresses the adaptive behavior needs of all students, whether they have disabilities or not.

This curriculum, although meant primarily for teachers functioning within a special setting, has the additional goal of assisting collaborative teams of teachers as they analyze and modify existing curricula, subsequently design individualized curricula (Individualized Education Programs [IEPs] and Individualized Family Service Plans [IFSPs]), and cooperate with other human service professionals and related human service agencies to meet the life needs of regular as well as special students.

Curricular areas have also changed. For example, vocational education, often associated with skill development and traditional "shop" programs, is now often defined in terms of work readiness, supported employment, and career education. Curricula in the area of leisure education have also gained prominence—a justified development given that free time continues to increase for most people in our culture. The problem of meaningful utilization of leisure time, especially for older people with disabilities, is particularly acute because many are chronically unemployed or underemployed, and therefore not only have expanded free time but also lack the financial resources required for the productive use of that time.

Safety, as a curricular entity, has also gained increasing recognition, especially as more and more programs emphasize community-based education, which entails greater and more numerous threats to safety than the traditional, classroom-based approach. Safety elements should pervade all curricular areas, and therefore have been included in the lesson plans and learning activities of this edition.

Unserved, underserved, and increasing populations of children with disabilities continue to enter educational programs at a rapid rate. Some of this change is a result of recent legislative mandates, such as P.L. 99-457 (Education of the Handicapped Act Amendments). Part H, reauthorized as P.L. 102-119, IDEA Amendments of 1991, mandates the provision of comprehensive early intervention and family services for infants and toddlers and their families (birth through age 2). School programs are also now serving children and youth with disabilities who were not often identified in the 1970s and whose numbers have drastically increased in the 1990s. Examples include children with fetal alcohol syndrome (FAS) and those who have been damaged prenatally (or perinatally) through maternal substance abuse, the AIDS virus, syphilis, or gonorrhea.

Technology continues to play an increasingly important role in educational practice. The instructional use of the personal computer and other instructional technology (including interactive television) is increasing at a rapidly accelerating rate. The use of technology has proven to be of considerable assistance in planning (development of IEPs), in managing teaching (recording of formal and informal assessment data), and in communicating with parents (progress reports and report cards). The personal computer, with its capacity for miniaturization, adaptations, and peripherals, is also moving rapidly to address the habilitative needs of individuals with disabilities. In the near future, as a result of research with neuromuscular feedback and computers, we can expect some individuals who cannot walk—to walk. Other technological advances will make it possible for those who cannot see—to see in some fashion, and those who cannot hear—to hear in some way from implant devices and as yet unknown technologies. The use of assistive technology will also expand as continuing efforts are made to assist students in meeting the demands of an increasingly complex and demanding postindustrial society.

The role of parents (or parent surrogates) is essential to the implementation of this curriculum. Parental participation in decisions regarding placement, IEPs, and needed related services is essential to a holistic approach to educating exceptional children. The parental role in providing pertinent information to teachers should not be minimized, because parents can provide information that is essential for assisting in identifying goals and objectives, establishing educational and programming priorities, and determining areas of interest. Parents have a unique advantage in instructing their children in activities that are best introduced and practiced in the home setting and also in the community. Parents can also serve as effective carryover agents who provide practice sessions and reinforce newly acquired skills as the child performs them within his or her reality contexts.

Because of these various trends and factors, it seems appropriate to now produce a new edition of the curriculum. Teams of teachers, students, parents, clinicians, and other related service staff have been surveyed to find out what needed to be addressed in these three new volumes. Our overriding goal continues to be the presentation of new information and material that will assist teachers, other professionals, and parents in facilitating the functional performance of children and youth with disabilities in the full variety of life situations and contexts. As in past incarnations, the present curriculum assumes that the reader possesses a basic understanding of teaching methods and a fundamental level of expertise in analyzing educational tasks so that they may be used as a framework for evaluating the child's current level of performance and as a means of focusing on specific behaviors requiring remedial or instructional attention. Emphasis continues to be placed on teaching students in reality situations in the home, community, and workplace. Whenever home-based or community-based education is not feasible, teachers must provide realistic classroom simulations that offer students with disabilities opportunities to practice life skills in functional contexts and settings. The past successes of the curriculum have supported our view that reality contexts can be effectively simulated in a classroom setting only if the entire behavior is demonstrated with all its applicable dimensions (psychomotor, affective, and cognitive) expressed as a total, integrated act.

Long-range goals and specific teaching objectives have been identified, in this edition, as "general goals" and "specific objectives" to indicate their relationship to the development and subsequent revisions of the Individualized Education Program (IEP) and the Individualized Family Service Plan (IFSP). Although we have provided readers with suggested activities viewed from an age and grade-level perspective, readers applying the curriculum must appreciate the essential relationship between informal and formal assessment data and the decisions they make as to the relevant goals and objectives to be addressed. Although specific objectives have generally been placed in their developmental sequence, known sequences have been considered only if they make functional sense. Developmental milestones and traditional educational tasks have been deemphasized and eliminated from this curriculum if the identified behavior does not contribute to functional success for the intended population (e.g., drawing a geometric shape or matching wooden blocks of different colors). Furthermore, developmental profiles are less important as children get older, whereas they are central for infants and toddlers.

The curriculum is intended as a guide not only for individuals with disabilities but also for individuals who may be experiencing learning problems but who have not been classified as having a disability. In fact, many high-level goals and suggested activities are included to encourage program implementors not to have restricted or limiting views. There are many nondisabled students and adults, students and adults with mild disabilities, and students and adults with no formally defined disability who are functioning at a lower-than-expected level who would also benefit from the activities in the curriculum. These high-level goals and suggested activities are also meant to guide mainstreamed and collaborating teachers in their modification of regular curricula, which should do much to make inclusion more successful for both the students who have disabilities and those who do not.

As with the first edition, this new edition has been designed as a guide to preservice and inservice teachers and other professionals who work directly as service providers to children and adults with disabilities. Parents, surrogates and foster parents, and other family members, as well as service coordinators (case managers), house parents in group homes/apartments or other alternate living arrangements, and counselors in activity centers and workshops should find this curriculum valuable as they interact with and instruct the individuals with whom they work and/or live.

The original curriculum also has had wide acceptance and use as a text for preservice teacher candidates and inservice teachers taking courses in curriculum development and teaching methods in special education at the undergraduate and graduate levels. The current edition has been updated to reflect the present needs of students taking these courses, especially as they interact in diverse practica experiences with previously unserved and underserved populations of individuals with disabilities.

The list of Selected Materials/Resources attached to each unit is relatively brief because many of the essential materials needed in teaching a functional curriculum are the ordinary materials of life that are invariably found in the home, school, community, and workplace, and because well-designed and well-presented teacher-made materials are usually more appropriate, better focused, and more motivating to students.

The Suggested Readings appended to each unit list not only recent publications but some older, classic materials as well. These classics have been included because they retain their immediacy and appropriateness and thus should not be automatically eliminated from lists of relevant professional literature out of a passion for newness.

This new edition of the curriculum continues to provide information and suggestions that have proven to be of value in the past. The suggested activities provided in this new edition, a direct response to user recommendations and reviews, have been separated into two major categories: Teacher Interventions and Family Interventions. Further, four distinct age/grade levels for each of these interventions have been developed to reflect content deemed appropriate for the following levels: infant and toddler/preschool, primary, intermediate, and secondary. The suggested activities for the infant and toddler/preschool level are meant to meet the functional needs of infants and toddlers (birth through 2 years) and preschool children (3 through 5 years). Additionally, attention needs to be directed to the several alternative settings for teaching children, especially where infants and toddlers are concerned, because they are frequently educated in their own homes and in day-care settings.

Finally, this curriculum does not address all the dimensions of a functional curriculum because to do so is neither practical nor possible. It does not provide all the possible instructional activities that are applicable or would be interesting and motivating to students and adults with disabilities. It does, however, provide a structure and format from which a creative professional can extrapolate additional instructional goals and objectives, design learning activities, and suggest possible responses to the multitude of challenging questions that will arise from the actual implementation of the curriculum.

Acknowledgments

We wish to express our appreciation to all those students, teachers, parents, and support staff who helped us define the objectives of functional academics, and especially to Carol Ann Baglin and Sheréa Makle, who spent unlimited hours on the refinement and editing of this volume.

General Goals

UNIT 1

I. The student will identify personal data that have been written by others when this personal information appears on documents.

II. The student will set clocks and timers and will identify time from numerals and markings on watches, clocks, and timers.

III. The student will operate tools, appliances, and equipment in response to written information and markings on buttons, switches, dials, and gauges.

IV. The student will respond appropriately to written information found on safety signs, size labels, price tags, and other signs and labels.

V. The student will carry out instructions written in simple notes.

VI. The student will locate and utilize information from simple charts, diagrams, maps, and menus.

VII. The student will locate and utilize information from directories, schedules, and bulletin boards.

VIII. The student will correctly carry out directions written on equipment, machinery, games, toys, and items that are to be assembled.

IX. The student will identify key words found on employment applications and other simple blanks and forms and will provide the requested information.

X. The student will locate and utilize written information found on bills, work time cards, check stubs, and store receipts.

XI. The student will locate and utilize information found in help wanted and other classified ads, printed advertisements, brochures, pamphlets, and other written materials.

XII. The student will seek the assistance of a responsible person to decode and explain, when necessary, printed and written material that he or she is unable to read.

UNIT 2

I. The student will acquire those perceptual motor skills that will facilitate effective written communication.

II. The student will write his or her personal data, needs, and thoughts with such clarity that they are communicated readily to readers.

UNIT 3

I. The student will acquire those basic arithmetic skills that facilitate independence in functional situations.

II. The student will acquire those skills necessary for participating successfully and independently in cash transactions.

III. The student will acquire functional measurement skills that facilitate independence in various measurement activities.

IV. The student will acquire those functional time measurement skills that facilitate time management.

Introduction and Curriculum Overview

A primary purpose of special education is to help students with disabilities lead successful and personally fulfilling lives now and in the future. A functional curriculum is designed to prepare students to function as independently as possible in an integrated society (Wheeler, 1987). A broad range of skills, therefore, must be included in the design of a functional curriculum for students with disabilities. It is axiomatic that the more severe the disability, the greater the educational need and challenge, and, thus, the more comprehensive the curriculum.

In addition, the skills needed by individuals with disabilities continue to expand as society becomes more complex. Moreover, with the renewed and increasing emphasis on inclusion and mainstreaming, it is imperative that curricula taught in these settings address the needs of students with disabilities who, given the nature of the traditional curriculum, are less likely to be expected to develop functional skills in these mainstreamed settings. Traditional ways of developing content for students with disabilities, such as through the watering down of the regular curriculum, do not work. If new entrants to the regular education mainstream are to be successfully integrated into the school and community, their programs must be modified in functional, real-life ways. In essence, *life is the curriculum.*

According to Gast and Schuster (1993), "A functional curriculum is a primary *external support* for children with severe disabilities" (p. 471). Gast and Schuster have identified a number of principles that should be observed in the development and implementation of a functional curriculum. These authors believe that the designer/instructor should:

> focus on teaching skills that are chronologically age-appropriate and immediately useful to the learner. Use ecological inventories and compile a community catalog of current and future environments that are important to the students. Define goals based on the prior step. Prioritize goals based on their potential for enhancing independence. Task analyze the skills needed to perform successfully. Conduct a discrepancy analysis to determine what the student can and cannot do. Use principles of applied behavior analysis. Provide instruction in integrated and community settings. (p. 471)

The need for acquiring functional skills has become the cornerstone for most programs involved in teaching special populations. Fortunately, for some mainstreamed students with disabilities, the principles and contents of this approach are increasingly being incorporated into regular educational programs.

DEFINING THE FUNCTIONAL APPROACH

The functional approach to educating students with or without disabilities is based on a philosophy of education that determines the format and content of a curriculum and that requires an instructional methodology emphasizing the application of knowledge and skills in reality contexts (Bender & Valletutti, 1985; Valletutti & Bender, 1985). Some authorities view this approach as being different from the developmental approach in that its emphasis is on teaching age-appropriate skills that are immediately applicable to diverse life settings (Gast & Schuster, 1993). Patton, Beirne-Smith, and Payne (1990), on the other hand, have posited: "The functional curriculum is a hybrid of the developmental and the behavioral curricula. It attempts to incorporate the best features of the two. Insofar as it emphasizes teaching interrelated classes of behavior and generalization within task classes, it is developmental, but it is behavioral in its emphasis on teaching skills that the infant or child needs now or will need" (p. 298). According to Kirk and Gallagher (1989), "Over the years, from research, common sense, and experience, a philosophy of teaching students with multiple and severe handicaps has evolved. Today our objective is to teach functional age-appropriate skills within the integrated school and nonschool settings, and to base our teaching on the systematic evaluation of students' progress" (p. 467).

Educators using the functional approach identify life skills, specified as instructional goals and objectives, and then seek to facilitate a student's acquisition of these skills. It is adult referenced in that it is a top-down approach, identifying behaviors essential to successful adjustment as a functioning adult rather than having a bottom-up design with its child-oriented focus (Polloway, Patton, Payne, & Payne, 1989). It fosters the development of skills that increase autonomy, as in self-care activities, and encourages constructive codependency, as in cooperative enterprises and mutual problem solving in the home, school, community, and workplace. It endeavors to make the individuals to whom it is applied as successful as possible in meeting their own needs and in satisfying the requirements of living in a community. It also strives to make the individual's life as fulfilling and pleasurable as possible (Cegelka & Greene, 1993).

The functional approach determines the nature of the instructional process. It requires that specified skills be taught in reality contexts. That is, skills are to be taught directly through typical home, school, or community activities, or, if a natural setting is not feasible, indirectly through classroom simulations (Brown, Nietupski, & Hamre-Nietupski, 1976; Polloway et al., 1989).

Conducting an ecological inventory has been suggested as a strategy for generating a functional curriculum that is community referenced. The steps involved in this process include identifying curricular domains (e.g., vocational and leisure), describing present and future environments, prioritizing the activities pertinent to these environments, specifying the skills needed to perform these activities, conducting a discrepancy analysis to determine required skills missing from the student's behavioral repertoire, determining needed adaptations, and, finally, developing a meaningful IEP (Brown et al., 1979).

A functional curriculum identifies *what* is to be taught, whereas the functional approach to instruction determines *how* a skill is to be taught. Whereas a functional curriculum is, in most cases, absolutely essential to instructional programs employed in special classes or special schools, it can also be particularly valuable to teachers of mainstreamed or inclusive classes. These teachers must make functional adaptations to existing curricula if life skills are to be addressed, despite the restrictions imposed by rigid adherence to the subjects traditionally found in school curricula. Teachers, therefore, must analyze the academically driven goals and objectives of traditional curricula and identify their potential practical applications.

DEVELOPING A FUNCTIONAL CURRICULUM

An analysis of the social roles that people play as children, adolescents, and adults can serve as the foundation for designing a functional curriculum (Bender & Valletutti, 1982; Valletutti & Bender, 1982). Social competency is thus primary in a functional curriculum. "Social competency dimensions are critical to the child's acceptability in the classroom, peer relationships, the efficiency and success of academic efforts, current life adjustment, and future social and vocational success" (Reschly, 1993, p. 232). Closely allied to the concept of a life skills curriculum is the concept of social competence, often referred to as "adaptive behavior." *Adaptive behavior* refers to the individual's effectiveness in meeting the demands and standards of his or her environment based on age and the cultural group to which the individual belongs (Grossman, 1983). According to Drew, Logan, and Hardman (1992), "Adaptive skills are necessary to decrease an individual's dependence on others and increase opportunities for school and community participation" (p. 257). Drew et al. specified that "adaptive skill content areas for school-age retarded children include motor, self-care, social, communication, and functional academic skills" (p. 258).

Curricular models based on the concept of career education emphasize effective participation by the individual in all of life's "occupations." Career education, thus, requires an educational program that starts early in the school career and continues into adulthood (Clark, 1979).

Brolin's (1986) Life-Centered Career Education (LCCE) model identifies 22 major competencies needed for effective functioning in school, family, and community. These skills are divided into three domains: daily living, personal/social, and occupational. Cronin and Patton (1993) have produced a life skills instructional guide for students with special needs. This guide provides information that addresses the importance of life skills instruction and insight as to how to identify major life demands and specific life skills. Professional sources such as these yield a wealth of information on ways of integrating real-life content into the curriculum.

Developers of reality-based curricula, whether identified as functional, life skills, adaptive behavior, or career education, must examine the situations faced by members of society and specify the behaviors expected of them as they function at different stages in their lives. The long-range orientation of education, however, requires that competencies needed by adults be given programming priority.

Functionally oriented curricula must have an adult-outcomes emphasis. This is especially true for those students with disabilities and their nondisabled peers for whom a higher education is neither desired nor appropriate. Adult-outcomes curricula have abandoned their vocational myopia and now deal more comprehensively and realistically with the many elements needed for successful personal and social adjustment in adulthood (Cronin & Gerber, 1982). Students categorized as having diverse learning and behavioral disabilities, as well as students who are at risk for school failure who have not been so classified, are more likely to be stimulated by learning activities that emphasize their present and future problems, needs, and concerns. Regardless of age or grade, students should be prepared for the challenges of life after they graduate or leave school.

If the social-role perspective is accepted, then teachers, parents, counselors, and other trainers must decide which competencies should be included in a curriculum with such a nontraditional approach. This task is not an esoteric or an insurmountable one, however. Through an examination of their own lives and the lives of other adults, educators can easily identify what life skills should be included in a functional curriculum. Moreover, listening and attending to the writings of the students themselves, especially during the adolescent years, will also prove a superb source of functional instructional goals and objectives (Polloway et al., 1989).

The process of selecting the goals and objectives and establishing the functional priorities of a life skills curriculum requires the designer to eliminate those traditional academic tasks that have little or no value. The determinant of inclusion is whether the skill in question is needed or may be needed by the individual now or at some time in the person's future. Patton, Beirne-Smith, and Payne (1990) have suggested that the selection should be governed by an objective's adaptive potential and its direct and frequent application to the individual's environment, the likelihood of its successful acquisition, its potential for improving the quality and level of services available to the individual, and its impact on the reduction of dangerous or harmful behaviors.

Once the functional curriculum has been developed, the student's IEP or IFSP must be formulated based on this general curriculum, with attention devoted to the establishment of instructional priorities. Priorities are determined, in part, on the basis of answers to the following questions:

- Will the acquisition of a skill with less-than-obvious functional relevance lead to the later development of a key functional skill? For example, will it be important to teach an individual to hop and skip because these movements will be incorporated in games, sports, and other leisure activities, such as dancing?

- Is the skill of practical or current value to the individual as he or she functions on a daily basis?

- Will the skill be needed by the individual in the future? A skill that is immediately needed must be assigned greater priority than a skill needed in the future. Age appropriateness is always to be honored whether it applies to the choice of suitable instructional materials or to establishing instructional priorities.

- Has the individual demonstrated an actual need for the development of a particular skill? Teachers, support personnel, and other instructors need to observe the individual to identify the areas in which he or she is experiencing difficulty and utilize these observations in setting programming priorities.

- Has the individual expressed the desire to acquire a specific skill? Students will often ask for needed assistance in acquiring a skill that has psychological importance. These self-identified needs should never be ignored and often will determine educational priorities.

- Do the parents believe that the acquisition of a particular skill will increase their child's adaptive behavior or performance in the home?

- Will the individual's acquisition of a specific skill improve his or her performance in school- and home-related tasks?

- Does the skill have survival value? Clearly, teaching a person how to cross a street safely has greater priority than teaching a youngster to chant or sing a nursery rhyme.

- Will the development of a particular skill facilitate the acquisition of skills pertinent to the goals of other human service professionals who are providing related services? (Valletutti & Dummett, 1992).

On the basis of the responses to these questions, and with essential input from parents and relevant human service professionals, teachers and trainers must develop the student's IFSP or IEP with its stated instructional priorities.

FUNCTIONALITY AS AN INSTRUCTIONAL PROCESS

In order to teach in a functional way, instructors must ask the questions, "Under what circumstances is this skill applied?" and "Why and when is this skill needed?" The answer to either question determines the functional scenario that structures the instructional plan and process. For example, if the short-term instructional objective is, "The student draws water from the sink," the response to the questions "Under what circumstances . . .?" or "Why and when is this skill needed?" may be, "when washing vegetables in preparing a meal," "when filling ice cube trays," or "when getting water to fill the fish tank." The responses to either of these two questions provide the creative vision out of which the lesson should emerge. The lesson might then involve making a meal for guests in which a salad is prepared and ice cubes are made for the meal's accompanying beverage.

Once the circumstances under which a skill is typically practiced have been identified, teachers, parents, and other instructors, if possible, should provide instructional activities in the skill's usual setting or, at a minimum, in its simulated setting. Whenever the realistic setting for a skill's application is the home, teachers must make the student's parents part of the instructional team by helping them to be effective teachers of their children, assisting them in carrying out functional "homework" assignments, such as doing simple household cleaning and home repairs. Teachers, of course, have primary responsibility for skills that are best developed in the school setting, such as teaching cognitive or academic skills in their functional applications. The community setting is the shared responsibility of both parents and teachers.

Whenever it is not possible to practice a skill in its reality context, learning experiences should be provided in classroom simulations. Instructional materials and equipment in a functional and functioning classroom also must be reality based. Furniture, decorations, appliances, and materials typically found in the home must then be found in the classroom as well. To simulate the community, the school might set up a mock traffic pattern in the gymnasium to practice safely crossing streets, establish a supermarket to practice shopping skills, and assign classroom duties as work tasks that mirror jobs available in the community.

THE SCOPE OF THE FUNCTIONAL CURRICULUM

A functional curriculum, if it is to meet the needs of students with disabilities, should be formulated in terms of the social roles people are required to play. Suggested instructional activities should be designed to assist students to fill these roles as successfully and productively as possible even when the curriculum is organized around traditional subject areas, and even when it is arranged around skill areas such as vocational, leisure, motor, communication, and interpersonal skills. Included among these roles are the individual as a

- socially competent person who works cooperatively with others for mutually agreed upon goals.
- capable student who learns from others, and, as a helper, assists others to learn.
- contributing member of a family unit.
- successful member of his or her own personal community (e.g., as a neighbor and friend).
- responsible and responsive citizen of the general community.
- skilled consumer of goods and services and participant in financial transactions.
- productive worker.
- skillful participant in diverse leisure-time activities.
- competent traveler who moves about the community while meeting all other social roles.

DEVELOPING INSTRUCTIONAL PLANS

Instructional plans serve as the blueprint for coordinating and teaching functional skills. In this curriculum, activities are presented in terms of Teacher Interventions and Parent Interventions. Subsumed under these interventions are four age and grade-level designations appropriate to teaching different age groups of children and youth with disabilities: infant and toddler/preschool, primary, intermediate, and secondary.

With its annual goals and their short-term objectives, the curriculum serves as the framework for systematically observing and assessing the student's performance in terms of both process and product. Evaluation occurs as the learner functions on a daily basis in natural settings and as he or she responds to structured and simulated activities. These observations, supplemented by more formally acquired data, aid in selecting what goals and objectives are to be placed, for example, in the student's IEP. Once these decisions are made, lesson planning can commence as follows:

- Lesson planning begins, based on instructional insights acquired from assessment data, with the selection of a priority *annual goal* and its associated *specific objective* from the student's IEP.

- Following this selection, a pertinent *lesson objective* is then constructed. The lesson objective, like the short-term instructional objective, is student oriented and has the dual purpose of structuring the instructional sequence and suggesting the assessment strategy and its performance criterion level. Toward these ends, a lesson objective has three key elements:

  - Clarification of the stimulus situation or conditions: "When given . . ." or "After being shown . . ."

  - Specification of a desired response: "The student will . . ."

  - Establishment of a performance level: "He will do so in four out of five trials" or "She will do so without assistance."

- Next, *materials and equipment* are listed even though a complete list is not really known until the total plan is developed. This segment is placed in the beginning of the plan, however, for ease in reading when the instructor skims the plan immediately prior to its implementation.

- The *motivating activity* is stated. Identifying an appropriate motivating activity may be a challenging task because it is not always easy to identify age-appropriate motivating activities that will capture the attention and encourage the involvement of the different age groups of students with disabilities who are functioning at depressed levels.

- *Instructional procedures* are then enumerated. These are instructor oriented and are sequenced in logical steps arising out of the motivating activity and leading to assessment. The instructional procedure itself is divided into four steps: initiation, guided practice, independent practice, and closure. Evidence that teaching is taking place must be carefully articulated in each of these steps. Demonstrations, assistance, and problem-solving challenges are ways of ensuring that instruction is occurring.

- The *assessment strategy* to be employed is then specified. This procedure should reflect the desired response and performance criteria indicated in the lesson objective. It is instructor oriented and should specify the method to be used in recording observational data.

- At this point, a proposed *follow-up activity or objective* is written to ensure that the sequence of instruction is honored. The hoped-for follow-up activity or objective is composed in positive terms because it can be pursued only if the student successfully meets the plan's lesson objective. If the learner fails to meet the lesson objective, a remedial lesson plan must be written on an ad hoc basis (because it is not possible to predict the reason for failure, especially given that the lesson was designed and taught with the likelihood of instructional success).

- A concluding section, *observations and their instructional insights*, is appended. This section is included in the instructional plan as one means of recording student data and for identifying one's insights as to programming implications for later reference and for use in completing checklists, writing progress reports, and designing and modifying the student's IEP.

Then, introductory information should be provided at the beginning of the instructional plan, such as the following:

- topic area
- name of the designer of the plan
- required time for implementation
- student(s) for whom the plan is intended
- relevant background information on the involved student(s)

Finally, an instructional (lesson) plan should be written in a simple and direct way and be relatively free from jargon so that parents, teacher aides, volunteers, and other appropriate instructors can readily understand it and implement it.

References

Bender, M., & Valletutti, P. J. (1982). *Teaching functional academics to adolescents and adults with learning problems.* Baltimore: University Park Press.

Bender, M., & Valletutti, P. J. (1985). *Teaching the moderately and severely handicapped: Curriculum objectives, strategies, and activities. Vol. 1: Self-care, motor skills and household management.* Austin, TX: PRO-ED.

Brolin, D. E. (1986). *Life-Centered Career Education: A competency-based approach* (rev. ed.). Reston, VA: Council for Exceptional Children.

Brown, L. F., Branston-McLean, M. B., Baumgart, D., Vincent, L., Falvey, M., & Schroder, J. (1979). Using the characteristics of current and subsequent least restrictive environments in the development of curricular content for severely handicapped students. *Journal of the Association for the Severely Handicapped, 4,* 407–424.

Brown, L. F., Nietupski, J., & Hamre-Nietupski, S. (1976). The criterion of ultimate functioning and public school services for severely handicapped students. In M. A. Thomas (Ed.), *Hey don't forget about me: Education's investment in the severely, profoundly, and multiply handicapped* (pp. 2–15). Reston, VA: Council for Exceptional Children.

Cegelka, P. T., & Greene, G. (1993). Transition to adulthood. In A. E. Blackhurst & W. H. Berdine (Eds.), *An introduction to special education* (3rd ed., pp. 137–175). New York: HarperCollins.

Clark, G. M. (1979). *Career education for the handicapped child in the elementary classroom.* Denver: Love.

Cronin, M. E., & Gerber, P. J. (1982). Preparing the learning disabled adolescent for adulthood. *Topics in Learning & Learning Disabilities, 2,* 55–68.

Cronin, M. E., & Patton, J. R. (1993). *Life skills instruction for all students with special needs: A practical guide for integrating real-life content into the curriculum.* Austin, TX: PRO-ED.

Drew, C. J., Logan, D. R., & Hardman, M. L. (1992). *Mental retardation: A life cycle approach* (5th ed.). New York: Merrill/Macmillan.

Gast, D. L., & Schuster, J. W. (1993). Students with severe developmental disabilities. In A. E. Blackhurst & W. H. Berdine (Eds.), *An introduction to special education* (3rd ed., pp. 455–491). New York: HarperCollins.

Grossman, H. J. (1983). *Classification in mental retardation.* Washington, DC: American Association on Mental Deficiency.

Kirk, S. A., & Gallagher, J. J. (1989). *Educating exceptional children* (6th ed.). Boston: Houghton Mifflin.

Patton, J. R., Beirne-Smith, M., & Payne, J. S. (1990). *Mental retardation* (3rd ed.). Columbus, OH: Merrill.

Polloway, E. A., Patton, J. R., Payne, J. S., & Payne, R. A. (1989). *Strategies for teaching learners with special needs* (4th ed.). New York: Merrill.

Reschly, D. J. (1993). Special education decision making and functional/behavioral assessment. In E. L. Meyen, G. A. Vergason, & R. J. Whelan, *Challenges facing special education* (pp. 227–240). Denver: Love.

Valletutti, P. J., & Bender, M. (1982). *Teaching interpersonal and community living skills: A curriculum model for handicapped adolescents and adults.* Baltimore: University Park Press.

Valletutti, P. J., & Bender, M. (1985). *Teaching the moderately and severely handicapped: Curriculum objectives, strategies, and activities. Vol. 2: Communication and socialization.* Austin, TX: PRO-ED.

Valletutti, P. J., & Dummett, L. (1992). *Cognitive development: A functional approach.* San Diego: Singular Publishing Group.

Wheeler, J. (1987). *Transitioning persons with moderate and severe disabilities from school to adulthood: What makes it work.* Menononie: University of Wisconsin Materials Development Center.

Functional Reading

Monday	
Tuesday	1
Wednesday	
Thursday	
Friday	

The implementation of a functional reading curriculum requires both the identification of the *specific content* of the reading program and the *instructional strategy* to be employed.

The *specific content* is the vocabulary that is to be read and understood. It consists of those symbols, numerals, words, phrases, sentences, and abbreviations that a person needs or is expected to read and comprehend as he or she moves through life.

Functional reading, however, should not be viewed simply as the reading and comprehension of numerals, words, phrases, sentences, and abbreviations. It should be viewed within a broader perspective as the "reading" of all visual stimuli in the physical environment that provide clues to behavior. These nonword clues include the identification of a store type by the objects in window displays, the reading of approaching weather conditions by patterns of clouds and sunlight, and the interpretation of rebuses and other symbols, such as those found on traffic lights and signs. For many students with disabilities, functional reading should begin with the interpretation of nonverbal visual stimuli, continue with the comprehension of rebuses and other written symbols, and culminate in the comprehension of numerals, words, phrases, sentences, and abbreviations.

The *instructional strategy* refers to the approach to be taken in teaching students with disabilities to identify and comprehend the nonverbal and verbal written "messages" found in the environment. The functional approach to teaching reading requires teachers and other trainers to provide their students with real and simulated experiences that capture those functional life situations in which the comprehension of diverse visual stimuli, including written materials, is important to the optimal functioning and even the very survival of the viewer/reader.

When implementing a functional reading curriculum, other methods of teaching reading may be used in conjunction with the functional approach. For example, phonics and other word identification techniques may be used in concert with this curriculum when they help facilitate the rapid recognition of words that the student either has not yet experienced or has not yet incorporated into his or her sight vocabulary repertoire. The various context clue approaches to word identification and comprehension are also appropriately employed in a functional approach to teaching reading.

The goals and their specific instructional objectives included in this functional reading curriculum were identified by the authors from their

- review of relevant professional literature and pertinent instructional materials and resources;

- observations of children, youth, and adults with disabilities as these individuals functioned on a daily basis in school and the community;

- consultations with parents and other caregivers;

- conferences with students with disabilities, especially former students who, as adults, are functioning successfully in the community; and

- analysis of the daily reading requirements of their own lives.

Throughout the process of identifying the sequence and scope of a functional reading curriculum, attention was directed to the various life settings in which individuals function on a daily basis and as they fulfill their various social roles—as a member of a family unit, a household, a community; as a learner; as a participant in leisure activities; as a consumer of goods and services; as a worker; and as a traveler.

Teachers, related professionals, parents, and caregivers who implement this section of the curriculum need to engage in their own exploration of additional functional instructional goals and objectives. This task is best accomplished as one explores and experiences the multitude of reading demands one faces in one's own life. It would be advantageous to fill a notepad with the host of visual stimuli and written messages that are found in the environment, as, for example, when one identifies the approaching bus stop from the topography and the buildings sweeping by and as one reads the street signs, the writing on packages of food and other items, the notes on posters and bulletin boards, and the warnings on medicine labels.

Not only might this curriculum development and expansion activity suggest other relevant life experiences and/or emphases; it is also likely to lead to a more fully realized appreciation for the ubiquitous nature of the written messages that abound in the lives of us all and that are likely to confuse, frustrate, and impair those among us who are not facile readers or interpreters of pertinent visual stimuli.

General Goals of This Unit

   I. The student will identify personal data that have been written by others when this personal information appears on documents.

   II. The student will set clocks and timers and will identify time from numerals and markings on watches, clocks, and timers.

   III. The student will operate tools, appliances, and equipment in response to written information and markings on buttons, switches, dials, and gauges.

   IV. The student comprehends and responds appropriately to written information, including symbols, words, and phrases that appear on labels.

   V. The student will carry out instructions written in simple notes.

   VI. The student will locate and utilize information from simple charts, diagrams, maps, and menus.

   VII. The student will locate and utilize information from directories, schedules, and bulletin boards.

VIII. The student will correctly carry out directions written on equipment, machinery, games, toys, and items that are to be assembled.

   IX. The student will identify key words found on employment applications and other simple blanks and forms and will provide the requested information.

   X. The student will locate and utilize written information found on bills, work time cards, check stubs, and store receipts.

   XI. The student will locate and utilize information found in help wanted and other classified ads, printed advertisements, brochures, pamphlets, and other written materials.

   XII. The student will seek the assistance of a responsible person to decode and explain, when necessary, printed and written material that he or she is unable to read.

GOAL I.

The student will identify personal data that have been written by others when this personal information appears on documents.

Name:_____
Address:_____
Telephone #:_____
Social Security #:_____

SPECIFIC OBJECTIVES

The student:

- ❐ A. Identifies his or her name when it appears in written materials.
- ❐ B. Identifies his or her address when it appears in written materials.
- ❐ C. Identifies his or her telephone number when it appears in written materials.
- ❐ D. Identifies his or her social security number when it appears in written materials.

SUGGESTED ACTIVITIES

 ## Specific Objective A

The student identifies his or her name when it appears in written materials.

Teacher Interventions

Primary Level. Place a photograph of the student with his or her name written below it on as many of the student's possessions as possible (e.g., desk, cubicle, and lunch box). After the student has consistently identified his or her possessions from the photographs, follow up by placing a large photograph of the student in a prominent place in the classroom.

Below the photograph place a 5″ × 8″ index card on which the student's first name has been printed. Capitalize only the first letter of the name. Point to the photograph, and ask the student to identify it. Then say the student's name aloud. Next, point to the name card, and say the name once more. Ask the student to point to his or her picture and then to his or her name written on the card.

Next, remove the name card, and ask the student to place it under his or her picture. If the student does so, add cards to the task in the following progression: a blank card, cards with nonletter shapes and figures, cards with words markedly different in appearance from the student's name, and, finally, cards with words that are quite similar to the name. In each instance, ask the student to find and make the "match."

Intermediate Level. Schedule reading "Roll Calls." Each school day during this instructional activity (and in subsequent reviews), show the student and his or her peers flashcards on which their names have been printed. Ask the students to raise their hands or to say "Present" or "Here" when their name cards are shown. Once a student consistently identifies his or her name card as the card that has only his or her first name written on it, add the student's last name to the card and proceed as described in the primary-level activity above.

Additionally, set up a number of favorite activities, and explain that each of the students participating must wait to take a turn when his or her name card is shown. Also, prepare surprise activity boxes with games, pictures, and toys enclosed. Print the student's full name on his or her assigned box, and tell the student to find his or her box from among all of the students' boxes. Give the student free time to open his or her box and play with its contents.

Secondary Level. Write the student's full name—or ask the student to write his or her name—on assignment folders, notes, and individual progress charts so that the student can monitor and regulate his or her own progress. Place all of the student's folders, charts, notes, and memoranda together, thus requiring the student to identify his or her own material. At a class party or special luncheon, ask students to find their seats by locating their place cards.

Family Interventions

Primary Level. Ask the parents to put their child's first name on all of his or her articles of clothing. Tell them to ask their child to locate his or her clothing from all the recently washed or laundered clothing and to put his or her clothing away in the appropriate drawers and closets. Encourage the parents to communicate in writing whenever possible, for example, putting the child's name on a gift and asking him or her to find it rather than simply saying, "Here is a gift for you!"

Intermediate Level. Ask the parents to identify the family name (when their child's last name is the same as theirs) by saying, "We are the O'Connors. Our last name is O'Connor." Tell them to make sure that their child identifies him- or herself by the full name (Sean O'Connor) before beginning to write the full name on possessions and on labels.

Once their child consistently comprehends and uses his or her full name, remind the parents to put the child's name on his or her birthday and holiday gifts, allowance envelope, closet or toy and game chest, and simple notes. Tell them that if their child is consistently identifying his or her name when it is written, they should initiate instruction in which the child is expected to write his or her own name in manuscript and in cursive (a signature).

Secondary Level. Ask the parents to ask their child to pick up the family's mail from the mailbox. Tell them to require the child to separate the mail by its intended recipient, including any letters or mail addressed to him- or herself. Encourage the parents to ask the student to locate his or her name on bills, medical reports, checks, and other documents that refer to the student. Tell them to also begin or to continue instructing the child in how to write his or her name in both manuscript and cursive.

 ## Specific Objective B

The student identifies his or her address when it appears in written materials.

Teacher Interventions

Primary Level. Once the student identifies his or her full name consistently, assist the student in identifying his or her address. Use manuscript letters in writing the words of the address. Begin with the house number. If possible, show the student copies of actual envelopes that have been sent to the home. Underline the house number.

Take a trip to the student's home, and match the number on the envelope with the one displayed on his or her house. Take a picture of the house with the number prominently shown. Tell the student that the house number is the house's "name." Post the photograph in the classroom, and put the student's name card below it.

Draw a picture of a house, and duplicate several copies. Leave a blank space where the house number would be. Tell the student that you are going to play a game called "Finding My Way Home." Then fill in the student's house number on one of the houses. Ask the student to find his or her home. If he or she does so correctly, write in a different number on another copy, then give the student both copies, and ask him or her to find his or her home once again.

As the student successfully achieves each step, gradually increase the difficulty of the task by adding house numbers to more of the drawings and by increasing the similarity of the house numbers.

Secondary Level.   Make a list of products, sports teams, clubs, associations, and so on that include the name of the town or city in which the student lives. Show the student emblems and other signs that include the town or city name. For example, say, "This is a *Baltimore* Oriole's cap. The stadium where the *Baltimore* Orioles play their home games is in *Baltimore*, just like your home, which is also in *Baltimore*. This is a picture of the entrance to the *Baltimore* Zoo. It is in *Baltimore*. You live at 695 Druid Hill Avenue; you live in *Baltimore*."

Then show the student envelopes on which his or her full address is written (or typed), and ask the student to underline the name of his or her city or town. Follow up by taking walks in the community and identifying places whose names include the name of the city or town—for example, the *Baltimore* Spice Company, Lady *Baltimore* Dry Cleaners, the *Baltimore* Chamber of Commerce, and the Bank of *Baltimore*.

Proceed by showing the student an outline map of the state. Print the student's town or city name in its proper location on the map. Explain that the state is made up of many towns and cities. Say the name of the state, and remind the student that he or she lives in Baltimore, *Maryland.* Show the student maps of the state, and assist him or her in locating the name of the city and state.

Take the student for trips in the community, and assist him or her in locating the state name on various buildings and business establishments, such as *Maryland* National Bank, *Maryland* Crab House Restaurant, or the *Maryland* State Teacher's Association. Finally, introduce the concept of the zip code, and assist the student in identifying his or her zip code as it appears on letters addressed to his or her home.

Family Interventions

Primary Level.   Ask the parents to show their child the street signs that name their street and the house numbers appearing on their home. Tell them to practice with their child until he or she is able to say the address correctly and consistently. Tell the parents to show their child letters, cards, magazines, and packages that have been mailed to their home and to point out and underline the house number and street name.

Intermediate Level.   Ask the parents to review the name of the city or town in which they live until their child is able to say it correctly and consistently. Tell them to show their child mail that has arrived at their home and to assist the child, if needed, in reading the street address and the name of the city.

Encourage them to follow up by taking their child for walks in the community to identify places where the town or city name is displayed. Tell them to point to the name and to explain that the owners of the shirt factory decided to call it the *Baltimore* Shirt Company because it is located in *Baltimore.*

Secondary Level. Ask the parents to review the name of the state in which they live until their child is able to say it correctly and consistently. Ask them to assist their child in identifying their zip code. Tell them to show their child mail that has arrived at their home and to assist the child, if needed, in reading aloud the entire address, including the zip code.

Tell them to also show their child outgoing mail and to ask him or her to read aloud the return address located on the envelope or package. Encourage them to take their child for walks in the community to locate business establishments and other buildings where the name of the state is included in the name of the business.

 ## Specific Objective C

The student identifies his or her telephone number when it appears in written materials.

Teacher Interventions

Infant and Toddler/Preschool. Engage the student in playing "telephone" by using toy or real telephones. The purpose of this activity is to play a "grownup" game and to practice simulating a telephone call.

Primary Level. Draw a picture of the student's home telephone dial or push-button panel. If the student has a push-button telephone, enlarge the taped strip that shows the telephone number (if one exists), and attach it to a real telephone. Tell the student to pretend that the telephone is his or her home telephone and that you want to make a call to his or her home. Then dial your own telephone while you say the student's telephone number aloud. Engage in a simple conversation.

Follow up by giving the student a small card on which his or her home telephone has been written, and then role-play the part of one of the student's family members while the student plays him- or herself calling you from somewhere other than home. Ask the student to say his or her home telephone number while dialing it.

Engage in various memory facilitation activities, and encourage the student to remember his or her phone number. Tell the student to keep the card with the telephone number in his or her wallet, so that it can be referred to easily if the student forgets his or her number while away from home and needs to contact someone there. Tell the student that it might be easier to remember the number if he or she writes it and says it in grouped patterns, for example, 555-19-96.

Complete the sequence by asking the student to use the number card to actually call home and speak to a family member. (Make sure that you arrange for someone to be at home to receive the call at the specified time.)

Intermediate Level.   Ask the student to make copies of his or her telephone number to give to classmates to keep in their wallets and/or put in their personal telephone directories. Also, write each student's telephone number on the chalkboard. Give out class assignments and assign duties to the students by pointing to the telephone number of the student written on the chalkboard rather than the usual way of pointing to the student's name.

Secondary Level.   Tell the student there will be various situations in which he or she might have to give a telephone number to others. Role-play such situations as being lost and showing a police officer the telephone number from a card listing key personal data. Assist the student in finding his or her telephone number in a public telephone directory. Explain that if the student forgets his or her telephone number and does not have a personal data card (see Figure 1.1) in his or her wallet, it might have to be looked up in a directory.

Collect several telephone bills belonging to different people (or use facsimiles), cross out all identifying information except for the account-holder's telephone number, and ask the student to locate his or her telephone bill.

Family Interventions

Infant and Toddler/Preschool.   Ask the parents to buy their child a toy telephone. Tell them to make pretend telephone calls, even if their child does not speak yet. Explain that, if their child is in the babbling stage, for example, they can have a "babbling" conversation in which they use normal vocal patterns while they are babbling.

Primary Level.   Ask the parents to point out their telephone number as it appears on the home telephone(s). Tell the parents to explain to their child that the number on the telephone is an important one for people to know if they want to speak to them from places outside the home.

Remind the parents to tell their child that it is an important number for him or her to know when he or she is away from home (e.g., while

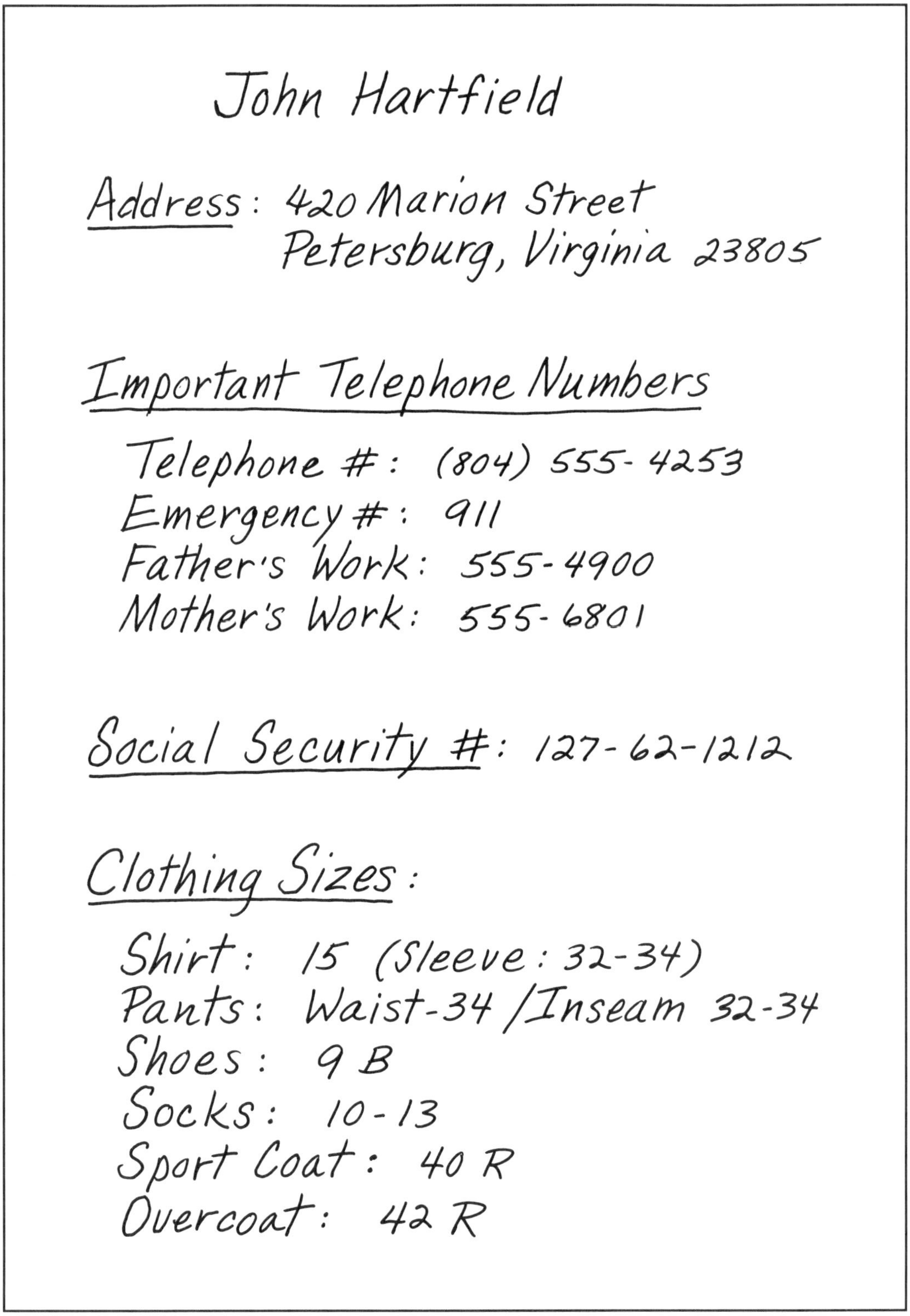

John Hartfield

Address: 420 Marion Street
         Petersburg, Virginia 23805

Important Telephone Numbers

Telephone #: (804) 555-4253
Emergency #: 911
Father's Work: 555-4900
Mother's Work: 555-6801

Social Security #: 127-62-1212

Clothing Sizes:

Shirt: 15 (Sleeve: 32-34)
Pants: Waist-34 /Inseam 32-34
Shoes: 9 B
Socks: 10-13
Sport Coat: 40 R
Overcoat: 42 R

FIGURE 1.1. Personal data card.

staying at Grandma and Grandpa's house) and wants to call them. Ask them to assist their child in dialing their home telephone number when they are not at home and are calling another family member who is at home. Tell them to put their child on the line to speak with the person who answers.

Intermediate Level. Ask the parents to take their child to the homes of various family members and friends. Tell the parents (with the host's permission) to tell their child to call someone at home to give that person a message. Tell them to give their child the family's personal directory and ask him or her to use it to phone home.

Secondary Level. Ask the parents to give their child a list of names and telephone numbers to put in his or her own personal telephone directory. Remind them to include the child's own telephone number without providing the accompanying name designation. Tell them to reward their child for putting his or her own telephone number in the correct place in the directory.

Tell the parents to give their child copies of their telephone bill and to ask him or her to locate the telephone number as it appears in various places on the bill.

 Specific Objective D

The student identifies his or her social security number when it appears in written materials.

Teacher Interventions

Intermediate Level. Show the student your social security card, and explain that a person's social security number is a very important part of his or her personal information and that there will be many times in life when the student must write his or her social security number and will need to check his or her card (or memory) to see whether the social security number appearing on documents is correct.

At this point, show the student samples of documents in which your social security number appears (e.g., driver's license [as in the state of Virginia], checkbook, payroll check stub, and income tax forms). Explain that you always check these documents to make sure that your number is written correctly. If the student does not have a social security card, assist him or her (with the parents' permission) in getting one.

Secondary Level.   Obtain various forms (e.g., voter registration forms, employment applications, and bank records) that require a person to record his or her social security number. Fill them out as they would apply to the student, with the social security number being correct in some instances and incorrect in others. Praise the student for verifying the correctness of the information and for correcting any errors.

Family Interventions

Intermediate Level.   Ask the parents to show their child various documents on which their social security numbers have been written. Tell them to ask their child to watch as they match the social security number on these documents with the number on their social security cards. Remind them to assist their child in obtaining his or her own card if the child does not already have one and they have not given you permission to do so as part of a class activity.

Secondary Level.   Ask the parents to collect documents on which their child's social security number has been written or printed. Tell them to supervise as the child verifies whether the number is correctly listed.

GOAL II.

The student will set clocks and timers and will identify time from numerals and markings on watches, clocks, and timers.

SPECIFIC OBJECTIVES

The student:

- ❏ A. Identifies and names the time by viewing different types and styles of clocks and watches (digital and standard).

- ❏ B. Sets a watch, a standard clock, and the clock on a clock radio.

- ❏ C. Sets and operates manual and electric kitchen timers and alarm clocks.

SUGGESTED ACTIVITIES

Specific Objective A

The student identifies and names the time by viewing different types and styles of clocks and watches (digital and standard).

See Unit 3, "Functional Mathematics," for suggested activities.

Specific Objective B

The student sets a watch, a standard clock, and the clock on a clock radio.

Teacher Interventions

Infant and Toddler/Preschool. Bring in a variety of watches, clocks, and clock radios to class. Show the student these items, and explain that people like different styles of watches and clocks but that they are all used by people to help them know what time it is.

Primary Level. Demonstrate setting the correct time on a watch that needs to be wound and on a standard clock that has run down. Then ask the student to set the correct time on the watch and clock. Show the student the correct time on a clock or watch that is running, and ask him or her to reproduce it (or copy it or make a match) on the watch and clock that he or she has been given. Do this for a variety of time settings and with a variety of watches, including battery-operated ones that do not need to be wound.

Intermediate Level. Repeat the primary-level activity. This time, expect the student to set the watch or clock without being shown a clock or watch with the correct time. In this case, tell the student the correct time, for example, "I just called the telephone company's number for the correct time, and the correct time is ___."

Secondary Level.   Review with the student where and how he or she might get the correct time when his or her own watch or a clock at home has stopped (e.g., from the radio, the time channel on cable television, or a friend). Give the student several watches and clocks that have stopped, and ask him or her to set them correctly. Also, role-play a situation in which time is important, and have the student ask someone, "Please, can you tell me what time it is?"

Family Interventions

Infant and Toddler/Preschool.   Ask the parents to show their child all the clocks in their home as well as any watches they possess. Tell them to demonstrate the process of setting a watch and a clock that have stopped without necessarily drawing their child's attention to the actual settings. Explain to the parents that the objective is to help their child acquire the concept that knowing the correct time is important to people.

Primary Level.   Ask the parents to show their child how they set a watch and a clock. At this level, tell the parents not only to stress the importance of having the correct time but also to draw their child's attention to specific settings.

Intermediate Level.   Ask the parents to repeat the primary-level activity with their child performing the actual setting of the watch or clock. Tell the parents to point out that the child needs to set the watch or clock in order to avoid being late for a specified activity such as joining friends for a recreational activity or to remind the parents that they promised to take him or her shopping for new shoes at 7:30 P.M.

Secondary Level.   Ask the parents to give their child the responsibility of setting the clocks in the home when they have run down. Tell the parents to also require their child to be in charge of excursions and other special activities and to inform them when they must get ready.

 ## Specific Objective C

The student sets and operates manual and electric kitchen timers and alarm clocks.

Teacher Interventions

Infant and Toddler/Preschool. Bring in a kitchen timer and several different types of alarm clocks to the classroom. Point them out to the student and draw attention to your hand as you set the timer for a classroom activity such as a simple arts and crafts project. Explain to the student that you are timing the activity so that when the timer bell rings, you both will know it is time to clean up. Do the same using an alarm clock to measure a longer period of time, such as when it is time to get ready for lunch.

Primary Level. Show the student the numerals and slash marks on a kitchen timer, and explain that they represent different times. Indicate that when the timer is set, we are able to measure the time as it passes by, for example, while something is cooking or baking. Tell the student that you are going to make a five-minute boiled egg and ask him or her to watch you as you bring the egg to a boil and set the timer for 5 minutes.

Draw the student's attention to the ticking of the timer by clicking with the tip of your tongue. Inform the student that the "tick-tick-tick" of the timer means that time is passing and the timer knob is moving back from 5 to 0. Tell the student that when the knob reaches 0, the timer will ring. When the timer bell rings, say, "Did you hear the timer bell? Time's up!"

Assign the student several timed tasks. Set the timer for the student after discussing the time required for the task, and tell him or her to periodically check to see how much time is left in order to monitor his or her own work. Once the student has mastered winding the kitchen timer, give him or her an alarm clock that requires manual winding. Demonstrate, using a second alarm clock, winding the alarm clock (which requires a clockwise movement rather than the counterclockwise movement of the kitchen timer). Tell the student to wind his or her alarm clock in a similar manner.

Intermediate Level. Assign the student a series of simple and quick tasks to complete in a short period of time. Give the student the time specification and tell him or her to set the time and monitor his or her progress by using the kitchen timer. Provide assistance as needed. If one is available in the school, point out the electric timer on a stove, tell the student that it is also a kitchen timer for cooking, and assist him or her in setting it and using it in food preparation.

Do the similar activities in which the student is expected to set an alarm clock for longer tasks and for the purpose of drawing attention to major events in the school day, such as the time for physical education, lunch, a playground activity, and dismissal. Be sure to review the various words and abbreviation clues that appear on alarm clocks as well as the various time designations, including numerals and markings.

Secondary Level. Review with the student the cooking and baking time specifications on food packages and in simple recipes. Supervise as the student sets the kitchen timer to the appropriate setting and then carries out the food preparation task. Join the student in enjoying the food. Continue by engaging the student in a discussion of the time he or she must get up to be at school on time. Include in the discussion the time needed for toileting, washing and other grooming activities, dressing, eating and/or preparing breakfast, and transportation (include the idea of leeway time).

Ask the student to set the alarm clock for his or her wake-up time. Continue by telling your wake-up time as well as hypothetical wake-up times for other people.

Family Interventions

Infant and Toddler/Preschool. Ask the parents to point out to their child the electric timer (if one exists in the home) and a kitchen timer (if available) and to demonstrate their use. Impress on the parents that the objective is not to identify numerals or markings but rather to develop the concept that time must be considered and measured in cooking and other activities. Tell them to do the same for an alarm clock, especially in terms of morning wake-up time.

Primary Level. Ask the parents to actively involve their child in various food preparation activities that have to be timed. Tell them to demonstrate setting timers and alarm clocks and to involve their child as an observer of the process.

Intermediate Level. Ask the parents to involve their child in a number of activities that require measuring time spent and time still left. Tell them, at this level, to expect their child to set the timer or alarm clock independently. Explain that they might need to demonstrate, provide assistance, and give their child sufficient practice for independent action to occur.

Secondary Level. Tell the parents that they must give their child greater responsibility in setting his or her own wake-up time and in food preparation and other tasks that need to be timed. Ask the parents to specify time constraints and to expect their child to properly set a timer to measure time needed, time spent, and time still left.

GOAL III.

The student will operate tools, appliances, and equipment in response to written information and markings on buttons, switches, dials, and gauges.

SPECIFIC OBJECTIVES

The student, in response to written information:

☐ A. Operates appliances and equipment involved in food storage, meal preparation, and meal cleanup activities (refrigerator, food scale, toaster, fry pan, microwave, stove, oven, blender, electric mixer, and dishwasher).

☐ B. Operates appliances and equipment involved in maintaining clothing and household linens (washer, dryer, and iron).

☐ C. Operates a telephone and a telephone answering machine.

☐ D. Operates appliances involved in grooming activities (hair dryer or blower and electric or battery-operated shaver).

☐ E. Operates equipment involved in recreational/educational activities (toys and games; television; radio; VCR; personal computer; and record, cassette tape, and CD players).

☐ F. Operates equipment and other objects involved in maintaining and monitoring his or her health (bathroom scale, heating pad, and thermometer).

☐ G. Operates appliances and equipment involved in heating and ventilation (thermostat, fan, air conditioner, and electric blanket).

☐ H. Operates tools and appliances involved in household maintenance and repairs (hand vacuum, vacuum cleaner, electric broom, and drill press).

☐ I. Utilizes that information as he or she travels in the community, including operating a self-service elevator and paying the correct fare as shown on a taxi meter.

SUGGESTED ACTIVITIES

 ## Specific Objective A

The student, in response to written information, operates appliances and equipment involved in food storage, meal preparation, and meal cleanup activities (refrigerator, food scale, toaster, fry pan, microwave, stove, oven, blender, electric mixer, and dishwasher).

Teacher Interventions

Infant and Toddler/Preschool. Bring in various toy appliances that can be used to role-play cooking and eating activities. Follow up by bringing to class the real appliances involved in meal preparation and meal cleanup activities. Ask the student to match the toy appliance with its real counterpart.

Name these appliances, and ask the student to point to the object named. Once the student is able to correctly and consistently point to the object, ask him or her to name each appliance as you point to it. Use these appliances to prepare tasty snacks and meals.

Primary Level. Bring in various meal preparation and meal cleanup appliances. Take the student to the place in the school where a refrigerator and a stove are located.

In the case of the refrigerator, show the student where the control dials are located, and set them while talking aloud: for example, "I am setting the dial to number ___ because it is getting warmer now that summer is here, and I want the refrigerator to be colder."

In the case of the stove and its oven, use each of the dials, and talk aloud about your decisions: for example, "I need to heat this food at 350°, so I must set this dial to that reading."

Use each of the food preparation appliances to prepare an appropriate food item, and talk aloud your behavior: for example, "I like my toast dark, so I am turning the light/dark dial [while pointing and gesturing] toward the dark side." Make sure to use as many different settings as possible to demonstrate to the student the results that occur from each of the different settings.

Intermediate Level. Involve the student in various meal preparation and meal cleanup tasks. Require the student to operate each appliance by talking aloud his or her actions: for example, "To turn on the front left burner of this stove, I must find the dial that has L/F written next to it and set it at the proper temperature [HI or LO and intermediate numerical settings]." In this case, it may be necessary to develop the concept of left and right along with their abbreviations. Similarly, the concept of high and low and their abbreviations may have to be developed.

Secondary Level. Plan a special luncheon or party, and invite another class or family members. Give the student various recipes involving the use of various food preparation appliances; show him or her videotapes of these processes as engaged in by you and skilled peers and, if possible, by chefs appearing on television; and expect the student to complete the tasks as independently as possible.

Make a videotape of the student engaging in these several processes so that he or she may monitor performance and progress. Include in this activity the need to use a food scale to measure food for a specific recipe or for a person who is on a special diet.

Family Interventions

Infant and Toddler/Preschool. Ask the parents to purchase toy sets of food preparation appliances and equipment as well as dishes and tableware and to pretend, in a game format, that they are being used for cooking, eating, and cleanup.

Tell the parents to introduce each food preparation appliance to their child. Encourage them to name the object, immediately use it, and join their child in eating the food item: for example, "This is a microwave. We use it to heat and to cook food. I am going to heat these apple cakes for our after-school snack."

Primary Level. Ask the parents to show their child the various buttons, switches, dials, and gauges that are in a refrigerator, on a stove, on a dishwasher, and on various household appliances used for meal preparation. Tell the parents to explain the markings, abbreviations, and words found on these appliances and equipment and to follow up by using the various settings to obtain different results.

Intermediate Level. Ask the parents to require their child to operate each of the pieces of equipment and appliances available in the home. Tell them to monitor their child as he or she performs specific tasks with these objects. Tell them, if possible, to take home videos of their child carrying out various tasks involving the use of these appliances.

Secondary Level. Ask the parents to give their child responsibility for preparing different food items for a family gathering, a picnic, or a family reunion. Tell the parents to give their child simple recipes to follow that involve the use of different appliances.

Specific Objective B

The student, in response to written information, operates appliances and equipment involved in maintaining clothing and household linens (washer, dryer, and iron.)

Teacher Interventions

Infant and Toddler/Preschool. Take the student to a laundry room that has a washer and dryer. Point to and name the washer first. Draw the student's attention to the door or lid and the control dial as the most important parts of the washer. Lift the lid or open the door, and ask the student to watch what you are doing as you perform the action. Start the machine. Be sure to point out the sound of the washer when it is running and the absence of sound when the wash is done.

Continue by pointing to and naming the dryer. Again draw the student's attention to the door or lid and the control dial. Then ask the student to watch what you are doing as you carry out the process. Follow up by using an electric iron to iron several pieces of clothing. Again, urge the student to watch as you set the dial and carry out the process.

Primary Level. Repeat the activities identified for an infant/toddler. This time, however, involve the student in identifying the markings, abbreviations, numerals, and words on the various dials. You may wish to make a chart (see Figures 1.2, 1.3, & 1.4) of the key words and phrases that appear on these appliances and use it for instruction and practice purposes. You may also wish to review the numerals from 1 to 10 by using flashcards for rapid recognition.

Intermediate Level. Ask the students to bring in clothing and other materials from home that need to be washed (check with the parents first for their permission). Explain that a pile of laundry needs to be separated into different piles for washing, such as whites only, dark clothing only, and colored clothing that can be washed together.

Show the student a video that demonstrates the several processes (washing, drying, and simple ironing). Assist the student in separating

| Warm | Perm Press | |
	Dry	Steam
Acetates	Polyesters	Blends of
Acrylics	Dacron	cotton and
Acrilan	Fortrel	polyesters
Creslan	Kodel	Wool
Orlon	Trevira	Wool with
Metallics	Rayons	cotton
	Silks	Nylons
		Triacetates

FIGURE 1.2. Electric iron settings.

the laundry, and expect him or her to carry out the several processes: washing, drying, and simple ironing (handkerchiefs and aprons).

Secondary Level. Expect the student to do some additional washing, drying, and ironing chores. At this level increase the complexity of the ironing task. Instruct the student in the tasks of ironing shirts, blouses, slacks, curtains, and other items.

Family Interventions

Infant and Toddler/Preschool. Ask the parents to have their child watch them as they engage in the total process of maintaining clothing and household linens: washing, drying, and ironing. Tell the parents to help their child remember the names of each of the appliances.

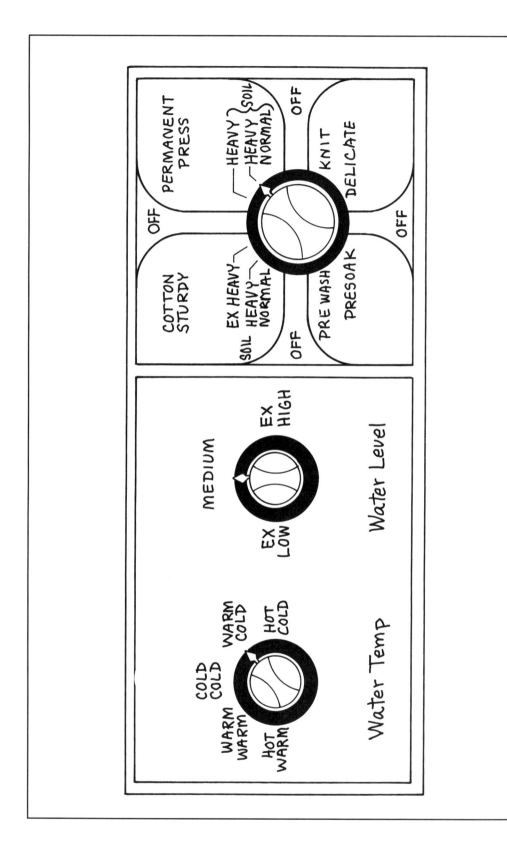

FIGURE 1.3. Washing machine controls.

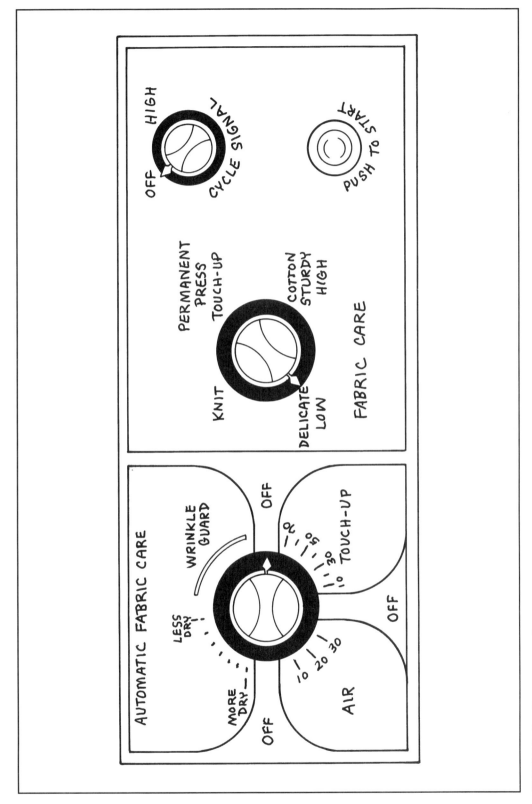

FIGURE 1.4. Dryer controls.

35

Primary Level. Ask the parents to involve their child in the washing, drying, and ironing of clothing and household linens by talking aloud the process as they carry it out. Tell the parents to comment about the various settings of the dials on these appliances and to model their decision-making process by speaking it aloud. Remind them to point out the words, phrases, numerals, and abbreviations on the dials.

Intermediate Level. Ask the parents to supervise their child as he or she operates the washer, dryer, and iron. Tell them to develop the concept that clothing and household linens must be separated in categories to prevent discoloration. Remind them also to only require their child to do simple ironing.

Secondary Level. Ask the parents to spend time with their child making him or her as independent as possible in doing more difficult ironing tasks such as ironing shirts, blouses, pants, and fancy curtains.

Specific Objective C

The student, in response to written information, operates a telephone and a telephone answering machine.

Teacher Interventions

Infant and Toddler/Preschool. Engage the student in pretend telephone conversations using toy or real telephones. The purpose of this activity is to role-play being an adult and to provide the student with practice in simulating a telephone call.

Primary Level. Role-play telephone conversations. Divide the class into groups of two. Assign each group a topic of conversation such as making arrangements to participate together in a recreational activity, discussing a sports team or event, or talking about a favorite television show.

Review the letters and numbers on the dial or keypad. Ask the student to practice dialing his or her home telephone number on a telephone that is not connected. (See Goal I, Specific Objective C.)

Explain and demonstrate how to contact the operator. Be sure to make clear those circumstances when the student should contact an operator. Continue by showing the student how to dial emergency numbers, such as 911.

Follow up by connecting the telephone and asking the student to call home to leave a message. (Arrange beforehand for someone to be home.) If needed, spend time familiarizing the student with dial tones, busy signals, and the sound of a telephone ringing on the other end. Conclude this activity by using a disconnected telephone to role-play calling the operator and emergency numbers.

Intermediate Level. Ask the student's parents for the telephone numbers of friends and relatives that the student should write in his or her personal directory. Using a disconnected telephone, ask the student to role-play dialing these numbers and holding a pretend conversation. If feasible, arrange for the student to actually call at least one of the persons listed in the personal directory.

Secondary Level. Bring to class a telephone answering machine. Play a sample of a recorded message you have put on it, and play some (screened) examples of calls that have been recorded. Explain the purpose of an answering machine, and then demonstrate how to operate it. If the parents have an answering machine, ask them to provide the student with practice in its use.

Family Interventions

Infant and Toddler/Preschool. Encourage the parents to play mock telephone conversations with their child using toy telephones. (There are a variety of toy telephones available in most toy stores.)

Primary Level. Ask the parents to use a disconnected telephone to assist their child in acquiring the skill of dialing his or her home telephone number. Tell the parents that once their child is able to do so, they should take him or her to a friend's or family member's home to call a family member who is at home.

Impress upon the parents the importance of teaching their child how to make emergency calls. If 911 is available in their community, ask the parents to use a disconnected telephone to role-play reporting household emergencies. Remind them to work with their child on developing the concept of an emergency versus a problem situation that is *not* an emergency.

Intermediate Level. Ask the parents to supply you with the telephone numbers of family members and friends whom their child might wish to call. Use these numbers to develop the child's personal telephone directory. Ask the parents to assist their child in calling these numbers when making actual calls and to encourage the child to do the dialing when he or she is able to do so independently. Remind the parents that their child can use the practice and therefore should make the calls.

Secondary Level. Ask the parents if they have an answering machine or an intercom system in their home. If available, encourage them to teach their child how to use this equipment.

Specific Objective D

The student, in response to written information, operates appliances involved in grooming activities (hair dryer or blower and electric or battery-operated shaver).

Teacher Interventions

Intermediate Level.   Bring a hair dryer or blower into the classroom. If applicable, show the student how to use this appliance after he or she has showered and washed his or her hair following a swimming activity or physical education. Make certain that you review the words and abbreviations on the dial. If it is not possible for the student to wash his or her hair in school, review how to turn the dryer on and off.

Ask the student to listen to the sound it makes when it is on and to feel the hot air as it emerges. If feasible, as part of grooming activities, assign the student a partner, and ask the partners to take turns washing and drying each other's hair using the dryer and blower. Videotape these sessions for later review and practice.

Secondary Level.   Bring in a variety of electric or battery-operated shavers. Review the ON and OFF and LOW-HIGH switches, as appropriate. After the male student has mastered the operation of a shaver and if he needs to shave and has one of his own, practice using it prior to a dress-up school event.

For female students, it may be necessary to practice using an electric shaver as part of grooming activities in which body hair is removed. (This activity should be carried out by a female teacher/aide or school nurse.)

Family Interventions

Intermediate Level.   Ask the parents to assist their child in using a dryer or blower to dry his or her hair after washing. Tell them to supervise their child to be sure that he or she is using it in safe places and in a safe manner.

Secondary Level.   Ask the mother to model using a shaver, if appropriate, and to assist her daughter in using an electric or battery-operated shaver, if needed or desired, to remove body hair. Ask the father, if appropriate, to model using a shaver and to assist his son in using an electric or battery-operated shaver to remove facial hair.

Specific Objective E

The student, in response to written information, operates equipment involved in recreational/educational activities (toys and games; television; radio; VCR; personal computer; and record, cassette tape, and CD players).

Teacher Interventions

Primary Level. Collect a variety of toys that have switches, dials, and/or levers. Demonstrate how to start and stop these toys. Follow up by assisting the student in operating and enjoying these toys. Encourage the student to bring in a favorite toy that has dials or switches to demonstrate to classmates and you during "Show and Tell" or "Sharing Time."

Continue by showing the student various equipment that is used in the home and school for recreational and/or educational purposes. Assist the student in identifying by pointing to and naming each of these pieces of equipment.

To develop each of the underlying concepts, turn on the particular piece of equipment and entertain the student while using the equipment and its requisite supplies and materials (e.g., CDs for a CD player and cassettes for a cassette player) to watch and/or listen to something that appeals to the student. Use, for example, tape cassettes with coordinated storybooks.

Intermediate Level. Assist the student in identifying the various markings, abbreviations, and words that appear on television sets, radios, record players, cassette players, VCRs, and so on.

Give the student directions, and expect him or her to operate recreational/educational equipment according to the specifications in your directions: for example, "Turn on the television set to Channel 3," "Put the videotape of *Peter Pan* on the VCR," "Make a videotape of your partner operating a washer and dryer so that you both can review the tape later on."

Secondary Level. Demonstrate to the student how to use a personal computer for recreational (computer games), educational, and communication purposes (word processing and the use of a voice synthesizer for a nonverbal student). Assist the student in using a personal computer. Assign the student daily computer time, and provide interesting recreational and educational software.

Family Interventions

Primary Level. Ask the parents to demonstrate to their child all the recreational/educational equipment available in their home. If family members and friends are willing to cooperate, ask the parents to visit friends and relatives who have equipment not available in their own home so that they may demonstrate additional equipment to their child.

Remind them that trips to specialty stores and to electronic departments of department stores can also provide an opportunity for them to demonstrate or see demonstrated recreational and educational equipment and materials.

Intermediate Level. Ask the parents to review with their child the various words and other written information on the various educational and recreational materials and equipment. Tell them to encourage their child to operate this equipment when he or she can do so safely and responsibly.

Secondary Level. Ask the parents, if they have a personal computer, to demonstrate to their child how to use it along with selected software.

Specific Objective F

The student, in response to written information, operates equipment and other objects involved in maintaining and monitoring his or her health (bathroom scale, heating pad, and thermometer).

Teacher Interventions

Infant and Toddler/Preschool. Ask if the student has ever had his or her temperature taken while ill or not feeling well. Follow up by showing the student a thermometer and a model (see Figure 1.5) of one with a silver sliding panel set at "normal" to show the height of "mercury" when the person is healthy.

Continue by showing the student a bathroom scale and asking him or her to name it and describe what it is used for. If the student is unable to do so, help him or her develop the concept.

Show the student a heating pad, and ask if he has ever seen one before. Plug in the heating pad and tell the student to place his or her hand on it to experience the heat generated. Explain that some people use a heating pad when a part of their body hurts.

Primary Level. Use the model of the thermometer, and set the "mercury" to assist the student in identifying the number where the silver sliding panel ends. After sufficient practice, help the student to "read" a real thermometer. If it does not embarrass or invade the privacy of the student and his or her classmates, make the student the "health monitor" and ask him or her to use a bathroom scale to record his or her weight and the weight of classmates.

Intermediate Level. Show the student the different settings of a heating pad. Tell him or her to try out the pad by feeling the heat (after 1 minute) to determine which is the lowest and which is the highest setting. Assist the student in identifying the several settings and in using the heating pad safely.

Secondary Level. Bring in a variety of thermometers, including weather and cooking thermometers. Show the student how to differentiate between each type and how to use each one.

Place a thermometer (see Figure 1.5) outside the classroom window in the shade, and ask the student to report on and record the daily temperature. Continue by showing the student an oven thermometer and asking him or her to point to the place where the needle should point if the food item is being baked, roasted, or heated at the temperature specified on the package or recipe card.

Family Interventions

Infant and Toddler/Preschool. Ask the parents to use a bathroom scale to weigh their child and to use a thermometer when their child is ill. Tell the parents to explain the reason for the use of these items when they are actually in use.

Primary Level. Ask the parents to show their child a heating pad and to explain its function and point out safety factors. If the parents actually use a heating pad, ask them to demonstrate its use to their child.

Intermediate Level. Ask the parents to explain to their child that there are various objects and appliances that help us when we are sick and when we wish to stay healthy. Ask them to discuss prevention of health problems by getting sufficient rest, eating proper foods, refraining from ingesting dangerous substances, and avoiding dangerous practices.

Have the parents tell the child that a thermometer is used when a person is ill or does not feel well in the home, doctors' offices, and hospitals. If possible, ask the parents to take their child to a clinical or hospital setting to see the various equipment and appliances found there. Tell them to check with a family doctor to see if he or she would be willing to show their child the instruments used in the office that must be read, such as a doctor's scale.

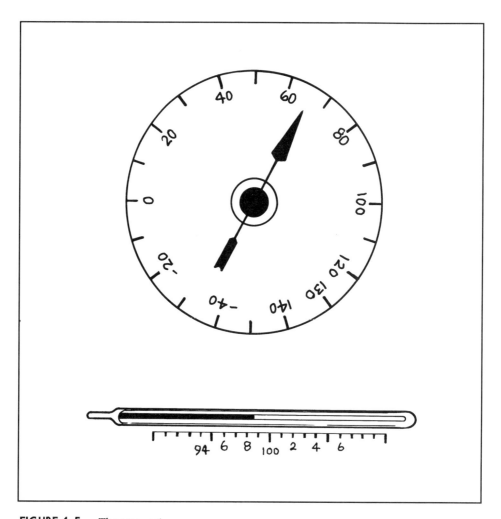

FIGURE 1.5. Thermometers.

Secondary Level. Ask the parents to show their child how to use an oven thermometer to monitor food preparation. Tell them to assign the student cooking and baking tasks for which he or she must follow temperature guidelines from recipes on packages, recipe cards, and cookbooks that are used in the home.

 ## Specific Objective G

The student, in response to written information, operates appliances and equipment involved in heating and ventilation (thermostat, fan, air conditioner, and electric blanket).

Teacher Interventions

Primary Level. Show the student any thermostats located in the classroom and school and any fans or air conditioners that are in current use. Explain their purposes, and, in the case of fans or air conditioners, tell the student to stand at a distance from them to feel the cool or cold air.

Intermediate Level. Show the student how to set a thermostat located in the classroom or school. It may be necessary to place a red dot on the number part of the thermostat to indicate the desired winter temperature and a blue dot to indicate the desired summer temperature. Demonstrate to the student how to line up the arrow on the movable dial with the dot on the number line. Discourage the student from "playing" with the dial.

Explain that setting the thermostat at a comfortable and healthy level saves the most energy and that during the cool and cold weather, people should supplement the heating system by wearing warmer clothes and during the warm or hot weather, people should help the cooling system by wearing lighter-weight clothes.

Continue by demonstrating the operation of an electric fan, an air conditioner, and an electric blanket. In each case draw the student's attention to the numbers and words that indicate speed or intensity level in the case of a fan and air conditioner (LOW, MEDIUM, HIGH) and the numbers and their relationship to the level of heat in an electric blanket (the higher the number the higher the heat or the hotter the electric blanket).

For the student who is having difficulty operating an electric blanket, it may be advisable to make a number line from 1 to 10 and put it on the wall at the student's eye level. Give the student a cardboard arrow, and tell him or her to point it to number 1 on the number line. Then tell him or her to move the arrow in the direction of "hotter."

Next, tell the student to place the arrow on the number 10 and move it in the direction of "cooler." Continue by having the student move toward "cooler" and "hotter" from the number 5. For the student who is experiencing difficulty, it may be necessary to color code the ON and OFF switch (buttons) and the various settings on a fan and air conditioner.

Secondary Level. Assign the student the job of being the class "heating and ventilation engineer," whose job it is to keep the classroom comfortably ventilated and heated at all times. If there is no opportunity for the temperature to be regulated from within the classroom, assign the "heating and ventilation engineer" the task of reporting to the school's custodian when changes need to be made in classroom temperatures.

Family Interventions

Primary Level. Ask the parents to show their child any thermostats located in their home as well as any fans or air conditioners that are in current use.

Guide the parents in assisting their child in comprehending and saying the names of these appliances.

Intermediate Level. Ask the parents to point out to their child the movable indicator dial on the thermostat, the arrow, the numbers that represent the degrees of temperature, and the words that indicate whether the system is ON or OFF and, when applicable, when it is on HEAT, COOL, or AUTOMATIC. Tell them to demonstrate setting the thermostat and then asking their child to do the same.

Ask the parents to show their child how to operate an electric fan, an air conditioner, and an electric blanket (during the cold weather) when they are available in the home.

Secondary Level. Ask the parents to take their child on a trip during the warm or hot weather. Tell them to demonstrate operating the ventilation and air conditioning system in the automobile (if available) and operating a motel room's air conditioning unit (when individual room units are available).

Encourage them to take their child on a trip during the cold weather. Tell them to demonstrate operating the automobile's heating system and operating a motel room's heating unit (when individual room units are available). Remind them that their child should do the various operations when he or she can do so independently or with minimal assistance.

 ## Specific Objective H

The student, in response to written information, operates tools and appliances involved in household maintenance and repairs (hand vacuum, vacuum cleaner, electric broom, and drill press).

Teacher Interventions

Infant and Toddler/Preschool. Show the student a hand vacuum, a vacuum cleaner, and an electric broom. Use these appliances to clean the floors. Point out the noise made by these appliances when they are on, and tell the student to feel the suction to help him or her understand their function.

Primary Level. Show the student the various settings on a hand vacuum, vacuum cleaner, and electric broom (including ON and OFF). Move the switch or dial to these various settings so that the student can experience the different functioning levels of these appliances.

Intermediate Level. Take the student to an area in the school where there is carpeting (e.g., a home economics suite or an office), and ask him or her to use the vacuum cleaner to clean the carpeting. Similarly, take the student to a noncarpeted area where he or she can experience using an electric broom.

Set up some small spills on floors and furniture that are best cleaned by using a hand vacuum. Ask the student to clean up these spills. Reward him or her for being a good "maintenance worker."

Secondary Level. Show the student a drill press. Point out the drill press wheel, and turn it to adjust the height of the drill. Point out the ON and OFF switch or treadle mechanism. Ask the student to find the words ON and OFF (these are usually designated by red and green buttons). Demonstrate how to use the drill press, and follow up by cautioning the student to use the drill press while wearing safety glasses. Assign him or her a task involving the use of a drill press.

Family Interventions

Infant and Toddler/Preschool. Ask the parents to show their child where they keep their hand vacuum, vacuum cleaner, and/or electric broom. Tell them to demonstrate their use during actual cleaning activities.

Primary Level. Ask the parents to show their child the different settings on their hand vacuum, vacuum cleaner, and/or electric broom and to demonstrate their differential use: for example, different settings for different carpet heights and textures. Tell them to follow up by requiring their child to participate in household cleaning activities in which he or she must use one or more of these appliances.

Intermediate Level. Ask the parents to draw up a cleaning and home maintenance schedule and to assign their child different tasks on several occasions so that he or she gets sufficient experience engaging in each of the various home maintenance tasks during regular cleaning times and special times such as spring and fall cleaning.

Secondary Level. Ask the parents to replicate the secondary-level Teacher Intervention activity with their child in the home setting.

Specific Objective I

The student, in response to written information, utilizes that information as he or she travels in the community, including operating a self-service elevator and paying the correct fare as shown on a taxi meter.

Teacher Interventions

Infant and Toddler/Preschool.   Take the student for trips in the community to department stores and office buildings where there are self-service elevators. Use these elevators to get to desired locations while pointing out that you have to operate the elevator by pushing the right buttons. If possible, on one of the trips take a taxi, point out the taxi meter to the student, and, as you pay the fare, say, "The meter says $__ . __; these numbers tell me how much the taxi ride costs."

Primary Level.   Use number and letter flashcards that have printed on them the letters B (for Basement), G (for Ground Floor), L (for Lobby), and so on, as well as the numbers that the student is likely to experience in the elevators found in his or her community. Make sure that the student is able to match the abbreviation with its reference word.

Also, construct an elevator push-button panel out of corrugated cardboard (see Figure 1.6). Paste on (or draw) buttons, and tell the student to push the buttons as you say them. Follow up by taking trips into the community and demonstrating how you use the buttons on the panel to get to a desired floor.

In addition, out of a cardboard box, wooden dowels, and paper, make a simulated taxi meter. On the paper write different amounts of fares, starting with the current basic rate in your community. Construct the simulated meter so that the fare shows through an opening in front of the box. Ask the student to identify the various figures as you change them. Pair the student with a classmate to take turns role-playing driver and passenger so that they gain experience in reading the meter and paying the fare.

Intermediate Level.   Prepare the student for a trip in the community (where you will operate a self-service elevator) by showing a facsimile of a sign that indicates the direction to walk to find the ELEVATORS. Review this sign, and add it to the student's sight vocabulary word bank when he or she identifies it consistently.

Also, review the specially constructed elevator control panel used in the primary-level activity (see Figure 1.6). Then add the special emergency buttons: EMERGENCY, STOP, and ALARM.

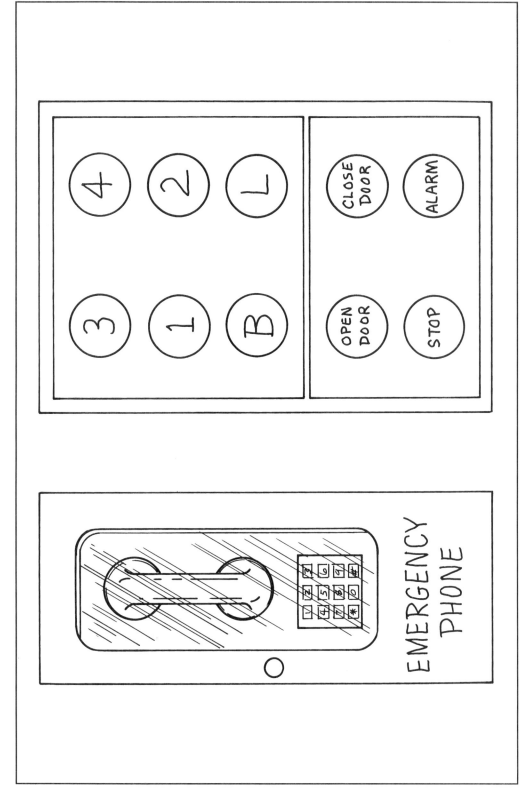

FIGURE 1.6. Elevator panel and emergency telephone.

Follow up by taking the student on trips in the community so that he or she can operate a self-service elevator. Ask the student to find any signs that indicate the location of elevators. Once an elevator has been found, show the student the outside call buttons, and review the words UP and DOWN and the up and down arrows. Practice with the student until he or she can locate elevators, call for them, and operate them to go to desired locations with minimal or no assistance from you.

Be sure to introduce the emergency telephones that are available in most elevators, making sure that the student is able to use them correctly and comprehends that they should only be used in an emergency.

Secondary Level.   Tell the student that he or she must act the part of a trip leader and take you and a classmate for a trip in the community to carry out an important errand. Make sure beforehand that a self-service elevator is available at the desired location. If possible, give the student the money for a taxi (including a tip), and send him or her to a local business that is hiring part-time workers (such as a fast-food restaurant or supermarket) so that the student and his or her friend can fill out job applications. Praise the student for each successful step carried out during the trip.

Family Interventions

Infant and Toddler/Preschool.   Ask the parents to take their child for a trip in the community when they must use a taxi. Tell the parents to point out the taxi meter and to say while paying the fare, "The amount shown on this meter tells us how much money we must pay for the cost of the taxi ride." Urge the parents to also acquaint their child with self-service elevators.

Primary Level.   Ask the parents to make flashcards with numbers and letters found in an elevator and to review this written information with their child. Tell them to take these cards with them to a self-service elevator and to match them with the words on the elevator inside panel.

Intermediate Level.   Ask the parents to take their child on trips in the community in which they play the "Robot Game," which requires the parents to play the part of robots responding to the directions of their child. For example, the child says, "Find an elevator, and take us up to the sixth floor." The parents must then follow the directions. If the child is able, ask the parents to occasionally make an error for the child to correct.

Secondary Level.   If feasible, ask the parents to arrange for a trip into the community for a stated purpose such as visiting a clinic. Tell the parents to require their child to arrange the trip, pay the taxi fare, find the elevators, and operate the self-service elevator to arrive at the desired location and to return home again.

GOAL IV.

The student comprehends and responds appropriately to written information, including symbols, words, and phrases that appear on labels.

Men's Ladies'

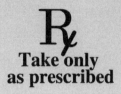

Take only
as prescribed

SPECIFIC OBJECTIVES

The student:

☐ A. Locates public bathrooms to use for washing and toileting.

☐ B. Using numeral and destination designations, identifies buses for traveling in and out of the community.

☐ C. Identifies and obeys traffic signs.

☐ D. Identifies and obeys warning signs and avoids places designated as being dangerous.

☐ E. Identifies warning words on packages and obeys their instructions.

☐ F. Follows instructions on cleaning labels that are found on clothing and other fabrics.

☐ G. Verifies size labels when purchasing clothing and household linens.

☐ H. Using information found on labels, identifies the contents of containers.

☐ I. Uses the size of packages and size notations to determine the quantity of food and other substances in the packages.

☐ J. Using price labels, tags, and store signs, identifies the prices of items being considered for purchase.

☐ K. Identifies the correct value of stamps needed to mail letters and greeting cards.

☐ L. Identifies and complies with signs that help direct people as they move about the community, such as arrows, detour signs, and signs that contain words such as PUSH, PULL, ENTRANCE, EXIT, IN, and OUT.

❏ M. Identifies the cost of admission at public facilities.

❏ N. Identifies the types of stores or businesses by their window displays and by key words on signs.

❏ O. Identifies and obeys storing and cooking directions found on food packages.

❏ P. Identifies and obeys storage and cleaning instructions found on packages containing laundry and housecleaning agents.

❏ Q. Locates the doorbells and mailboxes of friends and relatives.

❏ R. Locates signs on doors and store windows and then uses the information found there to identify the days and hours when the store or business is open.

❏ S. Locates public telephones and public telephone booths.

SUGGESTED ACTIVITIES

Specific Objective A

The student locates public bathrooms to use for washing and toileting.

Teacher Interventions

Infant and Toddler/Preschool. Place a photograph of a boy on the door of one of the boys' bathrooms in the school. Take the male student to that bathroom, and point to the photograph while saying, "See the picture of the boy on this bathroom door? That means all boys in the school may use this bathroom to wash or go to the toilet." Ask him if he is a boy. If he answers correctly, in some way (e.g., gesture, facial expression, and/or nod), say, "This is a bathroom you may use." If he does not answer correctly, review the concept of boy-girl. Do the same at the girls' bathroom door if the student is female.

Primary Level. Place a silhouette of a boy next to a photograph of a boy. Tell the student that sometimes a shape that looks like a boy is put on a public bathroom to let people know that it is a bathroom that all boys may use.

(Explain that the bathrooms in his home are *private*, not *public*, bathrooms. At this point, it may be advisable to develop the concept of private versus public.) Similarly, use a silhouette of a girl if the student is female.

Next, place the silhouette and photograph on the door of one of the boys' bathrooms directly above the written word. Then point to the written word and say, "In most schools, just the word BOYS is written on the door to let all the boys in the school know that it is a bathroom they may use."

Repeat these several steps with one of the girls' bathrooms, making sure that the student understands that he must not enter a bathroom that says GIRLS. Take the student on a tour of the school, and ask him to point out all the boys' and girls' bathrooms. Do the reverse of these steps if the student is female.

Intermediate Level. Explain to the student that most bathrooms in the community (public) for boys and men do not have the word BOYS written on the door, but rather they have the word MEN. Explain that the word MEN is written on the bathroom door to let people know that it is a bathroom for males only, that is, both boys and men. Make sure the student understands the concept of male and female. Explain, if necessary, and make certain the student understands the concept before continuing with this activity. Introduce the word WOMEN.

Take the male student to a nearby mall or other public place, and assist him in finding the men's room(s) and the women's room(s). Tell him to enter one of the men's rooms to check that it has urinals as well as commodes and to use it if needed. Stop him if he attempts to enter an inappropriate bathroom.

At this point introduce him to the sign REST ROOM(S). Also introduce him to the symbol and word that indicate that a toilet stall or facility is for the use of a person who is physically disabled and would have extreme difficulty in using the commode or be completely unable to do so. Do all of the appropriate steps if your student is female.

Secondary Level. Point out to the student that public bathrooms sometimes have other words on their doors besides BOYS, MEN, GIRLS, and WOMEN that indicate the sex of the people who may appropriately use them. Make sure that the student understands that the word *sex*, as in application forms (show the student samples of forms that require the applicant to indicate his sex), is a way to identify a very important characteristic of a person.

Make a chart (see Figure 1.7) of alternate ways that public bathrooms are labeled, for example, SEÑORS, SEÑORAS, BUOYS, GULLS, GENTLEMEN, and LADIES. Review the chart by asking the student to identify the "sex" of each of the bathroom door words.

Show the student photographs of actual bathroom doors found in the local community that have alternate words or other symbols on them. Show a videotape of a male volunteer locating an appropriate public bathroom after rejecting a bathroom with the wrong sex designation. Repeat this activity with a female volunteer.

Finally, tell the student that if he or she is confused by a strange label or symbol on a bathroom door, he or she needs to ask someone for directions. Practice saying, "Excuse me, can you please tell me where the rest rooms are located?" or "Excuse me, can you tell me where the women's room is?"

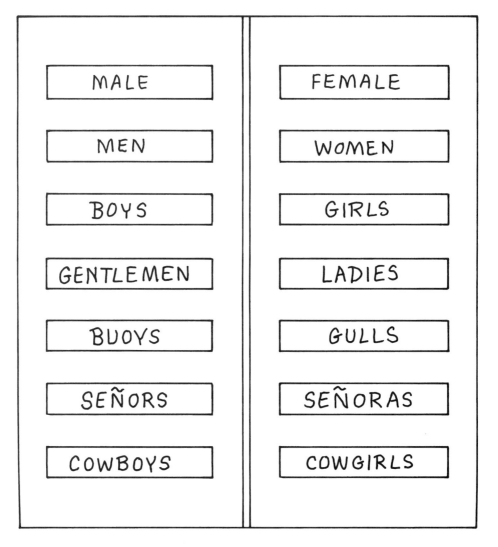

FIGURE 1.7. Labels on public bathroom and rest room doors.

Family Interventions

Infant and Toddler/Preschool. Communicate directly with the male student's father or other male family member. Tell him to take the child to a public bathroom, if available, where there is a silhouette of a male figure. Tell the male family member to remind the child that he is a boy and to comment that the shape of the figure on the door tells him that both of them can enter the bathroom. Ask him to stand outside the bathroom for awhile so that he can point out to the child that only boys and men are entering.

Tell him to then take the child into the bathroom and point out and comment on the presence of urinals as well as commodes and the boys and men who are there. Tell him to also point out to the child that there are no girls or women there because they must use a different bathroom. Have a female family member follow similar steps if the child is female.

Primary Level. Tell the father or other male family member to take the male child to school one day at a time when he is likely to need to use the bathroom. Tell the parent to take him on a tour of the building for the purpose of identifying all the appropriate bathrooms as well as all those that are not appropriate. Tell the family member to ask the child to locate an appropriate bathroom when one is needed.

Also, ask the father or other male family member to take the child to a public place and to introduce him to the words MEN and WOMEN. Ask him to repeat the activity outlined directly above for the infant/toddler, this time with the child identifying the bathrooms from the words written on the door. Have a female family member follow similar steps if the child is female.

Intermediate Level. Tell the parents to take their child to a public place, such as a shopping center, and ask the student to locate all the women's rooms located there (e.g., in the mall proper and within stores). Tell the parents to ask their child to point out all the men's rooms after the child has correctly identified all the women's rooms. Remind the parents to review the concept of male and female, if necessary.

Next, tell each of them to take turns asking their child to help them find a bathroom (or rest room) because they need to use one.

Secondary Level. Ask the parents to take their youngster on several trips into the community to identify any alternate labels that are used to designate appropriate-sex bathrooms. Tell them to make sure that the student understands why these alternate labels indicate the sex of the bathroom facility, for example, "This restaurant is a seafood restaurant, and BUOYS [while showing the student a picture of a buoy] has been written on the bathroom door because buoys are often seen in large bodies of water such as the sea, and the word looks like and sounds a lot like BOY, which we already know means that it is a bathroom that males may use." (In fact, one pronunciation for this word is /boi/.) Remind the parents to follow the same procedure for the designation GULLS.

 ## Specific Objective B

The student, using numeral and destination designations, identifies buses for traveling in and out of the community.

Teacher Interventions

Infant and Toddler/Preschool. Place numerals around the classroom or learning area. Place a different numeral, for example, on the clothes closet, the bookshelves, and the sink cabinets. When going to these places, point out the numerals and say, for instance, "See the number 1 on the clothes closet? That is a sign that helps us remember that we put our clothes in the closet behind this door," and "See the number 2 on the cabinets under the sink? That is a sign that helps us to remember that we keep our cleaning supplies in there." (Note: It is not necessary that the student identify these signs; the idea that numerals are used as a sign or signal is the point of this activity.)

Primary Level. Identify the public (or private) buses that stop near the school and that have local routes. (A call to the transit authority will help you identify these buses, their starting and finishing points, their stops, their route numbers, and the pattern of their routes.) Show the student a videotape of these buses as they arrive at, stop at, and then depart from bus stop(s) near the school, and point out numerals, words, and other identifying features.

Then, take the student to these bus stop(s), and comment on the fact that most buses for people who wish to travel in the community have numbers on them that match numbers that may be found on signs at bus stops where those particular buses stop.

Intermediate Level. Draw a pictorial map of the key destination points to which the student might travel in the community. On this map use photographs or draw pictures of the student's residence, school, post office, or place of worship (if appropriate). Draw heavy black lines down those streets that are used as bus routes. At the bus stop nearest the student's home, draw a picture of a bus. On this drawing, write in the numeral designation of the bus and its finishing point, for example, "5 Civic Center." Make sure that you include the bus that makes the return trip to the student's home.

Use this map to ask the student to indicate the various destinations in the community to which he or she might wish to go, the appropriate bus to be taken to get there, and the bus to be taken to return home.

Repeat this activity, this time with the school as the starting point for trips into the community. Ask the student to help you plan a local field trip, for example, to the Children's Museum, zoo, or similar high interest area. Follow up by taking the planned field trip.

Secondary Level.   Assist the student in making a chart (see Figure 1.8) of all relevant bus routes from his or her residence to various important (to the student, his or her family members, and friends) sites in the community, for example, the Motor Vehicle Bureau, a neighborhood clinic, a potential job site, a recreation center, or the unemployment office.

Review the chart with the student until he or she is able to identify the information located on the chart. Follow up by having the student make a wallet-sized card, if possible, of the chart.

Family Interventions

Infant and Toddler/Preschool.   Tell the parents to take their child into the community and point out numerals used on various signs. Explain to the parents that they should not expect their child to identify the numerals but should merely draw their child's attention to them.

Primary Level.   Ask the parents to take their child to bus stops near their home. Tell them to point out various clues that signal the location of a bus stop: a sketch of a bus or part of a bus on a sign, the words BUS STOP or TRANSIT STOP, the number of the bus route on a sign, the curb painted with a colored line, and so on. Tell them to engage in a game of "Find the Bus Stops."

Intermediate Level.   Ask the parents to take their child for bus rides to key locations in their community (e.g., a visit to a friend or relative, a place of worship, a shopping center, and a recreation site). Tell them to take follow-up trips in which their child is expected to lead the way, including locating the bus stop, identifying the correct bus by its numeral and destination designations, and identifying landmarks that indicate that they will soon have to signal the bus driver that they wish to disembark. Ask the parents to make videotapes of these trips as part of their collection of family "home movies."

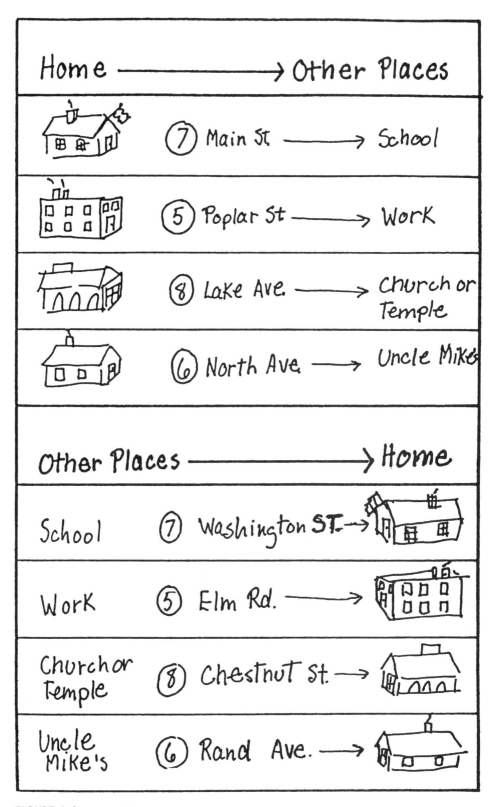

FIGURE 1.8. Bus chart.

Secondary Level. Ask the parents to take their child to the depot(s) of the bus line(s) that go to other towns and cities. Tell them to take their youngster on a tour of the depot and to point out various places and objects such as the announcement board, the bus schedule board, the waiting room, the ticket counter, and the information desk. Remind them to explain the purpose of each of these objects and places and to ask their youngster to listen for announcements of arrivals and departures.

Ask them to make sure they assist their youngster in identifying the numerals and destination designations found on buses and on signs that indicate departure and arrival lanes. Ask them to follow up with a visit to railroad stations and an airport if these are available in the community.

  ## Specific Objective C

The student identifies and obeys traffic signs.

Teacher Interventions

Infant and Toddler/Preschool. Take the student for a short walk in the community to an intersection where there is a traffic light with just two signal lights (red and green). Stop at this intersection, and comment on the traffic light. Tell the student to notice that the light changes colors (if the student is able to identify colors) or the light at the top sometimes is on, and, at other times, the light at the bottom is on.

Ask the child to point to the light when the light at the top (or red light) is on. Once the student does this successfully, switch to asking him or her to point to the light when the light on the bottom (or green light) is on.

Primary Level. Take the student for a short walk to where there is a traffic light. At the intersection, ask the student to notice the stopping and starting patterns of cars, trucks, buses, and other vehicles as well as the crossing and waiting-to-cross patterns of people (pedestrians). Point out that the lights are signals that have been put there to let people know when they can cross or should wait to cross and to let drivers know when they must stop or when they can move.

Explain that when the light facing the student is green (the bottom light), he or she usually may cross the street safely. Warn, however, that it may not always be safe to do so because bad, reckless, and drunk drivers will sometimes ignore or disobey the traffic light.

Also explain that emergency vehicles are allowed to disregard traffic signs because they must rush to help people or a person who needs help, and therefore people must not only follow the GO signal indicated by the bottom or green light but also pay attention to the traffic pattern. Additionally, explain that the safest time to cross is when the bottom or green light first goes on, as then there will be, more likely, enough time to cross the street safely.

Intermediate Level. Take the student on trips into the community. Ask him or her to practice obeying traffic lights and traffic patterns to cross streets. Introduce the white solid or dotted lines (zebras) that are frequently found at corners and at other locations to indicate a safety pedestrian zone. Indicate that these lines indicate safe crossing areas, and then demonstrate how to use them safely. Again, be certain that the student understands that some drivers disregard these safety zones.

Next, introduce other traffic signals such as WALK and DON'T WALK signs. Practice obeying any of the signs found in the community. Follow up with an in-class activity in which you set up a simulated intersection with mock traffic lights and with some students acting as pedestrians and other students acting as drivers.

Engage the student in crossing the street when both the traffic light and the vehicular pattern indicate that it is safe and in not crossing the street when the light and traffic patterns indicate it is not safe to do so. Once the student responds appropriately to traffic lights, including those with three signal lights (red, yellow, and green), introduce and develop the concept for the other traffic signs, such as STOP and YIELD signs.

Secondary Level. Ask the student to lead you on a hiking trip with the student acting as "tour leader." Reward the student for obeying traffic signs and for observing safety rules. Whenever an unfamiliar sign is encountered, be sure to explain its "message." Plan the trip so that a variety of signs may be experienced, including two-way, three-way, and four-way stop signs and other signs available in the community.

Family Interventions

Infant and Toddler/Preschool. Ask the parents to teach their child the concept of light. Explain that most infants/toddlers are fascinated by the "magic" of a light that is illuminated. Many parents enjoy the game of turning a light switch on, directing the child's attention to the now illuminated light by pointing to it, saying, "light," and then turning the light off and repeating the "game." Ask the parents to inform you when their child has begun to look at the light in anticipation of it being turned on when they say the word "light."

Primary Level. Ask the parents to take their child for a walk in their home community. Explain the Teacher Intervention activity suggested for the primary level, and ask them to do the same for several walks in their home community.

Intermediate Level. Ask the parents to arrange to take their child for several car rides in the community. Ask them to point out the various traffic signs from the viewpoint of the driver. Tell them to also comment on those pedestrians who are crossing streets safely and those who are not.

Secondary Level. Ask the parents to show their youngster a copy of the Motor Vehicle Bureau's driver's manual. Ask them to review the section on traffic signs. Tell them to help their youngster interpret these signs, first from the driver's viewpoint and second from the pedestrian's viewpoint.

 Specific Objective D

The student identifies and obeys warning signs and avoids places designated as being dangerous.

TEACHER INTERVENTIONS

Infant and Toddler/Preschool. Take the student on a tour of the school building, and point out tools and equipment that can be dangerous if not handled or used properly, for example, scissors in the classroom, knives in the cafeteria, power tools in a shop area, a stove in the home economics suite. Explain how these tools and equipment can be dangerous if they are not used carefully.

   The basic point of this activity is to introduce and develop the concept of "dangerous" and the idea of "caution."

Primary Level. Prepare for this activity by taking walks into the community to locate warning signs. Then follow up by taking the student for a walk into the community and on a variety of school-sponsored field trips. Point out any warning signs, and explain the specific dangers involved. Upon your return to the school, write an experience story and make an experience chart of the warning or danger words and the warning signs you discovered on your trip.

Intermediate Level. Make up a board game of "Caution—Danger Ahead!" that involves spinning a wheel to indicate the number of steps to be advanced and then advancing one's assigned or selected pawn (children, men, and women playing pieces) to various travel destinations, for example, the playground, the toy store, the bowling alley, and the community swimming pool.

Along with the "Go Ahead—You Are Keeping Away from Dangerous Places" notations printed on the board, write warnings such as: "Danger—Men at Work—Take the Detour Path to the Left" and "Stop! You Ignored the Sign to Keep Off the Grass! Return to Go!" Play the game as often as needed until the student is able to read and explain the warning signs.

Secondary Level. Present the student with a chart of warning signs (see Figure 1.9). Review each of them, and then ask the student to tutor a peer in identifying and explaining these words and signs. Tell the student to be sure to explain the possible outcomes of ignoring these signs, including possible bodily harm, serious injury, and problems with the law.

Family Interventions

Infant and Toddler/Preschool. Tell the parents to take their child on a tour of their residence and to point out tools and equipment found there that could be dangerous if not handled or used properly or safely, for example, the tools in the toolbox, knives, the stove, and other appliances. Remind them to pay particular attention to electrical equipment and items with sharp edges and points. Tell them that the main purpose of this activity is to develop the concept of "danger" and "dangerous."

Primary Level. Ask the parents to take their child for frequent walks into the community. Encourage them to point out any warning signs found there and to explain the possible dangers involved. Remind them to demonstrate the appropriate behavior and to require their child to model the behavior. Tell them to be sure they review the warning words and signs encountered on their walks.

Intermediate Level. Ask the parents to take their child on walks in the community with which he or she is familiar. Tell them to say to their child that he or she is the group leader on this trip and must get the family to its destination *safely*. Remind the parents to praise the child for being a good leader who obeyed all the warning signs and got them safely to their destination.

Secondary Level. Ask the parents to cut stories out of magazines and newspapers that depict accidents and tragedies that occurred because someone failed to heed warning signs. (You may wish to orient the parents to this activity by giving them one or two sample stories as a guide.) Tell them to give these stories to the student to read and discuss, if appropriate to their youngster's reading ability.

Warning Words

No	Private	Danger	Dangerous
Beware	Prohibited	Watch Out	Fragile
Do Not	Keep Off	Warning	Emergency

Warning Signs

IN THE COUNTRY
- No Hunting
- No Campfires
- Remember to Put Fires Out
- No Trespassing
- Private Road
- Private Property
- Do Not Drink the Water
- No Picnicking

FOR THE PASSENGER
- Fasten Seat Belts
- Watch Your Step
- No Smoking
- Emergency Door
- No Littering

AT BEACHES, LAKES, QUARRIES, AND OTHER BODIES OF WATER
- Swimming Prohibited
- Wading Prohibited
- Fishing Prohibited
- Diving Prohibited
- Keep Off the Rocks
- Polluted

IN BUILDINGS
- Hold on to Moving Hand Rail
- Watch Your Step
- Emergency Exit
- Elevator Out of Order
- Closing Times
- Warning—Elevators should not be used during fires!

FIGURE 1.9. Warning words and sign charts.

IN PARKS
AND ZOOS
{
Do Not Pick the Flowers
Do Not Feed the Animals
No Bicycling
Bicycling Prohibited
Keep Off the Grass
Keep Out
Closing Times
No Littering
No Standing up on Rides
}

FOR THE
PEDESTRIAN
{
Beware of Dog
Pedestrians Prohibited
No Trespassing
Keep Out
No Loitering
Quiet Zone
Curb Your Dog
No Dogs Allowed
No Hitchhiking
Danger — Men at Work
Danger — High Voltage
Don't Walk
Private
Railroad Crossing
Danger — Electricity
}

AT A LIBRARY { Quiet Please

ON
EQUIPMENT
AND
PACKAGES
{
Do Not Open Case
Do Not Remove
Fragile
Handle with Care
This Side Up
}

FIGURE 1.9. *Continued.*

If the youngster is unable to read the material independently or with minimal assistance, ask them to read the story to him or her and to engage their youngster in a discussion of the character's unsafe or unwise behavior and its serious or tragic consequences.

Specific Objective E

The student identifies warning words on packages and obeys their instructions.

Teacher Interventions

Infant and Toddler/Preschool. Paste Mr. Yuk labels on packages containing potentially dangerous substances. Show these labels to the student. Ask the student to look at you, and then imitate the Mr. Yuk face and say, "This face shows that there is something 'yucky' in this bottle [or box] that we should not put in or near our mouth or eyes or any other part of our face."

Follow up by asking the student to point to each of the Mr. Yuk labels and to join you in imitating the Mr. Yuk face.

Primary Level. Make a collection of items that are dangerous if ingested, used near the eyes, or stored or mixed improperly. Show the student each item, point to the words of warning, and indicate the dangers involved in as many ways as possible. Be sure to demonstrate the proper and safe way to use each of the items in the collection. Ask the student to use each item in turn and monitor and assist as needed. Emphasize the proper storage of each item. Make a safety videotape for instructional, monitoring, and review purposes.

Intermediate Level. Make a list of the key words and phrases of warning that appear on commonly used packages (see Figure 1.10). (Do not put all the possible words on this list as you, at a later time, will expect the student to add additional warning words that he or she discovers while experiencing new substances that contain warnings on their packages.)

Use the list as a guide for the student in exploring commonly used packages for warnings. Encourage the student to match the words and phrases on the list with the same or similar words and phrases found on packages.

Secondary Level. Engage the student in a variety of cleaning, repairing, and restoring processes that he or she is likely to encounter at home or on a job.

- CAUTION — Eye Irritant

- Harmful If Swallowed

- Keep Out of Reach of Children

- CAUTION — Not For Personal Use

- Do Not Use with . . .

- Not Recommended for Use on . . .

- CAUTION — Contents Under Pressure. Store away from Heat

- For External Use Only

- Do Not Exceed Recommended Dosage

- If Irritation Occurs Discontinue Use

- Shake Well

- WARNING — Keep This and All Medicines Out of Children's Reach

- WARNING — This Preparation May Cause Drowsiness. When Taking It, Do Not Operate Machinery . . .

- Poisonous

FIGURE 1.10. Chart of warning words on packages.

Present the student with the necessary items. Tell him or her that before beginning the project he or she must read the packages not only to discover the sequence of steps to follow but also to find out if there are any warnings that should be observed in carrying out these steps.

Demonstrate the safe use of the product, and monitor the student as he or she models your behavior. Encourage the student to proceed independently when he or she evidences both skill and appropriate caution.

Family Interventions

Infant and Toddler/Preschool.   Tell the parents to paste Mr. Yuk labels on packages (including medicines) containing potentially dangerous substances. Tell them to show these labels to their child and to ask him or her to look at them as they imitate the Mr. Yuk face. Remind them to say, "This face shows that there is something 'yucky' in this bottle [or box] that we should not put in or near our mouth or eyes or any other part of our face." Tell them to then ask the student to point to each of the Mr. Yuk labels and to make the Mr. Yuk face.

Primary Level.   Ask the parents to tell their child to help them carry out a household cleaning or repairing task. Tell them to demonstrate how they first read the instructions on the package and pay particular attention to the words and phrases of warning. Tell the parents to read these words and phrases aloud and to explain what they mean.

Remind them to demonstrate the appropriate behavior as it is governed by the warning words and phrases, for example, "I am wearing rubber gloves because the label on the package warned me that the contents of this package can burn my skin!"

Intermediate Level.   Ask the parents to tell their child to explain the warning words and phrases on a household cleaning or repairing product to a younger sibling or family member and to direct that "tutee" in safely carrying out a cleaning or repairing activity in the home involving the use of the materials. (If a younger family member is not available, ask the parent to role-play the part.) Remind the parents to monitor the process as needed.

Secondary Level.   Tell the parents that they should seek to involve their youngster, on a regular basis, in carrying out selected household tasks that involve the use of products that have warning labels. Tell them to supervise the activity as necessary and to reward their youngster for using the product safely and correctly, for storing the product in its appropriate storage area, and for completing the job satisfactorily.

Specific Objective F

The student follows instructions on cleaning labels that are found on clothing and other fabrics.

Teacher Interventions

Infant and Toddler/Preschool. Show the student examples of clothing and other fabrics (e.g., sheets, curtains, and tablecloths). Point to the soiled and dirty spots and say, "This needs to be cleaned before we wear or use it again."

Assist the student in discriminating between clothing and other fabrics that are clean and those that are soiled (based on visual evidence) and need to be cleaned. (The sole purpose of this activity is to make the student aware that clothing and other fabrics, at times, will need to be cleaned.)

Primary Level. Bring into the classroom clothing and other fabrics that need to be cleaned. After the student and you have established that they need to be cleaned, refer to the label on one of the items and read aloud the directions appearing on the label. Then comment on the fact that clothing and other fabrics frequently have labels with cleaning instructions. Ask the student to then find all the labels on the clothing and fabrics that are placed before him or her.

Make sure that you provide at least one sample of an item that can be machine washed, one that must be washed by hand, and one that needs to be dry-cleaned only. Explain these different cleaning instructions to the student.

Intermediate Level. Make a chart containing words and phrases with an accompanying rebus symbol for each of the items on the chart, for example, a picture of a pair of hands for HAND WASH and a picture of an iron with a big red X drawn across it to indicate DO NOT IRON. Make certain that you have included representative labels that are commonly found on clothing and fabrics.

Ask the student to find the cleaning labels on clothing and fabrics that you have brought to class. Ask the student to match the words and phrases on the labels to their counterparts on the chart. Revise the chart by removing each of the accompanying rebus symbols (see Figure 1.11) and work toward developing the student's ability to read and comprehend the cleaning directions.

Secondary Level. Set aside a wash day, and ask the student to bring his or her clothing and other fabrics that need to be cleaned. Ask the student to separate the clothing into three piles: those that can be machine washed, those that must be hand washed, and those that he or she must take home because they must be taken to a dry cleaner.

Wash Separately
Dry Clean Only
Drip Dry
Wash, Warm
Tumble Dry
Machine Wash, Warm
Line or Tumble Dry
Do Not Use Chlorine Bleach
Do Not Bleach
Hand Wash in Cold Water with Woolite
Lay Flat to Dry
Do Not Iron
Do Not Dry Clean
Hanger Dry
Do Not Dry in Direct Sunlight
Flame Retardant—Wash Before Wearing
Do Not Use Soap
Machine Wash and Dry
Wash Colors Separately
Dry Clean, Furrier Method Recommended
Hand Wash, Cold Water, Mild Soap
Sponge Spots with Damp Cloth

FIGURE 1.11. Label instructions chart.

Supervise the student as he or she hand washes those items that should only be hand washed and as he or she uses the classroom's or school's washer and dryer. Provide assistance when necessary while encouraging independent functioning.

Family Interventions

Infant/Primary. Ask the parents to include their child in those activities in which decisions are made relevant to the need to have a clothing or other fabric item cleaned. Tell them that the objective is simply to assist their child in determining when a clothing or fabric item needs to be cleaned.

Remind them to show their child how they hand wash an item and how they use a home washer and dryer or ones found in a laundromat. Tell them to set aside a storage area in the home for those items that must be taken to the dry cleaner.

Primary Level. Ask the parents to give their child chores that he or she must accomplish in the home. Tell the parent that, as part of the child's assigned duties, they should assign the task of identifying when an article of clothing or a fabric item needs to be cleaned. Tell them, whenever their child correctly identifies an item that needs to be cleaned, to deliberately and noticeably read the label and discuss the action to be taken as a result of reading the directions on the label.

Intermediate Level. Ask the parents to cut out cleaning labels from discarded clothing and other fabrics and paste them on index cards. Tell them to use these cards to play a match game (i.e., match the phrases to their pictures, as in DRY CLEAN ONLY and a picture or photograph of a dry cleaning store and as in USE COLD WATER ONLY and a picture of a glass of water with an ice cube in it). Tell them that they can also use these cards as sight vocabulary flashcards.

Secondary Level. Ask the parents to assign their youngster the task of separating clothing and other fabrics into piles for cleaning purposes based on the directions appearing on their labels. Remind them to reward the youngster for successfully carrying out this task. Tell them to follow up by requiring the youngster to clean those items that he or she can and to take the others to a dry cleaner.

 ## Specific Objective G

The student verifies size labels when purchasing clothing and household linens.

Teacher Interventions

Infant and Toddler/Preschool. Show the student several dolls of different sizes. Then show sample articles of doll clothing made for these dolls. Engage the student in a dressing session with these dolls. In each case match the right-sized garment to the doll just before dressing it and say, "This doll is much bigger than this other doll [while pointing to each doll in turn], so we must dress it with a larger-sized dress [or blouse or hat or sweater, etc.]."

Follow up by assisting the student as he or she puts the garment on the doll. Continue by changing the garment and replacing it with another garment of "the right size."

Primary Level. After checking with the student's parents to determine his or her clothing sizes and to ask their assistance by sending in samples of his or her clothing, review the student's sizes with him or her.

Then ask the student to locate his or her clothing from other articles of clothing in the classroom. After the student has located all his or her clothing, demonstrate how to find the size labels, and then read them aloud and say, "You sure know your own clothing! Yes, this is your shirt. You wear size ___, and this label says that this shirt is a size ___ shirt."

Assist the student in making his or her own personal size chart to serve as a reference when he or she goes shopping. (Update, when appropriate, as the child matures physically.)

Intermediate Level. Set up a mock clothing store in the classroom with racks, shelves, bins, and counters. Place different sizes of clothing (including shirts, jackets, suits, undershirts, shorts, socks, shoes, pants, and belts) in the store, including the student's current size in the store's inventory.

Tell the student (role-playing the part of a customer) to browse through the store and to locate articles of clothing that are his or her size. Ask the student to show you these items as you are playing the part of a salesperson. Make a videotape of the role-play for instructional, monitoring, and review purposes.

Secondary Level. Present the student with two hypothetical situations in which he or she must purchase household linens. One of these situations involves purchasing household linens for a new home and/or for new furniture. The other situation involves purchasing household linens as a gift.

Show the student how and where to find size notations on household linens themselves or on their packages. After the student has identified the sizes of the linens available, engage him or her in a role-play in which he or she must locate the correct sizes of linens (sheets, pillowcases, curtains, drapes, tablecloths, quilts, bedspreads, etc.) from a classroom mock store counter.

Family Interventions

Infant and Toddler/Preschool. Ask the parents to take their child along on family shopping trips to clothing stores or to clothing sections in department or discount stores. Tell them to comment on the fact that they must first look for the right size before making a decision on what to buy. Remind them to say such things to the salesperson as, "My daughter wears a size ___ sweater. Where can I find sweaters that will fit her?"

Primary Level. Ask the parents to accompany their child to a clothing store or to a clothing department in a department or discount store. Ask them to help their child find the sections of the store that have his or her size and to assist the child in first identifying the size from clothing labels and then making decisions based on color and style preferences and budgetary constraints.

Intermediate Level. Ask the parents to take their child to a store where he or she may purchase needed clothing. Tell them to find the clothing the child would like to purchase and to ask him or her to bring the selections to them to verify that they are the right size, are within their budget, and are appropriate in terms of colors and styles.

Secondary Level. Ask the parents to include their youngster in shopping trips involving the purchase of household linens (tablecloths, drapes, curtains, sheets, pillowcases, blankets, bedspreads, quilts, etc.) and less frequently purchased clothing items such as belts, boots, slippers, hats, and gloves. Remind them to assist their youngster in locating size notations as they appear on these items. Tell them to reward their child for all independent action.

 ## Specific Objective H

The student, using information found on labels, identifies the contents of containers.

Teacher Interventions

Infant and Toddler/Preschool. Bring in samples of food (vegetables and fruits) in its natural state and packages of these same food items in glass jars or bottles. Point to the unpackaged item and say its name. Then point to the picture on the packaged item, comment on its similar appearance to the item in its natural state, and repeat the name of the item.

Primary Level.   Set up a class store that is stocked with various food packages that have pictures that provide clues to the contents. Include bottles, jars, boxes with cellophane windows (e.g., pasta, beans, rice, etc.), boxes without a "window," and cans. Point to the pictures on the labels, and ask the student to identify the contents.

Follow up, over a several-day period, by asking the student to identify the contents of several of the packages, assisting him or her in opening the packages and pointing out the similarity of the contents to the pictures (and unpacked food items), and, finally, using the contents for a class snack or meal. Begin to assist the student in identifying the names of the food items on the labels. Make flashcards of these names and use them for rapid word recognition exercises.

Intermediate Level.   Assist the student in differentiating food and nonfood items from their labels. Make certain that a nonfood item such as dishwashing liquid that has a picture of a lemon is identified correctly as a nonfood item that should not be ingested. Ask the student to assist you in stocking the shelves of the school's or classroom's store, making sure that food items are stored separately from nonfood items.

Take the student to a nearby supermarket or grocery store to see that nonfood items are stored in different sections. Continue word recognition activities by making additional sight vocabulary flashcards of names appearing on labels. Ask the student to make a scrapbook or chart of labels on products that he or she uses. Make sure that the student uses words and pictures as found on these items.

Secondary Level.   Give the student a handwritten shopping list, and ask him or her to do the weekly shopping in the classroom or school store. Place on the list items that he or she must identify by package labels that have only word clues as well as items that have both picture and word clues to the contents. Add the dimension of specifying brand names when a brand distinction is deemed appropriate.

Family Interventions

Infant and Toddler/Preschool.   Ask the parents to show their child the packages they use in meal preparation. Tell them to comment on pictures appearing on the labels and to show their child the contents and to point out their similarity to the pictures on the label. Tell them to review this when the child is eating the snack or meal item by once again showing the child the picture on the empty (or partially empty) package.

Primary Level.   Ask the parents to take their child on trips to the supermarket or grocery. Remind them to "talk aloud" their shopping decisions, for example, "I need a can of peas to make the tuna casserole. Here is a can of peas; I can tell from the picture on the can." Tell the parents to then show their child the can selected and to point to the picture as they say, "Here is a can of peas that I was looking for!"

Intermediate Level. Ask the parents to involve their child in planning weekly menus and in conducting an inventory of food on hand. For example, tell them to say things such as "You and I have decided that we are going to have spaghetti on Thursday. Check the kitchen cabinet to see if we have any packages of spaghetti, tomato paste, and tomato sauce. Since we will also have broccoli, check the freezer to see if there is a package of frozen broccoli."

Tell the parents to assist their child in making up a shopping list for those items needed that are not on hand and must be purchased. Ask them to follow up by taking their child on the shopping trip and actually preparing the meals with their child's participation in the several food preparation processes, including storage before use, cleaning of any food items requiring washing, cooking, cleaning up after a meal, and storing leftovers, as appropriate to the situation.

Secondary Level. Ask the parents to give their youngster the responsibility of doing the weekly shopping, gradually increasing the complexity of the task by, for example, increasing the size of the shopping list; adding size, weight, and number specifications; and making brand name restrictions.

 ## Specific Objective 1

The student uses the size of packages and size notations to determine the quantity of food and other substances in the packages.

Teacher Interventions

Infant and Toddler/Preschool. Determine the student's preferred foods. Purchase these food items in several different-sized packages. Start with two maximally different sizes and introduce the polar concept of big-small. Open each of these packages, and fill a container with the contents. Point out that there was more of the item in the *big* box. When using three sizes, introduce the concept of *not big, big, bigger,* and *biggest.*

Primary Level. Make a meal-serving chart (see Figure 1.12) that shows the number of people who can be served with each size package of a specific food item. Introduce the terms *regular, family,* and *economy size.* Follow up by

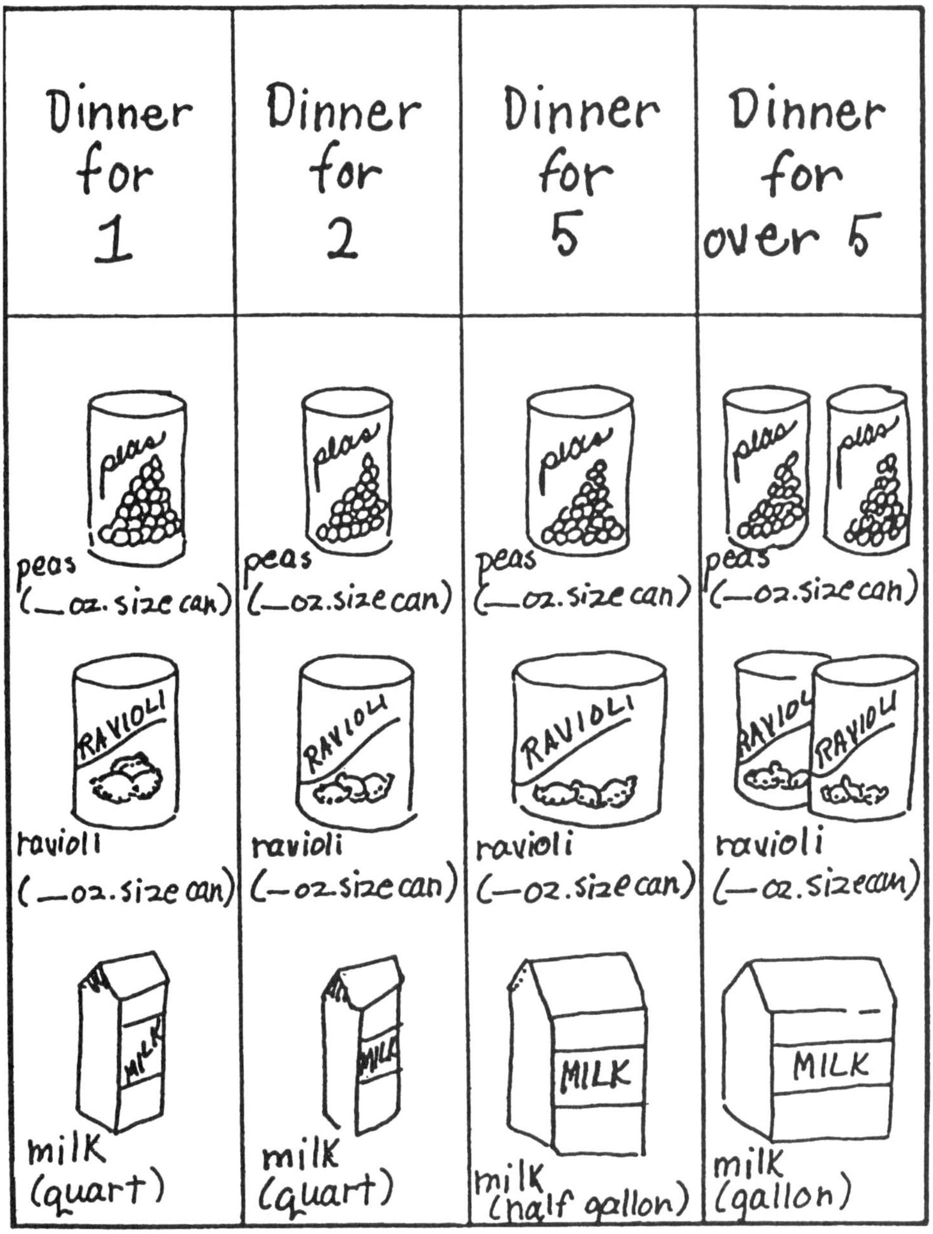

Dinner for 1	Dinner for 2	Dinner for 5	Dinner for over 5
peas (__oz. size can)	peas (__oz.size can)	peas (__oz. size can)	peas (__oz.size can)
ravioli (__oz. size can)	ravioli (__oz.size can)	ravioli (__oz.size can)	ravioli (__oz.sizecan)
milk (quart)	milk (quart)	milk (half gallon)	milk (gallon)

FIGURE 1.12. Meal-serving chart.

asking the student to assist you in planning a meal or class party based on recipe information that you read to him. Encourage the student to use his or her serving chart as a guide to making up a shopping list.

Intermediate Level. Make a meal-serving chart (see Figure 1.13) that shows the number of people who can be served with each size package (in this chart

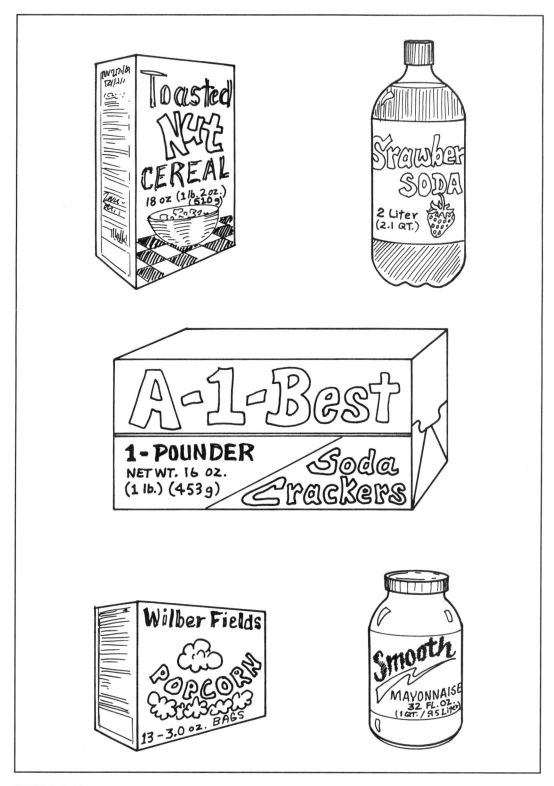

FIGURE 1.13. Weight, size, and quantity notations on food packages.

use not only size designations but also weight, volume, and quantity designations, if applicable as they appear on food items). Introduce the various size (economy), weight (___ -oz. size), volume (gallon), and quantity (24 Net Contents) designations appearing on labels. Show the student samples of food packages with various size and weight notations.

After sufficient review, ask the student to assist in planning a meal or class party by reading recipes and making up a shopping list with appropriate size and weight notations. Remind him or her to use the serving chart, if needed.

Secondary Level. After the student has made up a shopping list that includes size, weight, volume, and quantity designations, send him or her to the school or classroom store to purchase these items. Make certain that the store has a variety of sizes so that the student must make a number of decisions based on his or her shopping list specifications. Reward the student for being a good shopper if he or she is successful. If problems arise, reteach and review.

Family Interventions

Infant and Toddler/Preschool. Ask the parents to show their child different-sized packages of food and other items stored in their home. Tell the parents to make such comments as "This package of soap powder is bigger [or *larger*] than this package. There is a lot more soap powder in this box!"

Primary Level. Ask the parents to show their child different-sized food packages, to open these packages, to show their child the difference in quantity, and then to prepare the contents of each package separately. Remind them to show their child the results by saying, for example, "The small box of pudding only made enough pudding for your brother, your sister, you, and me. The big box made enough pudding for all of us plus Grandma, Grandpa, and Mommy [or Daddy]."

Intermediate Level. Ask the parents to assist their child in translating favorite family recipes into package size or quantity of packages needed to carry out the recipe. Tell the parents to vary this activity to cover the size and quantity of packages needed not only for the family but also for when different numbers of guests are involved.

Secondary Level. Ask the parents to require their youngster to make up a shopping list for a party or meal that he or she, without help, plans to prepare for the family and guests. Remind them to allow the youngster to carry out all the planning and executing of the party or meal without any assistance from them. If assistance is required, ask the parents to review the aspects of the task with which their youngster is experiencing difficulty.

Specific Objective J

The student, using price labels, tags, and store signs, identifies the prices of items being considered for purchase.

Teacher Interventions

Infant and Toddler/Preschool. Bring to class food, clothing, and other items that have price labels and tags on or attached to them. Show the student each of these items and their labels and tags while making such comments as, "I bought this sweater because it was exactly what I needed and wanted and when I looked at the price on the label [or tag] [while demonstrating the action of doing so], I decided the price was right, so I bought it."

Primary Level. Take the student for a trip to a local supermarket or grocery store and show him or her where the price labels are, whether on the package itself or on the shelf or counter. After you have done a few, ask the student to locate others on a variety of packages.

With the permission of store owners or managers, you may follow up with trips to stores in which prices are noted on price tags, such as furniture and clothing stores. Again, demonstrate locating the price tags and then asking the student to do so. At this point, assist the student in identifying the dollar sign ($), the cents sign (¢), and the decimal point.

Intermediate Level. Make a chart of price notations (see Figure 1.14), and ask the student to match price labels and tags appearing on actual food, clothing, tools, appliance items, and other items. You may wish to use the chart to play a Bingo type of game. Once the student correctly matches the item's price with the price on the chart, assist him or her in identifying and naming the prices appearing on representative labels.

Prepare flashcards of different money amounts, and require the student to correctly indicate dollar and cent values.

Secondary Level. Schedule a fair, white elephant sale, or flea market at which you plan to raise money for school equipment or for a charitable organization or cause. Whenever feasible, include items that the student has made in workshop and arts and crafts activities.

Assist the student, through a discussion, in making pricing decisions. Give the student price tags on which he or she must write the price of the item. Follow up by asking the student to place price labels on food and nonfood items before placing them on shelves in the school or classroom store.

PRICE BINGO				
$9.99	75¢	$29.01	34¢	$1.25
$1.00	50¢	$2.15	$7.00	62¢
$3.88	$6.77	FREE	$5.00	98¢
25¢	$19.98	85¢	$1.99	$12.15
$98.99	$103.77	$75.00	$70.00	$67.77

FIGURE 1.14. Price notations.

Family Interventions

Infant and Toddler/Preschool. Ask the parents to draw their child's attention to the price labels, tags, and signs appearing in the stores in which they shop. Explain to the parents that the purpose of this activity is just to begin to make their child aware that things they buy have prices that must be paid with money and is not meant to have their child identify prices.

Primary Level. Ask the parents to show their child items they have purchased. Tell them to introduce the idea that the price of the item was one of the things they considered in making the purchase. Encourage the parents to show their child the price tags and labels of some of the items and then to ask their child to locate the others.

Intermediate Level. Ask the parents to take their child on a variety of shopping trips and to locate price labels, tags, and signs. Tell them to read these aloud to their child and to point out the numbers and the dollar and cents signs (including the use of the decimal point). Ask the parents to make up a set of flashcards with price designations and to use these cards in drills with their child.

Secondary Level. Ask the parents to go to a store and check out the prices. Tell them to make up a shopping list that includes the prices of the items to be purchased and then to give the shopping list to their youngster.

Encourage them to then send their youngster into the store to make the purchases without their assistance. Remind them to reward their youngster for a successful experience and to provide assistance if needed. Ask them to repeat the activity after correcting any problems their youngster has.

Specific Objective K

The student identifies the correct value of stamps needed to mail letters and greeting cards.

Teacher Interventions

Infant and Toddler/Preschool. Bring to class envelopes from correspondence you have received. Show the student the stamps on these envelopes. Comment on the colors and designs of these stamps and how they contrast with the envelope itself.

Show the student samples of unused stamps, and tell him or her that you will use these stamps to mail letters and cards to family members and friends. Then prepare a letter or card for mailing, making sure that you emphasize attaching the stamp securely to the envelope.

Primary Level.   On special occasions such as Mother's Day and when a classmate is sick, ask the student to make a greeting card to be sent to the person concerned. Give the student a stamp in the correct amount that he or she must paste on the envelope at its appropriate location.

Bring to class stamps with different designs so that the student becomes aware that he or she must pay particular attention to the price notation as well as the design or picture so that he or she comes to realize that there are different designs for the same face value. Introduce the ideas (a) that the price of mailing a letter may change and (b) that the weight and size of a letter or card may require additional stamps or postage.

Intermediate Level.   Introduce the concept that there are different values of stamps to be used for different world locations. Show the student a map of North America and explain that North America includes the United States of America, Canada, and Mexico.

Review with the student that he or she lives in one of the states that make up the United States of America, and review the current rate for mailing in the United States. If the student is able, share with him or her the rates for the other countries in North America, and engage him or her in a "Geography Game" by giving the student locations in the United States, Canada, and Mexico and asking him or her to assist you in finding these locations.

Continue by indicating the value of the stamps needed. After the student is successful, show him or her maps of another continent, and tell the postage rate for that part of the world. Repeat the "Geography Game" for this continent, if the student is able to do so.

Secondary Level.   Set up a mock "work site" mailroom in the classroom in which the student must play the role of a "mail clerk" who is required to weigh letters and packages, check destinations, refer to postal rates, and indicate the value of stamps needed to mail the letters and packages.

Family Interventions

Infant and Toddler/Preschool.   Ask the parents to show their child letters and other correspondence that comes to their home. Tell them to comment on the stamps by speaking of the colors, pictures, and designs on them. Remind them to tell their child that letters usually must have stamps on them in order for them to be delivered to their home.

Primary Level. Ask the parents to take their child to the post office (or supermarket or other location where they can purchase postage stamps) whenever they buy stamps (including when they use post office vending machines). Ask the parents to show their child how they paste stamps on letters and greeting cards. Tell them to point out the numerical value on the stamps used.

Intermediate Level. Ask the parents to include their child in special mailings such as holiday cards and to give him or her the job of sealing the envelopes and pasting on the stamps (using water and sponges rather than licking them). Remind them also to expect their child to write to family members and friends who are out of town and to send greeting cards on happy occasions (such as birthdays) and sad occasions (such as illnesses). Ask the parents to assist their child in setting up a personal directory of important addresses.

Secondary Level. Ask the parents to give their youngster the responsibility of purchasing books of stamps and independently placing the stamps on family correspondence and then mailing letters, cards, and packages at both mailboxes and post offices.

Specific Objective L

The student identifies and complies with signs that help direct people as they move about the community, such as arrows, detour signs, and signs that contain words such as PUSH, PULL, ENTRANCE, EXIT, IN, and OUT.

Teacher Interventions

Infant and Toddler/Preschool. If there are signs in the school that indicate student traffic patterns or room locations, point these signs out to the student. Explain that the tip of the arrow, for example, points the way to the lunchroom and the red tiles on the floor and wall indicate that the classroom is nearby. If there are any other signs that direct movement in and around the school, also point them out.

Primary Level. Take the student for a trip in the community where there is an abundance of signs that assist people as they move about. (A shopping mall is an ideal location.) Point out these signs, explain their meaning, and ask the student to watch people as they, for example, approach and enter through the supermarket doorway marked ENTRANCE to "enter" the store and as they approach and leave through the supermarket door-way marked EXIT when they wish to "exit" the supermarket.

Repeat this activity for all the other signs that direct people's movement, concentrating on the development of the concept that there are signs that assist people as they move about the community. If there are locations in the community where construction activities are under way, point out the various detour and caution signs found at these sites and explain how they are telling people which way to walk or move.

As part of your review process, make a videotape of a trip in the local community in which signs are seen and obeyed by the individuals in the film.

Intermediate Level. Take the student on walks in the community to locate the various signs located there that direct people's movements. Model reading these sounds by first saying them aloud, then explaining what behavior they are requiring, and next carrying out the behavior. Proceed to expecting the student to execute the same behaviors with your guidance and then with independent practice as you move through and about the community. Be sure to include the concept that when attending public places and events, especially where there are likely to be large crowds, the student should locate the EXIT signs in case of emergencies.

Secondary Level. Arrange for a field trip into the community in which the student is expected to supervise and lead you and others. Explain that as the leader of the trip, the student is responsible for the safety of the group and that the safety of the group depends to a great extent on the student's observing and obeying the signs that guide people safely about the community.

Also, ask the parents to indicate a trip the student needs to take in the community for an individual or family purpose such as going for a job interview or meeting a visiting relative at the bus depot. Tell the student to take you on a "trial run" to the specified location. Videotape this "trial run."

Family Interventions

Infant and Toddler/Preschool. Ask the parents to take their child for trips in the community and to model identifying signs that direct their movements, by saying such things as, "The arrow on the sign is pointing in this direction [while using their arm and hand to replicate the arrow's pattern] in order to tell us that we should move this way [using the appropriate gesture] if we are going to avoid getting hurt while the sidewalk is being repaired."

Explain to them that they must then carry out the required movements while explaining, for example, "This sign is saying PUSH, so if I want to go into this store, I must push this handle, and it will help me enter."

Primary Level. Ask the parents to arrange to take their child for a car ride in the community when they will point out the various signs that direct vehicular patterns. Explain to the parents that this activity is not meant to teach the signs themselves but to develop the concept that there are signs that are placed in the community to guide the movements of cars, trucks, buses, and even bicycles.

Intermediate Level. Ask the parents to take their child for frequent trips in the community to carry out various recreational, work, consumer, and community-related activities. Tell them to explain the various signs that direct people's movement, for example, when they go shopping, go to an amusement center, go to vote, visit a care provider such as a physician, or go to pick up a paycheck. Remind them to begin to expect their child to start identifying these signs and explaining their purpose.

Secondary Level. Ask the parents to expect their youngster to independently take trips in the community to carry out various personal and family-related goals. Tell them to phase in this independent action by first going along as a "silent" observer who only provides assistance and guidance when needed and, finally (when the youngster gains consistent competence in observing signs as well as the other necessary task elements), by sending or allowing the student to take trips into the community on an independent basis.

 ## Specific Objective M

The student identifies the cost of admission at public facilities.

Teacher Interventions

Infant and Toddler/Preschool. Take the student to a recreational site in the community in which admission is charged. Take him or her with you to the ticket booth, comment on the price of admission, and draw attention to the exchange of money. Explain that in order to enjoy the recreational activity, there is a price to be paid just as there are prices on food and other goods that we use.

Primary Level. Take the student for a walk in the community. Point out movie theaters, bowling alleys, skating rinks, sports stadiums and arenas, museums, and other recreational and cultural facilities that charge admission. Read the admission prices aloud to the student, and then ask him or her to say them with you and then alone.

Point out the words posted at these ticket counters and booths: for example, PAY HERE, PLEASE PAY CASHIER, ADMISSION PRICE. Help the student acquire the concept of the word *admission* by showing its relationship to the root word *admit* and by acting it out. Review the words by showing the student a videotape of the trip and, also, by putting them on flashcards and striving for rapid recognition.

Intermediate Level. Bring to class the amusement/entertainment section of a local newspaper. Explain the words *amusement* and *entertainment*, relating them to the concept of recreation and leisure. Look with the student through this section while pointing out any listed admission prices for movies, theaters, ball games, arts and crafts shows, flea markets, pet shows, and so on.

Encourage the student to identify leisure-time pursuits of interest and to identify the key information in the advertisements and announcements, including dates, times, places, and costs of admission.

Secondary Level. Plan field trips to a variety of recreational/entertainment facilities that require admission. Give the student a memo or flyer for the facility in advance of the event. Make certain that the price of admission is specified in the memo or flyer. Tell the student to put aside the admission price and to bring money with him on the day of the outing. Tell the student to pay his or her own admission and to verify any change received.

Family Interventions

Infant and Toddler/Preschool. Ask the parents to take their child to various recreational facilities in the community such as a Children's Zoo (or petting zoo) or a Children's Museum that are likely to be of interest to a very young child. Tell the parents to make sure that they comment to their child that money must be paid so they can enter or be admitted to the facility. Remind them to then pay the admission price and to join their child in the fun experience.

Primary Level. Ask the parents to take their child to recreational/entertainment facilities and to point out price notations on signs at ticket counters and booths. Tell them to comment to each other and their child about the cost of admission and to share the decision-making process as to whether to "go in or not." Tell them to share with their child the elements they consider in deciding whether to go, such as budgetary and time constraints, interest factors, and appropriateness of the activity.

Intermediate Level. Ask the parents to engage their child in discussions at home related to family outings and to possible participation in recreational events based on information seen in newspapers, heard over the radio, seen and heard on television, shared by friends and relatives, and read in announcements seen on bulletin boards and posters and received in the mail.

Tell them to review with their child any print materials available, such as announcements and advertisements. Remind them to emphasize the price of admission as a key element in the decision process along with family interests and preferences.

Secondary Level. Ask the parents to encourage their youngster to participate with friends and family members of similar ages in community recreational activities appropriate to their age and interests. Tell them to make certain, in planning for the activity, that the youngster determines the approximate costs of the total outing, including the cost of admission, so that he or she brings sufficient money.

Specific Objective N

The student identifies the types of stores or businesses by their window displays and by key words on signs.

Teacher Interventions

Infant and Toddler/Preschool. Take the student for walks to shopping centers and malls. Tell the student to join you in looking at window displays. Say, "Tell me something you see in this window." Add to anything the student says by stating, "I see men's suits, jackets, shirts, and pants. This must be a store that sells men's clothing. It must be a men's clothing store."

Repeat this activity with other specialty stores such as pet stores, bookstores, and video stores. Be sure to end the activity by going into the store and verifying that you have "read" the window display correctly.

Primary Level. Make a chart (see Figure 1.15) of key words written on and over store windows and buildings that are likely to appear in the names of stores and businesses and that communicate their specialty. For example, BEAUTY PARLOR, BAKERY, RESTAURANT, FURNITURE, and CAFETERIA are likely to be part of the name of a store or business. Review these key words and their underlying concepts.

Then go on a trip into the community to find representative shops and businesses. Reward the student for locating and identifying these words on actual shops and businesses. Make a videotape of this trip for later review.

FIGURE 1.15. Keys words appearing over and on store windows.

Intermediate Level. Make a chart of the supermarkets; department, convenience, and discount stores; restaurants; and other businesses that exist in the student's community and near the school. Ask the student to identify those that he or she is able to, and provide help as needed in identifying those he or she cannot. Ask the student to point to the names on the chart when the names are said and to point to them also when shown advertisements and flyers that refer to these stores and businesses.

Give the student a shopping list that includes stops at several different stores and businesses, and tell him or her to tell you where he or she would go for each separate location on the shopping list.

Secondary Level. Accompany the student as he or she makes various stops at stores and businesses in the community based on reading and comprehension of a shopping itinerary, including, for example, stops at a restaurant for lunch, a stop at the post office, and a stop at the dry cleaner's. Only provide assistance when needed. Whenever assistance is provided, review and provide additional practice.

Family Interventions

Infant and Toddler/Preschool. Ask the parents to take their child on trips into the community during which they stop at different stores and businesses. Tell them to notice store signs and to say such things as "This is the Bargain Supermarket. I must stop here to buy some bananas. They are on sale today," and "This is Ruby's Restaurant. Let's stop here for lunch. It has the best meat loaf in town. I know it is your favorite, so let's go in and order the meat loaf platter." Remind them to then enter and carry out what they said they would do.

Primary Level. Ask the parents to point out to their child the various stores, restaurants, and other businesses in their community. Tell them to follow up by visiting and touring these businesses and checking out the interiors—the counters, stock, equipment, displays, and so on.

Intermediate Level. Ask the parents to make up, in concert with their child, shopping and activity lists from various advertisements and announcements. Tell them to identify each shopping and activity list (going to the bowling alley, seeing a movie, etc.) by its destination label. Tell them to include stops (activity list) for lunch or snacks and stops for service (shoe repair, haircuts, clothing repair, etc.) as well as for the purchase of goods. Encourage them to actually carry out these consumer-oriented and leisure-time activities.

Secondary Level. Ask the parents to send their youngster on an actual shopping trip in which he or she is responsible for doing the weekly shopping for needed goods and services. On the first several occasions, suggest that they accompany the youngster to provide needed assistance until he or she can perform such tasks independently.

 ## Specific Objective O

The student identifies and obeys storing and cooking directions found on food packages.

Teacher Interventions

Primary Level. Set up a food storage area in the classroom, including food shelves, a refrigerator, and a freezer (or refrigerator with a freezer compartment). Take the student on four separate trips to the school store or to a nearby supermarket. On each of the first three trips buy only one kind of item (in terms of the place it is to be stored). Compare the way it is stored in the supermarket to the way it is to be stored in the classroom.

While in the supermarket say such things as "These cans of food are stored on shelves here, and when we get back to school and unpack, we will put them on shelves in our classroom until we are ready to use them."

Upon returning to school, involve the student in the unpacking and storing of the items. Repeat for foods that should be refrigerated and then for foods that should be stored in the freezer (or freezer compartment of the refrigerator). On the fourth trip, purchase all three types of food.

Next, add the dimension of modifying the storage area in specific cases, as, for example, with produce that needs to be refrigerated if it is not to be used soon and with meat that is not to be used for some time and needs to be frozen before it is defrosted and used.

Intermediate Level. Continue developing the concepts involved in storing foods before they are used. At this level, add the dimension of storing partially used foods (e.g., boxes of rice and pasta of which only some of the contents have been removed for cooking and mayonnaise, mustard, and condiments that are only partially used when seasoning other foods) as well as storing leftovers. Also, begin work on the reading and comprehension of storage and food preparation directions appearing on food packages. Make a chart of common words and phrases appearing on food packages that refer to storage practices.

Secondary Level. Make flashcards of the abbreviations, words, phrases, numerals, and symbols that are typically found on food packages, for example, TBSP., DIRECTIONS, PREHEAT, BOIL, ADD, SHAKE WELL BEFORE USING, 3/4 CUP, and 350° F (see Figure 1.16).

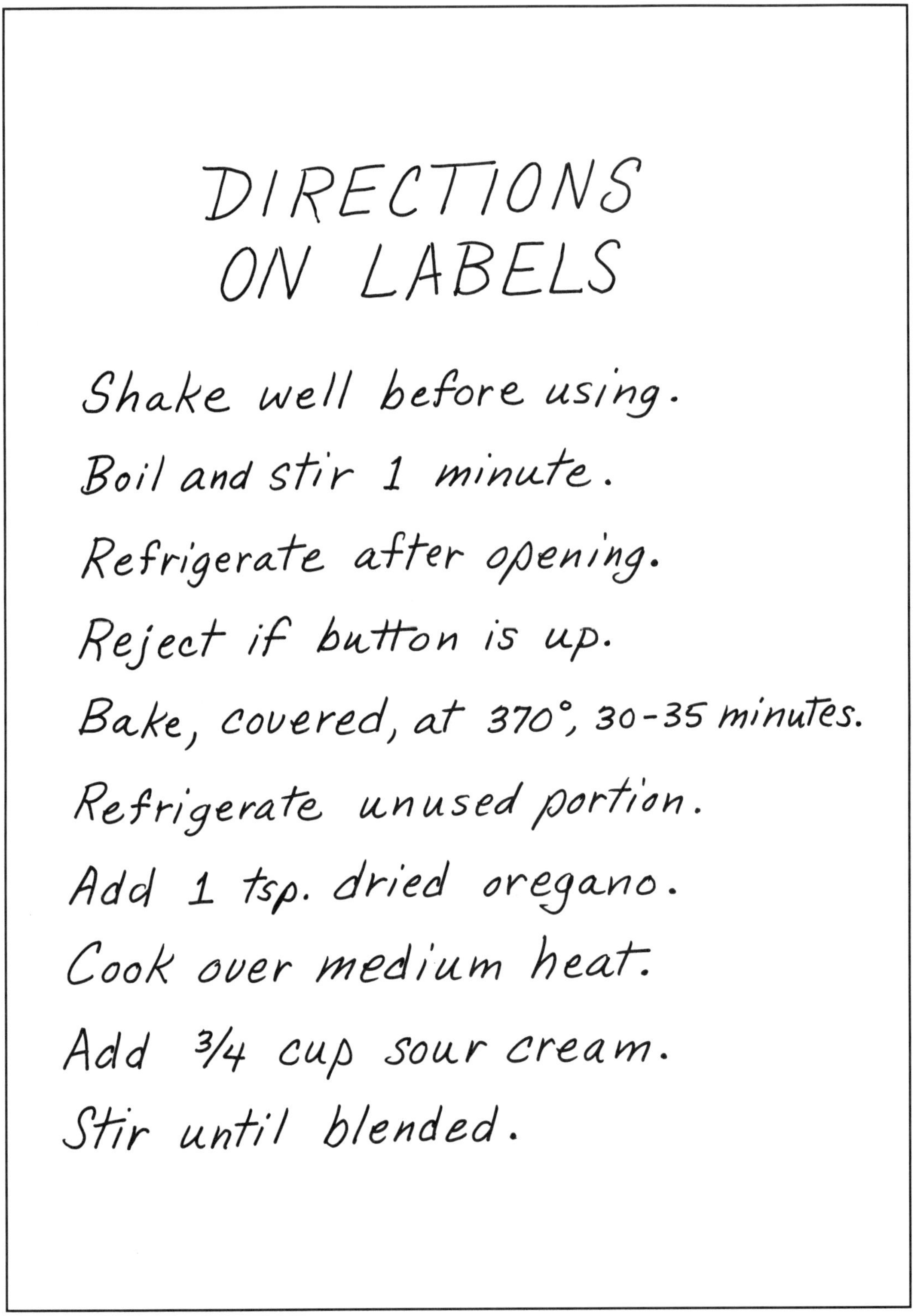

DIRECTIONS ON LABELS

Shake well before using.

Boil and stir 1 minute.

Refrigerate after opening.

Reject if button is up.

Bake, covered, at 370°, 30-35 minutes.

Refrigerate unused portion.

Add 1 tsp. dried oregano.

Cook over medium heat.

Add ¾ cup sour cream.

Stir until blended.

FIGURE 1.16. Key words and phrases on food packages.

After the student demonstrates some skill in identifying and comprehending these words, abbreviations, phrases, numerals, and symbols, give the student a cooking assignment in which he or she must prepare a snack, a part of a meal, or a complete meal from the directions appearing on the packages. Remind the student to refrain from asking for help unless he or she is experiencing difficulty.

For the student who is unable to read, prepare pictorial directions for the preparation of simple snacks and meals taken from recipes appearing on food packages (see Figure 1.17). Put these recipes on index cards to be kept in the kitchen for quick reference. Paste a picture of the prepared food item on the first index card so that the student can identify the pack of cards as the recipe for that specific dish.

Family Interventions

Infant and Toddler/Preschool. Acquaint the parents with the infant/toddler activity suggested for Teacher Interventions. Then ask the parents to engage in this same activity with their child while using the food storage areas of their home.

Primary Level. Ask the parents to take their child with them on actual shopping trips and to give their child the task of assisting them in putting the groceries away.

Intermediate Level. Ask the parents to demonstrate storing food containers in the refrigerator after they have been opened although they were not refrigerated before using them (e.g., mayonnaise, jellies, olives). Ask the parents to also involve their child in storing foods that are leftovers. Remind them to explain the nature of leftovers and how they are used in planning future meals and in living within a family budget.

Secondary Level. Ask the parents to require their youngster to prepare a variety of snacks, parts of meals, and meals for breakfast, lunch, and dinner and for special occasions such as barbecues and picnics from the directions found on food packages. Tell them to provide assistance only when it is needed.

 ## Specific Objective P

The student identifies and obeys storage and cleaning instructions found on packages containing laundry and housecleaning agents.

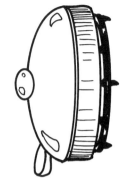

1. Combine mix and 2 tablespoons butter or margarine in large skillet. Sauté over medium heat, stirring frequently until golden brown.

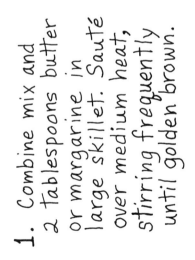

2. Stir in 2½ cups HOT water and contents of seasoning packet; bring to a boil.

3. Cover, reduce heat. Simmer 15-20 minutes or until liquid is absorbed and rice is tender. Stir before serving.

FIGURE 1.17. Recipes on food package.

Teacher Interventions

Infant and Toddler/Preschool. Bring representative packages of laundry and house-cleaning agents to the classroom. Use these products, following necessary precautions, to do simple laundering and cleaning. Explain each safe behavior as you use the product. Tell the student that each of these items must be stored in special places—away from food items, away from heat sources, and so on.

Paste Mr. Yuk stickers on these containers, and explain that they must never be ingested, put near the eyes, or played with because they can hurt people. Make a safety videotape of both proper use and safe storage practices.

Primary Level. Show the student representative packages of laundry and house-cleaning products, and point out any pictures on labels that provide clues to their function.

Then introduce key words (orally) that specify both storage directions and directions for the product's use. Use housecleaning items for such activities as washing the floor, dusting furniture, washing windows, and cleaning sinks. Explain that you are doing maintenance work. After sufficient demonstration, ask the student to be your "maintenance assistant."

Follow the same procedure with laundry items. Ask the student to be a "laundry worker" just like you as he or she imitates washing and drying clothing and linens.

Intermediate Level. Once the student comprehends oral directions for housecleaning and laundering activities, relate these words to their written counterparts appearing on packages. Indicate that you do not always have to read the directions if you remember them but that it is a good idea to review the directions and wise to check the directions when you are not sure.

Secondary Level. When the student is able to follow the storage and process directions appearing on labels of laundry and housecleaning products that have been used in the classroom for general maintenance and for clothes-washing activities, give the student unfamiliar brands, and ask him or her to engage in the various maintenance activities. Provide assistance, when needed, and reward the student for being a safe worker.

Family Interventions

Infant and Toddler/Preschool. Tell the parents to involve their child in various laundry and housecleaning chores. Tell them to talk aloud the safety rules that apply, for instance, "I am using rubber gloves to protect my hands," "I am keeping this cleaning fluid away from my mouth and eyes since I don't want to get sick or burn my eyes," "I am storing these containers in a locked cabinet so that they are out of reach of children who do not know how to use them safely."

Primary Level.   Ask the parents to help their child to differentiate packages of cleaning products from packages that contain food. Tell them to point out warning signs (such as a skull and crossbones) and words of warning that appear on cleaning and cleansing products. Remind them to put Mr. Yuk signs on nonfood and dangerous items and to have their child assist them in attaching these labels. Tell them to arrange the activity so that their child must discriminate between food and nonfood items and only put Mr. Yuk labels on laundry and housecleaning products.

Intermediate Level.   Ask the parents to involve their child in various household maintenance tasks. Tell them to begin by reading the directions to the child and asking the child to repeat and explain the directions. After their child explains the directions, ask them to supervise as he or she performs the task.

Secondary Level.   Ask the parents to assign their youngster specific household chores involving the use of laundry and housecleaning products. Tell them to supervise their youngster until he or she is consistently using these products safely and correctly.

Specific Objective Q

The student locates the doorbells and mailboxes of friends and relatives.

Teacher Interventions

Infant and Toddler/Preschool.   Explain to the student that when you visit relatives or friends, you must let the people you are visiting know that you have arrived at their home so that they can invite you in if they are at home. Indicate that this is why there are doorbells (or door knockers) on the front doors of houses and on apartment doors.

Show the student drawings or photographs of houses and apartments where the doorbell is prominently shown. Ask the student to point to the doorbell. Show the student the school's doorbell if there is one.

Primary Level.   Arrange for a visit to the student's home. When you arrive there, ask the student to ring the doorbell. If the student is unable to reach the bell, ask him or her to show you where it is. Go in for a short visit in which the student shows you his or her room or a new toy and/or introduces you to family members. If possible, make a videotape of the student taking you to visit his or her home and family members.

Intermediate Level. Take a trip into the community (previously arranged) to visit the home of a classmate or a classroom volunteer. Explain that sometimes doorbells are out of order and people put a sign up to that effect so that visitors will know to knock instead. Ask the parent of the classmate or the volunteer to place a sign on the doorbell that reads, DOORBELL OUT OF ORDER! PLEASE KNOCK. Reward the student for obeying this hand-printed sign.

Secondary Level. Take the student to multiple-dwelling houses and apartment buildings. When applicable, show the student that he or she must find the bell of a friend or relative by locating that person's name on a mailbox or on a directory. Make a chart that contains the pictures of friends and relatives whom he or she might visit (check with the student's parents). Underneath each picture, print the name of the person.

Use this chart to play a game in which you say the name of a person depicted on the chart and the student points to the picture. Follow up with a new chart in which only the names appear.

Family Interventions

Infant and Toddler/Preschool. Ask the parents to show their child the doorbell (or door knocker) of their home. Tell them to ring the doorbell so that their child is able to see them do so and hear the bell ring. Tell them to have previously arranged for a friend or relative to visit their home very soon after this demonstration.

When the friend or relative rings the doorbell, tell the parents to invite the visitor in for a pleasant visit in which the relative or friend plays with the child and joins the family in a snack.

Primary Level. Ask the parents to take their child for visits to the homes of family members and friends. Tell them, on the first visit, to show their child where the doorbell is. Encourage them to expect the child to ring the doorbell on future visits.

Intermediate Level. Ask the parents to make an "Electric Doorbell" game using a bell, batteries, and wire. Tell them to place, on one side of the game board, pictures of friends and family members and, on the other side of the game board, the corresponding names written in manuscript.

Tell them to attach the wires in such a way that if the child plugs the end of one wire into the socket next to the name and then plugs the second wire into the socket underneath the correct person's picture, the bell will ring.

Secondary Level. Ask the parents to assign their youngster the task of placing notes in the home mailboxes of friends and relatives, inviting them to visit or join the family in a recreational activity or giving them other important information because they could not be reached by telephone. Ask the parents to pay particular attention to friends who live in multiple-dwelling houses and apartment buildings as this is a more complex task than it is with a single-family residence.

Specific Objective R

The student locates signs on doors and store windows and then uses the information found there to identify the days and hours when the store or business is open.

Teacher Interventions

Infant and Toddler/Preschool. Take the student for a walk into the community, stopping at banks, stores, and offices of health care providers. Show the student the words that indicate the days of the week, the numerals that indicate time, and the key words that indicate hours and days of operation.

At this level, the student is not expected to read the signs but only to be aware that they exist and where they are likely to be found.

Primary Level. Review the days of the week with the student. Make sure that he or she can say them in order. Once the student is able to consistently say them in sequential order, introduce him or her to their written counterparts as both words and abbreviations. For example, show the student the words and abbreviations on a variety of calendars.

Next, place the days of the week and their abbreviations on flashcards and use them to facilitate rapid recognition.

Intermediate Level. Make flashcards of the words OPEN; CLOSED; COME IN; WE'RE OPEN; YES, WE'RE OPEN; OFFICE HOURS; and so on. Practice with these flashcards until the student is able to rapidly identify them. Take photographs of these signs as they appear in the community or prepare facsimiles of them, and use them for reading instruction.

Next, proceed to an activity in which the student must tell you when a specific place is and is not open for business.

Secondary Level. Take the student for trips in the community where he or she must identify the days and hours of operation of those places that were practiced at previous levels of instruction. In addition, expect the student to provide you with the information for places that were not reviewed previously.

Family Interventions

Infant and Toddler/Preschool. Ask the parents to take their child with them on various business trips in the community. Tell them to go at times when the place is not open. Tell them to look for the days and hours of operation, point out to their child when and where they find them, and share their disappointment by saying, for example, "Oh! Oh! The bank is closed now. I will have to return tomorrow!"

Primary Level. Ask the parents to take their child to various locations in the community. Tell them to ask their child to find the signs on doors and windows that give information to people concerning what days and hours they are open.

    Tell them also to review the names of the days of the week in sequence and to make certain there is a wall calendar somewhere in the home so that they can show their child the words and abbreviations for the days of the week.

Intermediate Level. Ask the parents to write daily plans for themselves that are headed by the words and abbreviations for the days of the week. Tell them to show the student these activity sheets ("Things to Do"), emphasizing the words for the days of the week. Encourage them to assist their child in making his or her own daily activity sheets, if he or she is able.

Secondary Level. Ask the parents to ask their youngster to go to selected places in the community and to report to them the hours and days of operation as posted on the windows and doors. Remind them to accompany the youngster on his or her initial attempts and to urge him or her to do it alone when competence is consistently demonstrated. Remind them that they should use their discretion at all times as to when it is safe for the youngster to move about the community safely.

 ## Specific Objective S

The student locates public telephones and public telephone booths.

Teacher Interventions

Infant and Toddler/Preschool. Take a walk in the community, and point out telephone booths located on the streets and in buildings. Tell the student to observe as people use the telephones to make a call. Make a call of your own to the school secretary to tell him or her that your walk in the community is proceeding safely.

Primary Level. During trips into the community, announce to the student that you need to make a telephone call. Seek the student's assistance in locating telephones and telephone booths. Make the telephone call, and thank the student for helping you find a public telephone.

   Follow up by assisting the student in making a telephone call to his or her home or to a relative or a friend. (Arrange beforehand for the individual to be at home to receive the call.)

Intermediate Level. Help the student compile his or her own personal telephone directory. Follow up by taking a trip into the community and asking the student to make a call to three different persons listed in his or her directory. (Arrange beforehand for someone in the directory to be on the telephone so that the student will experience a busy signal, for someone to be out so that the ringing is not answered, and for someone to be home.)

Secondary Level. Ask the student to take a walk with you so that various public conveniences may be noted. Include such things as mailboxes, fire alarm boxes, water fountains, trash receptacles, and telephone booths. Ask the student to independently identify and then specify the purpose of each of these public conveniences.

   Make sure to review the words that appear on public telephones, telephone booths, and informational charts that are found in telephone booths.

Family Interventions

Infant and Toddler/Preschool. Ask the parents to take their child for trips into the community and to locate a public telephone. Tell them that while they are there they should make a telephone call to one of their child's favorite relatives or friends and allow the child to hold a brief conversation if he or she is able or, at a minimum, to listen to the favorite person talking to him or her.

Primary Level. Ask the parents to take their child on trips into the community. Tell them to mention to their child that they need to make a telephone call and need his or her help in finding a telephone. Tell them to reward their child for helping them locate a public telephone.

Intermediate Level. Ask the parents to help their child differentiate between objects found in the community that are similar in appearance to a public telephone. These objects may include small-sized public mailboxes, police call boxes, road and highway emergency telephones, and fire alarm boxes. Also, ask the parents to introduce their child to OUT OF ORDER signs that appear on telephones, vending machines, public bathrooms, elevators, and other objects.

Secondary Level. Ask the parents to give their youngster the task of making several telephone calls, using the parents' or his or her own personal telephone directory, while they are moving about the community. Tell them to also assist their youngster in locating telephone numbers not in their own directory by using a public directory.

GOAL V.

The student will carry out instructions written in simple notes.

Note for You

Please . . . .
. . . .

Mom and Dad

SPECIFIC OBJECTIVES

The student:

- [ ] A. Identifies the written names and/or relationship names of family members.
- [ ] B. Identifies the written names of important objects found in and around his or her school and home.
- [ ] C. Identifies frequently used action words when they are written.
- [ ] D. Identifies frequently used prepositions when they are written.
- [ ] E. Identifies the numbers 1 through 12 when they are written.
- [ ] F. Identifies time notations.
- [ ] G. Identifies money designations when they are written as numerals.

SUGGESTED ACTIVITIES

Specific Objective A

The student identifies the written names and/or relationship names of family members.

Teacher Interventions

Infant and Toddler/Preschool. Ask the parents to send in photographs of the student's family members. Review them with the student by referring to the parents and grandparents by their preferred relationship names (e.g., "Mommy" and "Daddy"), to siblings by their first names (or nicknames, e.g., "Susie"), and to other family members by both their relationship and first names (e.g., "Aunt Rose").

Review the names until the student is able to point to each photograph when it is named and/or can name the photograph when it is referred to.

Primary Level. Place the photographs used in the infant and toddler/preschool activity on a chart or in a photo album. Under each photograph, print the name (on a card that can be removed) of the individual as described in the infant and toddler/preschool activity.

Give the student index cards upon which the name of the family members are printed. Ask the student to match the name cards with the names written under the photographs.

Repeat this activity. This time, however, place a card below each photograph that has the signature of the family member. Follow up by giving the student matching signature cards and encouraging him or her to make the match.

Intermediate Level. Show the student photographs of key family members, and ask him or her to identify them orally with names and/or relationship designations.

Play a simple game of Concentration with the student in which the object is to make photograph and printed name pairs.

Play the game once again. This time the student and you are expected to make combinations of three items: the photograph, the name written in manuscript, and the name in cursive.

Secondary Level. Write a variety of simple notes that a family member might leave for another family member. Show these notes to the student, and ask him or her to underline the signatures or printed names. Then, read the notes to the student, and ask him or her to tell you whom the notes are from.

Ask the parents to send in sample notes from family members and copies of greeting cards that have been signed by them. Use these to assist the student in identifying the written names of family members (both manuscript and cursive).

Family Interventions

Infant and Toddler/Preschool. Ask the parents to work with their child until he or she is able to identify close family members (especially those who live within the home) when their names and/or relationship designations are spoken.

Primary Level. Ask the parents to put name cards on the possessions of family members (e.g., "Mommy" on Mommy's jewelry box). Tell them, once their child is able to identify these cards, to remove them and to expect their child to place the name cards in their correct locations.

Intermediate Level. Ask the parents to collect copies of the signatures of close family members and to show their child the relationship between the signature and its printed counterpart. Tell the parents to prepare flashcards of the names of the family members and to expect their child to rapidly identify them.

Secondary Level. Ask the parents to write notes to their youngster and to encourage other family members to send the youngster notes as well. Tell them to begin by writing the youngster notes setting directions to be followed when they are not at home—for example:

Dear Joseph,

We have gone to visit Aunt Susie, who is in the hospital. Please wash the breakfast dishes and put them away. We will be home around 5 o'clock.

Love,
Mom and Dad

Specific Objective B

The student identifies the written names of important objects found in and around his or her school and home.

Teacher Interventions

Infant and Toddler/Preschool.   Make a list of objects found in the student's home and in the classroom. Ask the student to assist you in making a noun chart containing pictures of these objects. Use this chart to develop the concept for each of the objects and to facilitate oral comprehension and expression.

Primary Level.   Using the chart developed for the infant and toddler/preschool level, print the name of each object directly under its picture (see Figure 1.18). Give the student index cards with the name of each object written in manuscript. Ask the student to match the card to its picture. Cover the words on the chart, and ask the student to once more match the index cards to their pictures.

Intermediate Level.   Make flashcards of the words represented on the chart used in the infant and toddler/preschool activity. Use these cards for rapid recognition and to stimulate the student to use the words in sentences describing each of the object's functions or uses, for example, "Stove: We use the stove to cook our meals."

Continue by making a matching game worksheet (see Figure 1.19). Divide the worksheet into two columns. Place the nouns written on the student's chart in the left-hand column and pictures of a number of objects, including the ones that represent the nouns, in the right-hand column. Ask the student to draw a line from the noun to the picture it represents.

Secondary Level.   Write some notes in which you use the nouns found in the charts (see Figures 1.18 and 1.19). Underline each noun, and ask the student to name it without referring to the chart. Give the student permission to use the chart only if he or she is experiencing difficulty. Once the student identifies a noun, read the entire sentence to him or her so that he or she can see the reason for its use in the note (see example at top of page 103).

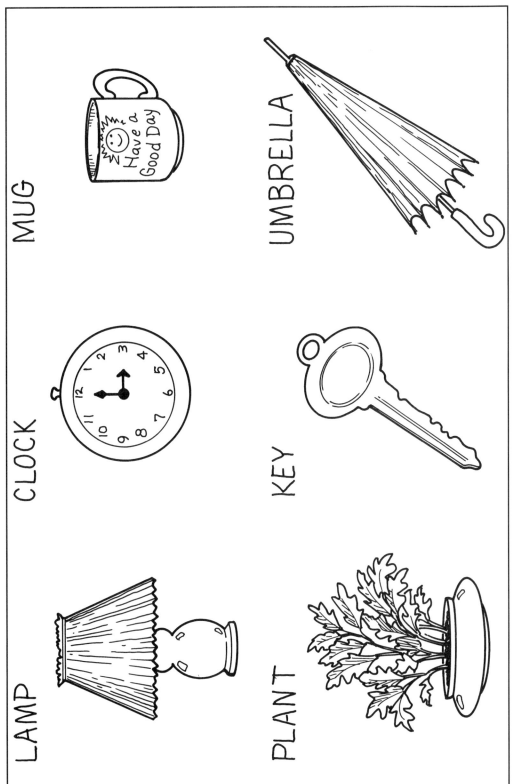

LAMP   CLOCK   MUG

PLANT   KEY   UMBRELLA

Have a Good Day

FIGURE 1.18. Noun chart.

101

FIGURE 1.19. Noun-matching game.

Dear Tyrone,

I have gone with Aunt Rose to the supermarket to buy some eggs. Please give the car keys to your father when he comes home, and put the turkey in the oven. Set the oven for 350 degrees. Thanks! You are a dear!

Aunt Martha

Family Interventions

Infant and Toddler/Preschool. Ask the parents to take their child on tours of their home and to point out objects found there. Demonstrate to the parents how they may develop comprehension and oral expression of the names for these objects. Ask the parents to provide regular reviews of this information until their child consistently and correctly identifies important objects found in the home environment.

Primary Level. Ask the parents to put name cards on objects found in the home. Tell them to give their child duplicates of these cards and to ask him or her to place his or her own cards over the cards they placed there.

Tell them to supervise their child while he or she is engaged in this activity and to provide immediate correction as needed and immediate praise when appropriate. Tell the parents to continue by removing the cards they placed on the objects and asking their child to place the cards without the written clue.

Intermediate Level. Ask the parents to write simple sentences using the names of the various objects that were reviewed. Tell them to underline the names and to ask their child to read the names aloud.

Secondary Level. Ask the parents to write simple notes to their youngster in which they give him or her directions—for example:

> Dear Juan,
>
> Your mother and I will be at the unemployment office. Please give your brother, Tony, his roller skates (they are in the upstairs closet), since he is going skating with friends. Also, change the bulb in your lamp and water the plants.
>
> Dad

Specific Objective C

The student identifies frequently used action words when they are written.

Teacher Interventions

Infant and Toddler/Preschool. Perform some basic action, and ask the student to imitate what he or she just saw. Once the student is able to perform the actions, name these actions, and proceed by asking him or her to perform the actions in response to your commands.

Play action games such as Simon Says, and sing action songs like "If You're Happy and You Know It, Clap Your Hands."

Primary Level. From the list of action verbs developed in the infant and toddler/preschool activity, draw up a written list (in manuscript), and ask the student to help you construct a chart containing photographs or drawings of people engaged in the specified actions.

Write the imperative form of the appropriate verb as a caption underneath each picture. Continue by saying an action verb and asking the student to point to the picture and then to the word written underneath. Then give the student cards upon which you have printed the verbs, and tell him or her to match his or her own card with the appropriate picture.

Next, cover the captions on the chart, and ask the student to use his or her cards to identify each of the actions depicted in the chart.

Intermediate Level. Make a matching-game worksheet. Divide the worksheet into two columns, with the words in the left-hand column and their corresponding pictures in random order in the right-hand column. Tell the student to draw a line between the word and its picture.

Continue by showing the student verb-noun combinations in phrases that might be found in simple notes that request actions of the reader—for example, "Iron the shirt!" "Boil the eggs!" or "Peel the potatoes!"

Ask the student to read these phrases aloud and/or to act them out in simple pantomimes, then say them, and next actually carry out the directions.

Secondary Level.   Write some representative notes that might be left by parents to the student. In these notes emphasize actions to be carried out—for example:

Dear Peter,

We have taken your baby sister to the doctor. After having your after-school snack, please do the following chores:

1. Make your bed.
2. Take the chicken out of the freezer.
3. Boil and then mash the potatoes.
4. Cut up 2 onions in small pieces.
5. Slice 3 tomatoes.

Thanks for being such a good helper and worker.

Mom and Dad

If the student is able to, ask him or her to write "pretend" notes with simple instructions to be carried out by a hypothetical reader (see Unit 2, "Functional Writing," Goal II, Specific Objective H).

Family Interventions

Infant and Toddler/Preschool.   Ask the parents to play action games such as Simon Says, sing action songs such as "The Eensy Weensy Spider," and act out nursery rhymes such as "Jack and Jill" with their child. Urge them to go to the library and take out children's books containing finger plays and action poems. Suggest that they buy children's records that encourage children to sing along and to join in the action.

Primary Level. Ask the parents to assign household chores to their child that he or she must carry out in response to oral commands. Remind the parents to demonstrate the actions, guide their child in carrying out the necessary actions, and provide him or her with sufficient practice in performing the assigned tasks.

Tell them to continue with playing action games, making sure that the task is more demanding and complex than when they played it earlier at the infant and toddler/preschool level.

Intermediate Level. Ask the parents to write on flashcards simple phrases with noun-verb combinations that were used orally at the primary level and to use these cards in a game format in which their child must respond to each flashcard by pantomiming and/or carrying out the command.

Secondary Level. Ask the parents to write simple notes to their youngster that contain instructions to be performed while they are out of the home. Ask the parents to identify household tasks that their youngster is able to perform independently and to write notes in which they say, for example, "Walk the dog," "Water the plants," "Dust the furniture," or "Empty the dishwasher."

 ## Specific Objective D

The student identifies frequently used prepositions when they are written.

Teacher Interventions

Infant and Toddler/Preschool. Demonstrate frequently used prepositions that indicate the position of an object. Give the student instructions in which he or she must put familiar objects *on, in,* and *under* his desk, *next to* the book, and so on. Use a variety of objects, locations, and situations.

Primary Level. Make a list of prepositions that are frequently used in instructions and commands. Ask the student to help you make a chart (see Figure 1.20) that illustrates these prepositions. Show a picture of a book *on* a shelf, a car *in* a garage, a toy *under* a table, or a ball *next* to a chair. Write the appropriate preposition underneath each of the pictures. In addition, you may wish to use rebuses, for example, for *in, on, under, over,* and *next.*

Make a flashcard-matching game in which the student must match picture, word, and rebus. Use these flashcards as a cooperative learning

1. Put the book _____ the shelf.

2. The ball is _____ the chair.

3. The ring is ____ the box.

4. The toy is _____ the table.

FIGURE 1.20. Preposition chart.

activity in which the student gets one set (e.g., the word *flashcards*), and he or she must locate the student with the rebus flashcards and another student with the picture flashcards. Together the three must make all the correct sets.

Intermediate Level.   Write some simple messages that include the prepositions found on the chart developed in the primary-level activity. Ask the student to underline all the prepositions in the messages while referring to the chart. Tell him or her to say each underlined word after locating it on the chart.

   Follow up by showing the student verb-noun-preposition-noun combinations that you have written to illustrate typical school-setting instructions or commands, for example, "Put the flowerpot on the windowsill," "Put the box of crayons in the closet." Ask the student to carry out the instructions.

Secondary Level.   Write the student simple notes in which he or she is given instructions for various classroom chores and activities, for example, "Mark the day on your personal calendar," "Sharpen your pencil," "Water the plants," "Feed the fish." For each day of the week, require the student to complete different classroom tasks.

Family Interventions

Infant and Toddler/Preschool.   Ask the parents to have their child watch them as they perform different household tasks. Tell them to perform the action(s) involved and to simultaneously say the action(s), for example, "I am putting the pair of scissors back in its drawer," "I am removing the frozen vegetables and putting them on the counter," "I am putting this dish under the flowerpot so that the table doesn't get wet."

Primary Level.   Ask the parents to make a list of prepositions that they frequently use in instructions and directions they give their child. Ask the parents to make flashcards that illustrate these prepositions, for example, show a picture of a clock *on* a mantle, a vacuum cleaner stored *in* a closet, a placemat *under* a table setting, an ottoman *in front of* an armchair, a floor lamp *next to* a couch.

   Tell them to write the appropriate preposition below each of the pictures. Tell them to use the flashcards for fast-recognition drills.

Intermediate Level.   Ask the parents to write some simple messages to their child. Tell them to use noun-preposition-noun combinations that they have written to illustrate typical home-setting instructions or commands, for example, "Unpack the groceries, and put the canned goods on the closet shelf," "Pick up your toys and put them in the toy chest," "Put your dirty laundry in the laundry bag."

Secondary Level. Ask the parents to write their youngster simple notes in which they ask him or her to engage in various household chores, for example, "Put the table pad *on* the dining room table," "Put the storage boxes *under* your bed," "Move the lamp *next to* the bookcase." Tell them to require their youngster to complete different household tasks on different days of the week.

 ## Specific Objective E

The student identifies the numbers 1 through 12 when they are written.

See Unit 3, "Functional Mathematics," Goal IV, for suggested activities.

 ## Specific Objective F

The student identifies time notations.

See Unit 3, "Functional Mathematics," for suggested activities.

 ## Specific Objective G

The student identifies money designations when they are written as numerals.

See Unit 3, "Functional Mathematics," for suggested activities.

GOAL VI.

The student will locate and utilize information from simple charts, diagrams, maps, and menus.

SPECIFIC OBJECTIVES

The student:

    ❏ A. Using a calendar, identifies the date, approaching dates, and previous dates.

    ❏ B. Uses a hand-drawn map to find his or her way around the school building and uses floor plan maps located in stores and office buildings.

    ❏ C. Uses a hand-drawn map to find his or her way around the community.

    ❏ D. Uses public transportation maps.

    ❏ E. Uses diagrams to assemble objects.

    ❏ F. Uses diagrams to make simple constructions and other arts and crafts projects.

    ❏ G. Locates key information on posters and other informational charts.

    ❏ H. Locates and records information on charts used for instructional and behavioral management purposes, including those used to assist the student in monitoring his or her progress.

    ❏ I. Uses menus to order meals and snacks.

SUGGESTED ACTIVITIES

Specific Objective A

The student, using a calendar, identifies the date, approaching dates, and previous dates.

Teacher Interventions

Primary Level. Engage in activities that assist the student in saying the days of the week in sequential order. A song like "Here We Go 'Round the Mulberry Bush" and simple rhythmic chants in which the student joins you in chanting the days of the week can be helpful.

    Try to identify each day with a significant event in the life of the student and the student's family. For example, "We visit Grandma and

Grandpa on Sunday!" Encourage the student to listen to radio and television news programs that announce the day of the week.

Write the name of each day and its abbreviation on a flashcard. Tell the student to put the seven cards in the correct order. If he or she is experiencing difficulty, show the student a colorful wall calendar.

Prepare a second set with only the names of the days and a third set with only their abbreviations. Use these two sets of cards for both matching and sequencing tasks. Continue by pointing out the key words for the names of the months on the wall calendar. Ask the student to identify the month of his or her birthday. Proceed through the calendar to identify something significant about each month—holidays, the start of school, the end of school, the birthdays of family members, and so on.

Intermediate Level. Show the student the year designations on wall calendars, on desk calendars, on appointment book covers, and on calendars that appear in checkbook registers. Underline the last two numbers to assist the student in identifying the year when it is written in an abbreviated numerical form (e.g., 2/3/99 and 9-23-98). Ask the student to use one of the calendars to tell you what day of the week a future date will fall on, for example, Thanksgiving or the student's birthday.

Periodically during the school year, ask the student to locate today's date on the calendar and to underline the month, draw a box around the day of the week, and draw a circle around the number of the day. Continue by asking him or her to shade in the previous day (or days after a weekend or a holiday) to indicate that it is (they are) now in the past. Demonstrate how to identify tomorrow's date by today's: "Today is Wednesday, so tomorrow must be Thursday!"

Secondary Level. Discuss with the student alternate ways of finding today's date, such as the date listed on store receipts, a bus or subway transfer, a time card. Engage the student in planning future class activities and school special events. For example, tell the student that there will be a special concert next week on Thursday, and ask him or her to write it on the classroom's wall calendar in the appropriate box and to tell you the date of the concert. Also, tell the student that your class is scheduled to go on a field trip to the planetarium on May 4th, for example.

Ask the student to find the day of the week you will be going by using the wall calendar or his or her own personal calendar (appointment book). Remind the student to make a notation on the calendar so he or she will remember. Follow up by role-playing telephone messages in which doctors' and other appointments are told to the student, and he or she must record the appointment on a wall or personal calendar.

Also, show the student how to use the calendar to record the due dates copied from bills and dates when deliveries are expected. Prepare a hypothetical page of a calendar on which you have written scheduled events and activities, appointments, due dates when bills must be paid, and dates when orders are expected to be delivered. Ask the student to look over the calendar and indicate what will be occurring on each day on which you have written a notation.

Family Interventions

Primary Level. Ask the parents to teach their child songs that mention the days of the week. Tell them to greet the family members each morning with a "Good morning, this is ___ day!" and to preview the events and tasks of the day, for example, "Tonight when you come home from school, Joshua, you are to bring in the garbage cans. Tonight the family is going to eat at ___'s Restaurant since the Monday special is ___, and when we return, we will watch our favorite Monday night show, "___.""

Intermediate Level. Ask the parents to demonstrate to their child how they use their home wall or desk calendar to write down future appointments, the due dates of bills, and the expected delivery of ordered materials. Tell the parents to also show their child how they look ahead each week to determine the activities and requirements they must meet as the days pass.

Secondary Level. Ask the parents to give their youngster an appointment book and to periodically indicate some future dates that he or she should record in his or her personal calendar. Ask the parents to occasionally remind the student to check his or her calendar to make sure not to miss any important dates or appointments. If appointment cards are received on visits to doctors, dentists, and other care providers, tell them to remind the youngster to record the appointments on a calendar.

 ## Specific Objective B

The student uses a hand-drawn map to find his or her way around the school building and uses floor plan maps located in stores and office buildings.

Teacher Interventions

Primary Level. Draw a map of the classroom. Explain that the map is a special way of "drawing" the room. Ask the student to identify each item on the map by finding its counterpart in the classroom.

Intermediate Level. Take a tour of the school building, and point out important locations (e.g., the cafeteria, the library, the office of the speech pathologist). As you pass each location, sketch it on your map. When you return to the classroom, finish drawing the map. Then ask the student to use the map to retrace the trip around the school.

Follow up by scheduling a "Treasure Hunt" in which the student is expected to find interesting games and objects that you have penciled in on a "Treasure Map" of the school building and the school grounds.

Secondary Level. Take the student on trips to department stores and office buildings where there are floor plan maps. Demonstrate how to use these maps to plan movements to get to a designated location. After the student shows sufficient skill in using such a map independently, ask him or her to lead you to a desired location.

Family Interventions

Intermediate and Secondary Levels. Ask the parents to take their youngster along when they take trips to stores and office buildings where there are floor plan maps. Ask the parents to demonstrate how to use the maps and to eventually require their youngster to lead them to desired locations while referring to such maps.

Specific Objective C

The student uses a hand-drawn map to find his or her way around the community.

Teacher Interventions

Primary Level. Take the student to interesting or important places in the community. Take along paper and pencil to sketch a map of the landmarks passed on the way to a designated location. Use the preliminary sketch as a guide for the return trip.

Upon your return to school, finish the map, and ask the student to use the map on the next school day to return to the location. Tell him or her to point to the landmarks as they are pictured on the map and as they are passed along the way (see Figure 1.21).

Intermediate Level. Obtain walking tour maps of the community and/or nearby communities. Take the student on a walking tour, using the map to locate sites of community and/or historical interest. Take another walking tour with the student using the map and acting as tour guide.

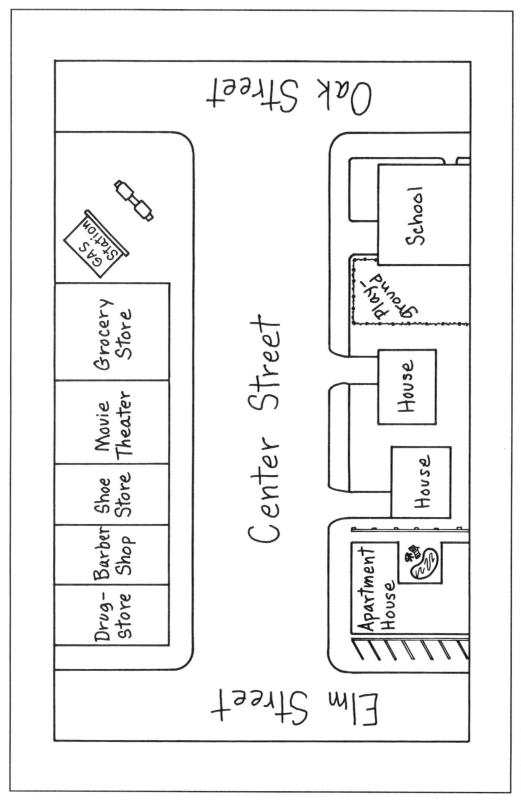

FIGURE 1.21. Community map.

Secondary Level. Show the student copies you have obtained of floor plans of apartments and houses, museums, parks and playgrounds, amusement parks, zoos, and so on. Show the student how to identify various items and locations depicted in these plans and maps.

Follow up by taking one or more trips to community locations while the student uses a map to serve as tour guide. In addition, show the student various hand-drawn maps that people provide to individuals invited to weddings and other celebrations, especially when the person invited lives in another area.

Family Interventions

Intermediate and Secondary Levels. Ask the parents to take their youngster on trips in the community and on vacation trips to other locations of interest (e.g., Disneyland and Epcot Center). Tell the parents to take time to show their youngster how to read the maps and to use them to find desired locations.

Tell the parents that they may wish to draw maps of the walking and transportation routes to visit relatives and friends and to use these maps with their youngster as an aid in finding his or her way to their homes.

 ## Specific Objective D

The student uses public transportation maps.

Teacher Interventions

Intermediate Level. When applicable, ask the transit authority in your community to provide you with copies of bus and subway maps (or obtain copies at specific transit locations in the community). Use these maps to plan and take trips involving public transportation.

Make videotapes of these trips, and use them for instructional, review, and monitoring purposes.

Secondary Level. Use public transportation to take trips in the community. When applicable, show the student maps displayed on buses and subway cars and platforms that depict transportation routes. Demonstrate using these maps to verify routes, determine transfer points, and check on the number of stops before getting off.

Family Interventions

Intermediate and Secondary Levels.   Ask the parents to use public transportation, when available, to take their youngster for trips in the community. Tell the parents to demonstrate how to use transportation maps to plan a trip and to monitor the trip as it is under way. Encourage them to use public transportation, when appropriate, on vacations and other trips to different communities, as other locations might use different route designation codes (e.g., color, number, and letter codes). Ask the parents to make videotapes of these trips as part of their collection of "home movies."

Remind the parents to assist their youngster in reading these maps on subsequent trips and in using them to lead the family to its various destinations.

 ## Specific Objective E

The student uses diagrams to assemble objects.

Teacher Interventions

Primary Level.   Give the student an interesting toy that needs to be assembled. Provide the student with a simple diagram, and assist him or her in reviewing the diagram and in talking out the various steps in the assembly. Take apart the toy and ask the student to reassemble it.

Intermediate Level.   Give the student assembly tasks as part of assembly-line or workshop activities. Demonstrate using a simple diagram to put the several parts together. Match the components to their sketched counterparts. Draw the student's attention to connecting points and to screws, nuts, and bolts that are used to join the parts together.

Put the fully assembled item in front of the student as a model, and ask him or her to make one just like it while reviewing the diagram.

Secondary Level.   Give the student an assembly kit for a piece of equipment that he or she might purchase at some future date, such as an outdoor grill, a swing set for a young sibling, or a stand for a television set. Assist the student in using the enclosed diagram to assemble the object.

Encourage the student to talk each step aloud, to match parts to the sketches in the diagram, and to follow specified sequences and identified size specifications for the different parts. Follow up by taking the equipment apart and asking the student to reassemble it.

Family Interventions

Intermediate and Secondary Levels. Ask the parents to involve their youngster in any assembly tasks resulting from purchases of equipment and other objects that need to be assembled. Ask the parents to provide a model of patience and of carefully following the diagram's sequence and size specifications. Remind the parents to pay particular attention to parts that closely resemble each other in shape and size.

 ### Specific Objective F

The student uses diagrams to make simple constructions and other arts and crafts projects.

Teacher Interventions

Primary, Intermediate, and Secondary Levels.   Collect a variety of arts and crafts magazines and books. Show the student photographs of finished projects, accompanying diagrams, and instructions appearing in these magazines and books. Ask the student to identify an object that he or she would like to make for his or her own use, to give as a gift, or to sell in a school-sponsored fund-raising activity.

Assist the student in reviewing the diagram and instructions and in completing the construction or project. If possible, work alongside the student as you also engage in the project. Practice using a variety of diagrams.

Assist the student, depending on his or her level, in selecting items to be made that are within his or her capabilities. For those students at the secondary level, a more complex craft such as crocheting or knitting might be appropriate, while those students at the primary level might do simple sewing tasks such as sewing an apron. A student at the intermediate level might be expected to work on making toys and other functional objects of wood.

Family Interventions

Primary, Intermediate, and Secondary Levels.   Ask the parents, if possible, to include arts and crafts and other construction projects in their leisure-time activities. Urge the parents to model engaging in arts and crafts projects as part of their own leisure-time activities.

Tell them to encourage their youngster to pursue his or her own interests in this area. Encourage them to assist their youngster by locating and purchasing appropriate magazines and kits that can be used to make the desired items. Remind the parents to assist their youngster in selecting projects that are appropriate to his or her age and level of functioning as well as those projects that are of interest to him or her. Ask the parents to provide assistance in interpreting diagrams and instructions as needed by their youngster.

Specific Objective G

The student locates key information on posters and other informational charts.

Teacher Interventions

Primary Level. If there are poster contests in the school or the need to develop posters to inform the entire school of an upcoming class activity, assist the student in designing and executing a poster to submit in the contest or to post in the school building.

Intermediate and Secondary Levels. Take the student for walks in the community, and point out billboards (giant posters) and posters placed on bulletin boards in supermarkets and department stores, in store windows, and in other places in the community (e.g., garage sale and political campaign posters on telephone poles, trees, etc.).

Review with the student any pictures appearing on these various posters as a means of determining the poster's message (see Figure 1.22). Continue by assisting the student in identifying the key information on the posters such as dates and times, prices, the names of events, and product names. Be sure to discuss both the informational content and the way the posters attempt to persuade the reader to attend an event, purchase a product, vote for a candidate, and so on.

Family Interventions

Intermediate and Secondary Levels. Ask the parents to draw their youngster's attention to posters and billboards in the community that attract their attention because they provide information of interest. Tell the parents to assist their youngster in identifying the information on these posters and then following up the information with the required action. For example, "I am glad we saw this poster. I didn't know that the ___s were giving a concert on Saturday, June 3rd. That is something we want to buy tickets for."

FIGURE 1.22. Sample poster.

 ### Specific Objective H

The student locates and records information on charts used for instructional and behavioral management purposes, including those used to assist the student in monitoring his or her progress.

Teacher Interventions

Primary, Intermediate, and Secondary Levels.   For the student who needs charts to remind him or her of key information that governs his or her behavior (clothing size chart, pictorial meal plan chart, etc.), begin by making large charts for use in the classroom instruction, and then follow up by making wallet-sized replicas of these charts for the student's use at appropriate times as he or she functions on a daily basis.

In addition, construct a variety of charts that the student should use to monitor his or her progress in academics, other curricular areas, and behavioral control (see Figure 1.23). Demonstrate how to record progress on these charts, and tell the student that he or she must take the responsibility of maintaining these charts.

Family Interventions

Primary, Intermediate, and Secondary Levels.   Suggest to the parents that they develop progress charts for their youngster to monitor progress, specifically for activities in the home and community. Also encourage the parents to require their youngster to use any wallet-sized charts developed individually for them (see Teacher Interventions above) rather than permitting the youngster to avoid the use of these charts by seeking assistance from them.

 ## Specific Objective I
The student uses menus to order meals and snacks.

Teacher Interventions

Primary Level.   Review with the student his or her favorite foods and beverages and favorite restaurants and fast-food establishments. Ask the student to tell you about any of the occasions when he or she has been to cafeterias and restaurants and to tell you what he or she ordered and enjoyed or even did not enjoy. Use the information from the discussion in activities that involve the use of menus.

Intermediate and Secondary Levels.   Ask local restaurant, cafeteria, and fast-food-restaurant managers and owners to give you copies of old menus. Use these menus to review course descriptors (appetizers, entrees, vegetables, desserts, beverages, etc.), specific food and beverage items within course categories, and prices. Begin by using menus that have pictorial clues as might be found in lower-priced or economy restaurant chains.

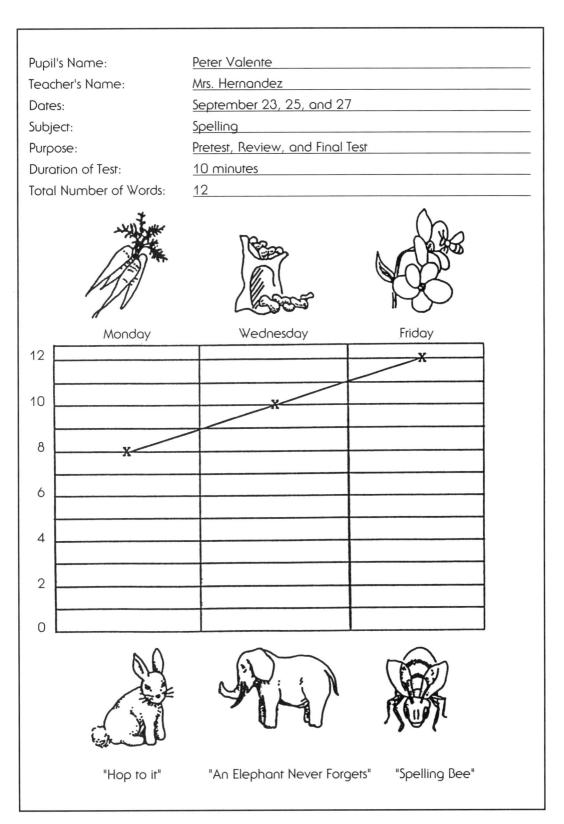

Pupil's Name: Peter Valente

Teacher's Name: Mrs. Hernandez

Dates: September 23, 25, and 27

Subject: Spelling

Purpose: Pretest, Review, and Final Test

Duration of Test: 10 minutes

Total Number of Words: 12

Monday   Wednesday   Friday

"Hop to it"   "An Elephant Never Forgets"   "Spelling Bee"

FIGURE 1.23.   Progress chart.

For each food or beverage item identified in a menu picture, assist the student in finding the words on the menu. Proceed to identifying the words found in representative menus.

Role-play the part of a server, with the student acting as a customer and being shown menus and ordering food. In the role-play pretend that you have been newly hired and are therefore unfamiliar with the menu so that you have to ask the student to point out the item ordered so you can write it down on your order pad.

Follow up with trips to some of the restaurants whose menus you have used for instructional purposes. If the student is not able to identify words on a menu successfully, provide him or her with alternate strategies for ordering, such as ordering items that are likely to be found in most restaurants and asking the server for help. Plan and take class trips to restaurants, cafeterias, and fast-food restaurants. Assign the student the task of making videotapes of these community-based activities.

Family Interventions

Primary, Intermediate, and Secondary Levels. Ask the parents to take their youngster to cafeterias, restaurants, and fast-food restaurants in their community whenever their budget allows. Tell the parents to give their youngster increasing responsibility for ordering his or her own meals as progress in reading menus is realized.

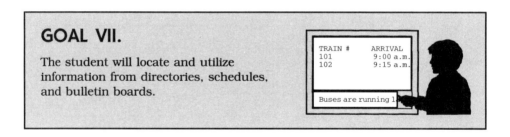

GOAL VII.

The student will locate and utilize information from directories, schedules, and bulletin boards.

TRAIN #	ARRIVAL
101	9:00 a.m.
102	9:15 a.m.

Buses are running 1

SPECIFIC OBJECTIVES

The student:

❐ A. Locates telephone numbers in his or her personal telephone directory.

❐ B. Locates apartments by using directories located in apartment houses and other homes with multiple living units.

❐ C. Locates a desired floor from a department store directory.

❏ D. Locates offices and other locations in various buildings by using their directories.

❏ E. Identifies times of mail pickup on mailbox schedules.

❏ F. Finds the locations of foods and other items from supermarket directories.

❏ G. Identifies foods and food prices from cafeteria and fast-food bulletin boards.

❏ H. Locates departure and arrival times from bus, train, and airline schedules, bulletin boards, and television monitors.

SUGGESTED ACTIVITIES

Specific Objective A

The student locates telephone numbers in his or her personal telephone directory.

Teacher Interventions

Intermediate Level. Help the student to make a personal telephone directory. Ask the parents to assist by informing you of telephone numbers of relatives and friends they believe should be included. (For the student who is unable to read the names of individuals, it may be necessary to use a notebook in which you paste photographs of important individuals with their telephone numbers placed alongside [see Figure 1.24].)

It is best, when feasible, to engage in activities in which the student telephones these individuals, for example, to invite them to visit the school for a special event (e.g., a display of arts and crafts projects or a class play). Remember to include emergency numbers on the inside of the front cover of the directory. Use symbols or pictures of the emergency service or agency (e.g., a police car, a fire engine, an ambulance).

Secondary Level. Encourage the student to periodically update his or her directory. Explore together the service agencies in the community that might be of present or future service to the student. Include governmental and private agencies such as the state employment office, the social services department, Blue Cross/Blue Shield, and the Better Business Bureau.

Assist the student in comprehending the purposes and objectives of these agencies, locating their telephone numbers, and recording these numbers in his or her personal directory.

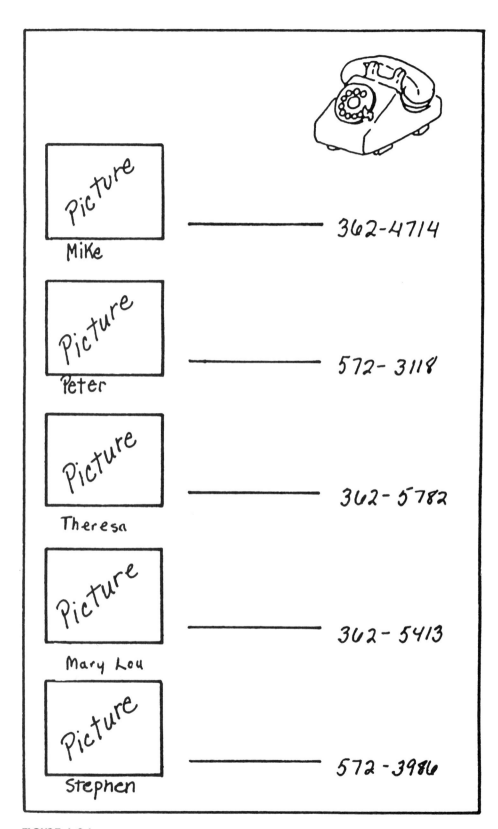

FIGURE 1.24. Personal telephone directory.

Family Interventions

Intermediate and Secondary Levels.   Ask the parents to assist their youngster in using his or her personal telephone directory, which they have helped make in collaboration with you, to make telephone calls to relatives and friends. Tell the parents to ask their youngster, "Please call Uncle Angelo and invite him and his family for dinner on Sunday. It is his birthday. After you finish talking to him, put me on the line since I would like to talk to him as well." Remind them to make sure their youngster updates the directory as he or she makes new friends and as telephone numbers change.

Specific Objective B

The student locates apartments by using directories located in apartment houses and other homes with multiple living units.

Teacher Interventions

Primary Level.   Discuss the different kinds of residences with the student. Include the various types of residences found in the community, including single-family houses, homes with multiple living units, apartment houses, and mobile homes. Ask the student to tell you about the homes or residences of his friends and relatives. Explain that it is sometimes more difficult to find the residence of someone who lives in an apartment house or a home with more than one living unit.

Intermediate Level.   Set up a simulated apartment house directory. Put the names of the student and classmates on the directory, and assign each one an apartment number. (This activity is also valuable in providing initial or review instruction in identifying odd and even numbers.)

In addition, make a mural of the inside of an apartment house with doors cut in such a way that, when the student reads the apartment number and opens the door, he or she sees a photograph of the student who "lives" in the apartment. Proceed by asking the student to read the directory and locate the apartment number, then go to the door, ring the pretend doorbell, and open the door to see if he or she has found the right apartment.

Using the same directory and mural, change the names and photographs to those of friends and relatives.

Secondary Level.   Visit an apartment house and/or a home with multiple living units, and ask the student to locate the apartment of someone who has previously agreed to a visit from the student and you. Videotape the trip, and use it for instructional, review, and monitoring purposes.

Family Interventions

Intermediate and Secondary Levels. Ask the parents to take their youngster, if possible, to friends and relatives who live in an apartment building or in a home with multiple living units. Tell the parents to draw their youngster's attention to the directory and to indicate to the student that the information obtained is necessary to determine the floor and to find the apartment when on the appropriate floor.

Remind them to point out any signs on walls and at corridor intersections that are placed there to help people locate apartments.

Specific Objective C

The student locates a desired floor from a department store directory.

Teacher Interventions

Intermediate Level. Take the student on trips to department stores. Help the student find any directories located in the stores. Go over the categories listed in the directory, and discuss the items that are usually included in each of the categories.

Upon your return to the classroom, write an experience story and make an experience chart (see Figure 1.25) that lists the categories found on the directory and their floor designations. For each category, list the items that are likely to be found there. Use the chart to play the "Categories" game in which you name an item to be purchased and the student names the listed category and identifies the floor where the item is likely to be found.

Secondary Level. Give the student a short shopping list that he or she will be using to take notes on the prices of these items as part of a comparative shopping exercise. Accompany the student to at least three (if possible) department stores with which he or she is not familiar, and ask the student to take notes on the prices of the items on the list. Reward the student for using the directory to successfully identify the categories and floors where he or she will find the items on the list. Videotape these sessions.

Upon your return to school, review the videotape, and ask the student to go over the prices and to identify, for each item on the list, the

Lacy's Department Store

Bakery	1	Ladies' Clothing	1
Bedding	2	Lawn and Garden	B
Boys' Clothing	1	Linens	2
Computers	2	Mens' Clothing	1
Cosmetics	1	Musical Instruments	1
Credit Office	2	Personnel Office	B
Draperies	2	Pharmacy	1
Electronics	2	Photography	B
Exercise Equipment	1	Sporting Goods	B
Games and Toys	2	Stationery	1
Gift Wrap	1	Tools and Accessories	B
Girls' Clothing	1		
Gourmet Foods	1	Restaurant	2
Household Appliances	2	Rest Rooms	2
Jewelry	1		

FIGURE 1.25. Department store directory.

store that has the lowest price. Conclude by asking the student to identify which he or she might buy if it were an actual shopping list.

Family Interventions

Intermediate and Secondary Levels. Ask the parents to involve their youngster in comparative buying activities at department stores in which there are directories. Tell the parents to assist their youngster in identifying the categories that they need to look up for specific purchases (e.g., a teakettle—HOUSEWARES; a notebook—STATIONERY; an end table—FURNITURE).

Specific Objective D

The student locates offices and other locations in various buildings by using their directories.

Teacher Interventions

Intermediate Level. Set up a simulated building directory. Write the names of professional offices, firms, and agencies that are currently important to the student and those that are likely to be important to his or her successful functioning in the future (Division of Vocational Rehabilitation, Legal Aid Society, Family Planning, Social Security Administration, etc.). Give the student slips of paper with the name of each of the offices listed on the simulated directory (see Figure 1.26), and ask the student to tell you each firm's office number and probable floor.

Secondary Level. Take trips into the community to visit office buildings and other buildings, such as a hospital or library, where there might be a directory. (It might be advisable to clear this activity with the building manager prior to the visit, especially if you are taking a large group.) Ask the student to identify those firms in the building that might be of importance to the student and to specify their location. Provide assistance as necessary.

Family Interventions

Intermediate and Secondary Levels. Ask the parents to take their youngster with them when they visit a doctor's, dentist's, lawyer's, or other professional's office. Tell the parents to explain to their youngster how to use

MONUMENTAL STATE BUILDING — Office Directory

A – L

Alberta Arcale, M.D.	302
Sara Chan, D.D.S.	201
Robert Dolite, D.O.	103
Marc Evans, P.T.	105
Florida Enterprises	304
Graham Motors, Inc.	306
Harbor Lighting Co.	301
Robert Irving, CPA	102
Japanese Cultural Center	203
Kids' Corner Toys, Inc.	303
London Importers and Exporters	308

M – Z

Nail Emporium	206
Oval Office Supplies	101
Pipe Fitters' Union	202
Quaker Home Furnishings	104
Roger's Restaurant	106
Social Services Dept.	107
Toys, Inc.	309
Unicorn Magic Supplies	307
Angelo Valente, M.D.	205
Wings Airline	207
Xantippe Greek Foods	305
Zebra Children's Books	108

FIGURE 1.26. Office building directory.

the directory to identify the location of the office. Encourage the parents to do the same when they visit firms, go to a multilevel library, visit sick relatives or friends who are hospitalized, and so on.

Specific Objective E

The student identifies times of mail pickup on mailbox schedules.

Teacher Interventions

Primary Level. Take the student for a walk, and assist him or her in identifying mailboxes. Help the student differentiate between those that are mail pickup stations and those that are for storage. (Those used for mail storage are usually of a different color and are without an opening at the top.) At each of the mailboxes encountered, drop in a letter or a card.

Intermediate Level. Make up a simulated copy of a mail pickup schedule that might be posted on a neighborhood mailbox. Point out the key words, relating them, when applicable, to calendar notations (e.g., SATURDAYS, SUNDAYS, HOLIDAYS) and key abbreviations such as A.M. and P.M. Explain the meanings of words and abbreviations. Give the student a copy of a second mailbox schedule, and ask him or her to tell you the mail pickup times.

Proceed by playing the "Mail Carrier" game in which the student must get his or her mail to the mailbox before you, playing the part of the mail carrier, arrive at the mailbox.

Secondary Level. On special occasions when the student needs to write notes and/or mail cards to friends and relatives (on happy occasions such as birthdays and special days such as Father's Day and on sad occasions when someone is ill or there has been a death in the family), implement a lesson in which the student makes a personal card or writes a simple note and then mails it according to the schedule of a nearby mailbox.

Family Interventions

Intermediate and Secondary Levels. Ask the parents to take their youngster with them when they mail letters and other correspondence. Tell them to set up situations in which they are too late for a specific mailbox and have to seek out an alternate mailbox or go to a post office to mail their correspondence.

 Specific Objective F

The student finds the locations of foods and other items from supermarket directories.

Teacher Interventions

Primary Level. Set up a class or school store in which the student is expected to identify food and other items by pictures on their labels and the prices of these items by price labels. Make certain that the student knows the concept of what an aisle is. It may be necessary to develop the concept by relating it to the aisles in the classroom and to aisles that the student can name that are found in movie theaters and in sports stadiums.

Intermediate Level. Set up a large simulated supermarket directory for the items found in the class or school supermarket. Set up aisles in the classroom with desktops serving as shelves. In each aisle place at least one representative item within a food category.

List the major categories of foods, and write the designated aisle number (or letter) next to each category. Name a category and list some representative foods that belong to the category: for example, meat—chicken, pork chops, steak; fruit (or produce)—oranges, apples, peaches; dairy—milk, cheese, sour cream. Then make a food category chart (see Figure 1.27).

Use this chart to play a "Categories" game in which you name a food item and the student names the category. Make a copy of an actual directory that is found in a community supermarket, and use it to practice identifying the aisles in which food and other items may be found. Once the student develops skill in using both the simulated and reproduced directories, take him or her to the supermarket whose directory you have copied. Give the student a shopping list on which he or she must write the aisle number where the item is likely to be found.

Secondary Level. Give the student a comparison shopping list that he or she must use to investigate the prices of foods and other items at a minimum of two supermarkets (if available in the community). Take the student to these stores, and ask him or her to write down the aisle number and

(a) Fruit (b) Vegetables (c) Meat

____ apples   ____ celery
____ pork chops   ____ tomatoes
____ potatoes   ____ ham steak
____ grapes   ____ grapefruit
____ cherries   ____ bacon
____ lettuce   ____ corn
____ leg of lamb   ____ chicken
____ bananas   ____ beans
____ carrots   ____ hamburger
____ oranges   ____ pears
____ roast beef   ____ strawberries

FIGURE 1.27. Category game worksheet.

Bargain Supermarket

Baked Goods	4	Greeting Cards	2
Beverages	4	Household Cleaners	7
Candy	10	Household Supplies	7
Canned Fruit	3	Meat	8
Canned Vegetables	3	Medicines	5
Cookies	10	Paper Goods	7
Cosmetics	5	Pet Foods	9
Dairy	6	Snacks	10
Frozen Foods	8	Vegetables	1
Fruit	1	Vitamins	5

FIGURE 1.28. Supermarket directory.

price of each of the items (see Figure 1.28). Because there are some supermarkets that have aisle signs rather than or in addition to directories, assist the student in using these signs to locate desired items.

Conclude by planning a class activity such as a celebration of various ethnic groups that requires shopping for needed food and paper goods, and ask the student to draw up the shopping list and to do the shopping. Videotape the activity and then review the videotape in class. Praise the student, as appropriate, for being an efficient shopper who uses his or her time well by going to the right aisles for the different items on the list.

Family Interventions

Intermediate Level. Ask the parents to take their child on shopping trips to the supermarket. Tell the parents to take a tour of the supermarket and point out to their child that, for example, all the fresh fruit and fresh vegetables are often called "produce" and are located in Aisle 1. (Tell them they may have to develop the concept of what an aisle is.)

Tell them that they should then refer to the directory to verify that it has correctly listed PRODUCE as being in Aisle 1. Encourage them to repeat this activity for each of the major categories of food and nonfood items.

Secondary Level. Ask the parents to give their youngster a family shopping list that he or she must fill. Tell the parents to take their youngster to a supermarket with which he or she is not familiar. Ask them to observe their youngster to make certain that he or she uses the supermarket directory as part of an efficient and organized shopping plan.

 ## Specific Objective G

The student identifies foods and food prices from cafeteria and fast-food bulletin boards.

Teacher Interventions

Primary Level. Make a list of the student's preferred foods. Include snacks as well as foods that are parts of meals. Place pictures of the food items next to the words to assist the student in identifying the words. Remove the pictures as soon as the student is able to identify the words without the picture clues.

Set up a simulated cafeteria or fast-food bulletin board that lists these preferred foods and their prices. (Remember to use realistic prices.) Ask the student to tell you what foods are available in the restaurant and how much each of the items costs.

Intermediate Level. Expand the list developed as part of the primary-level activity to include a wider range of food options that are typically found in cafeterias and fast-food restaurants. Use this bulletin board in a role-play in which you play the customer who orders a meal and the student hits the "keys" of a mock cash register on which the names of the food and beverage items are written (see Figure 1.29).

```
Fast-Food Cash Register

Hamburger        ☐   Cheeseburger   ☐

Colossoburger    ☐   Bacoburger     ☐

Large Fries      ☐   Small Fries    ☐

Mashed Potatoes  ☐   Baked Potato   ☐

Coleslaw         ☐   Garden Salad   ☐

Coke             ☐   Pepsi          ☐

Coffee           ☐   Orange Juice   ☐

Milkshake        ☐   Frozen Dessert ☐
```

FIGURE 1.29.   Sample fast-food cash register.

Secondary Level.   Arrange for a number of long field trips during which lunch must be eaten out. Take the student to a cafeteria or fast-food restaurant with which he or she is not familiar, and observe him or her ordering lunch. Videotape the trip, and review it with the student.

Family Interventions

Primary Level.   Ask the parents to take their child to cafeterias and fast-food restaurants when feasible. Tell them to demonstrate their ordering process to their child by talking aloud their decision-making process, for example, "I see that they have roast chicken, and half a roast chicken is on special today for $3.99; since I am on a diet I'd better order that instead of the fried chicken!"

Intermediate Level. Ask the parents to take their child to a cafeteria or fast-food restaurant and to expect the child to share his or her decision-making process just as they did in the primary-level activity. Encourage the parents to assist their child whenever he or she makes errors in the process, such as misidentifying the food item or its price.

Secondary Level. Ask the parents to observe their youngster as he or she orders food in a variety of settings. Remind them to only provide assistance if their youngster is experiencing difficulty in decoding the menus or item and/or price information on cafeteria and fast-food bulletin boards (see Goal XII, Specific Objectives A and B).

 ## Specific Objective H

The student locates departure and arrival times from bus, train, and airline schedules, bulletin boards, and television monitors.

Teacher Interventions

Primary Level. Take trips to intercity bus and train stations and to airports (if they are located in or near the community). Point out arrival and departure bulletin boards and television monitors on which arrivals and departures are displayed. Ask the student if he or she knows why these items are found at bus and railroad stations and airports. If necessary, assist the student with developing the concept that both passengers who are going on a trip (departing) and people waiting to pick up arriving passengers need this important information.

Intermediate Level. When they are easily available, send away for intercity bus and train schedules. Point out the words ARRIVAL(S) and DEPARTURE(S) and the abbreviations A.M., P.M., ARR., and DEPART. Explain the meaning of each of the words and abbreviations. Ask the student to point to these words and abbreviations when you say them.

Follow up by pointing to each of them and asking the student to say them aloud, to tell you what they mean, and to use each word in a sentence. Continue by making a chart (see Figure 1.30) of an airport television

ARRIVALS

Airline	Flight	From	Gate	Time
USAIR	167	NY: La Guardia	16	3:45
TWA	245	Boston	20	4:40
AA	154	Maine	8	Delayed
KLM	409	Amsterdam	12	12:15
TWA	308	St. Louis	—	Canceled
USAIR	324	Baltimore	14	Delayed

DEPARTURES

Airline	Flight	Destination	Gate	Time
USAIR	123	Philadelphia	11	9:45
AA	316	Las Vegas	9	2:30
TWA	504	San Diego	7	10:25
ELAL	289	Tel Aviv	8	Canceled
USAIR	743	Washington	2	Delayed
AA	470	Hartford	10	8:20

FIGURE 1.30. Airport TV monitors.

monitor that includes gate information and the words CANCELED and DELAYED, and has the abbreviations for airlines and their flight numbers. Use this chart to ask the student to give you information on specified flights.

You may wish to engage in a role-play in which the student pretends to be an airport public address announcer who is announcing the information on the chart (simulated monitor).

Secondary Level. Discuss with the student places he or she has visited, and ask him or her to tell what means of transportation were used to get to these places. Ask the student whether there are any cities, states, or countries he or she would like to visit in the future. After the student has named a number of locations, obtain travel brochures (see Goal XI, Specific Objective C) for these places and any bus, train, or airline schedules. Ask him or her to plan several trips and to indicate possible arrival and departure times.

Family Interventions

Intermediate and Secondary Levels. Ask the parents to take their youngster to bus depots, train stations, and airports in order to pick up visitors and on trips for which they must take intercity buses, trains, or airplanes (if feasible and practical).

Tell the parents to demonstrate how they use bulletin boards and television monitors to identify key information such as the location of the bus, train, or airplane (common carriers) and the times of arrival and departure. Urge them to have their youngster use the schedule information to report to them on arrival and departure times and the locations of these common carriers.

GOAL VIII.

The student will correctly carry out directions written on equipment, machinery, games, toys, and items that are to be assembled.

SPECIFIC OBJECTIVES

The student:

☐ A. Operates vending machines.

☐ B. Operates coin-operated washers and dryers.

    ☐ C. Follows directions written on packages of food, household cleaning products, and other packages and containers.

    ☐ D. Follows the directions provided with toys and games.

    ☐ E. Follows the directions provided with objects to be assembled.

SUGGESTED ACTIVITIES

 ## Specific Objective A
The student operates vending machines.

Teacher Interventions

Primary Level. Take the student to an area in the community where there are vending machines that sell food and beverage snacks. Demonstrate operating the various styles of vending machines, including those with push buttons and pull-out knobs. Pay particular attention to those with number and letter push buttons by drawing an analogy to a push-button telephone.

    Talk aloud your decision-making process: for example, "I want orange juice, and it is marked with the letter B and the number 6 and costs 75 cents, so I must put three quarters in the coin slot and press the B and 6 buttons." Carry out the process, and ask the student to observe you as you go through each of the steps in the process. Make sure you point out the words INSERT COIN and COIN RETURN. Follow up by assisting the student in obtaining his or her own snack from the same vending machine.

Intermediate Level. Make flashcards on which you have written 5 CENTS, 10 CENTS, 25 CENTS, 50 CENTS, and $1.00 and NICKEL, DIME, QUARTER, and DOLLAR. Give the student a quantity of nickels, dimes, quarters, and dollar bills, and tell him or her to place the coins on the appropriate flashcards. Collect boxes of the same size, and cut coin slots in their lid.

    Ask the student to pretend that these boxes are vending machines. Put cards with varying money amounts (depending on the costs currently found on vending machines in the community) on the lids, and ask the student to use exact change only.

    After the student successfully performs this activity, engage in a role-play in which the student does not have the exact change and you play the part of a vending machine that dispenses the change. Ask the student to verify the change received. Deliberately make some mistakes to check that the student is verifying change received.

Vary this role-play by giving the student only dollar bills and pretending to be a vending machine that has a dollar bill changer. Again, urge the student to verify change because "the machine is defective and sometimes makes mistakes." Follow up with trips in the community in which the student uses vending machines to make purchases of food and beverages.

Secondary Level. Take trips into the community to identify vending machines that sell items other than food and beverages. Review these machines and their items with the student. (Note: A female teacher might take a female student to a bathroom to show her a sanitary napkin vending machine while a male teacher, when appropriate, might take a male student into a bathroom to show him a condom vending machine.)

Family Interventions

Primary, Intermediate, and Secondary Levels. Ask the parents to demonstrate the operation of vending machines to their youngster. Tell the parents to gradually increase the complexity of the task by beginning with exact change only, proceeding to change verification, dollar bill changing with change verification, and vending machines that dispense items other than food, such as books, articles of clothing, and sanitary napkins.

Specific Objective B

The student operates coin-operated washers and dryers.

Teacher Interventions

Intermediate and Secondary Levels. Take the student to a laundromat. Show the student various parts of the machines: the washer (lid or door, control dial, agitator, coin slot, etc.) and the dryer (the door or lid, timer, temperature dial, starter button, coin slot, etc.). Point out the numbers and words appearing on these appliances.

Make a quick sketch of the control dials, and on your return to the school, construct large cardboard washer and dryer control dials (see Figures 1.31 and 1.32), and ask the student to read the numbers and words aloud. Provide help as needed. Follow up by taking the student back to the laundromat, and supervise him or her using the washer and dryer to wash his or her gym clothes (or other dirty clothes that the parents have agreed to send in for this activity).

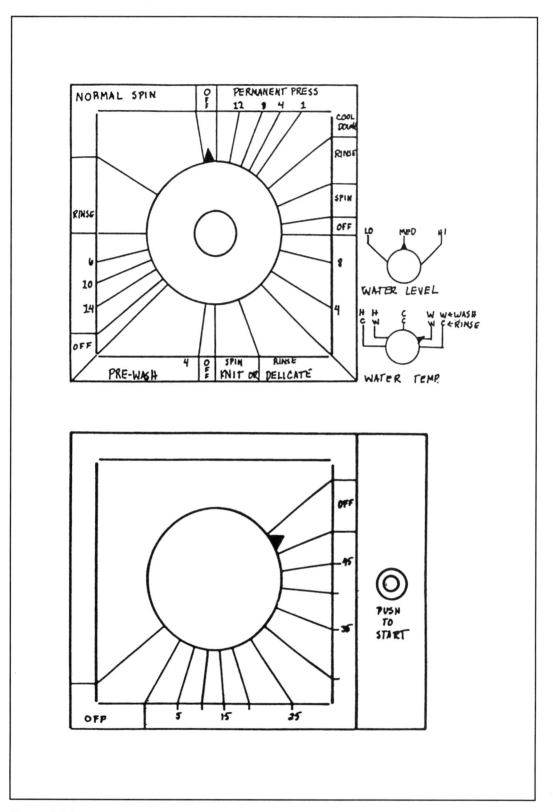

Figure 1.31. Washer and dryer control dials.

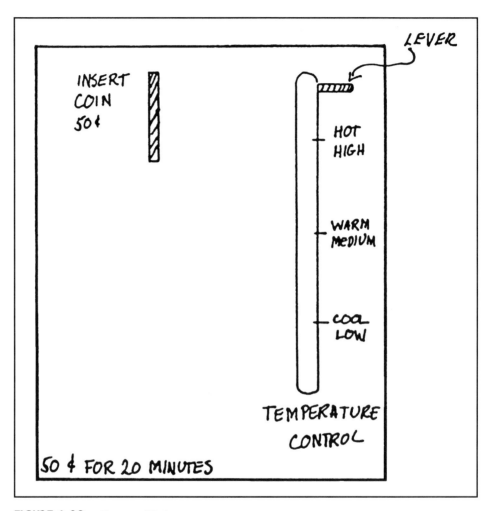

FIGURE 1.32. Dryer with lever.

Family Interventions

Intermediate and Secondary Levels. Ask the parents to pretend that their washer and dryer are not working properly (and/or take advantage of a real malfunction) and take their youngster to a laundromat. Tell the parents to pay special attention to the color and nature of the clothing and the implications of setting control dials. Encourage them to provide their youngster with a variety of clothing and linens so that he or she has an opportunity to experience the various settings.

Specific Objective C

The student follows directions written on packages of food, household cleaning products, and other packages and containers.

Teacher Interventions

Primary Level. Take the student to a supermarket or grocery, and purchase a variety of packaged foods that have cooking instructions written on them.

Upon your return to school and as you unpack the bags, demonstrate reading aloud the cooking directions, and comment on these directions and when you are going to use them. For one of the items, immediately follow the directions and prepare the food and join the student in enjoying it as a treat later in the day.

Intermediate Level. Ask the parents to tell you what food packages they use in the home, and then review these packages for any written cooking or preparing directions.

Next, make flashcards of the fractions, whole numbers, abbreviations, words, and phrases that you find on these food packages, such as DIRECTIONS, PREHEAT, STIR, BOIL, ADD, 3/4 CUP, 350° F, 25–30 MIN., SHAKE WELL BEFORE USING, BLEND, and MIX. Use these flashcards with the student for rapid recognition.

Once the student is able to read these packages with facility, engage him or her in the preparation of food items in which the student follows the directions under your supervision or the supervision of a classmate.

For the student who is unable to read the words, numerals, abbreviations, and phrases, develop pictorial directions for simple food items (see Figure 1.33). Put these pictorial directions on index cards and keep them in the student's recipe box.

Once the student is able to follow the cooking and preparation directions on food packages, assist him or her in reading and following through on the directions appearing on packages of household cleaning products and other products that come in packages and containers.

Secondary Level. Help the student to plan a variety of nutritious snacks and meals (breakfasts, lunches, and dinners) that he or she might prepare for a weekly menu for his or her family. Ask the student to shop for the items needed for the weekly menu and to ask his or her parents for permission to make the breakfasts and dinners for the week and the lunches over the weekend. Assign the student the task of making lunches during the school week.

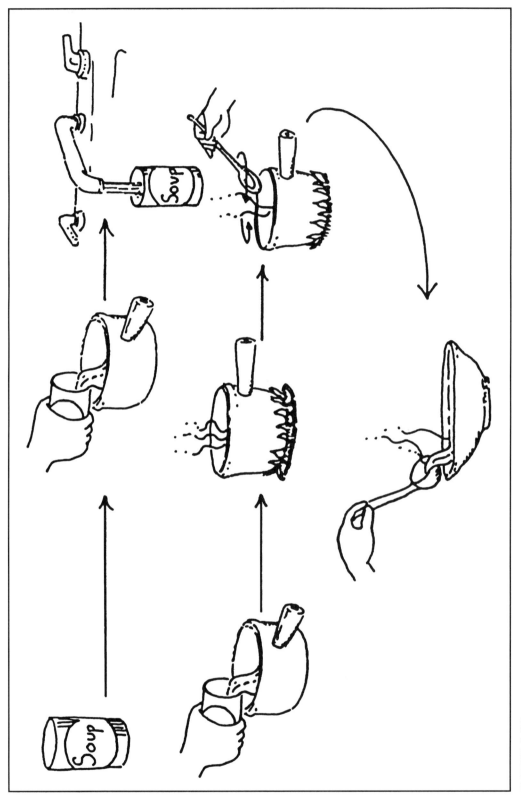

FIGURE 1.33. Pictorial directions for preparing soup.

Family Interventions

Intermediate and Secondary Levels. Ask the parents to demonstrate to their youngster how they use the directions on food packages, household cleaning packages, and other packages and containers involved in various food preparation, cleaning, household repair, and household maintenance tasks. Tell the parents to assist their youngster in reading the directions and carrying them out successfully in the specified order.

Specific Objective D

The student follows the directions provided with toys and games.

Teacher Interventions

Primary, Intermediate, and Secondary Levels. Bring a selection of games and toys that are appropriate to the student's interest and ability levels. Locate the playing directions on package inserts or on the box itself. Read the directions aloud to the student as you demonstrate the specified steps. Ask the student to read the directions alone and to demonstrate the steps to a classmate or classmates.

It may be necessary to make flashcards of the key words often found in game directions (e.g., SPIN, TAKE A TURN, ROLL THE DICE, TAKE A CARD, MOVE THREE SQUARES, MISS A TURN, GO BACK). Use the flashcards to practice with the student until he or she is able to explain the directions in games that have these words to someone else.

During free time provide the student with a choice of new games and toys that he or she might wish to play with a classmate or classmates. Praise him or her for figuring out how to play them without your assistance.

For the student who is unable to follow the written directions provided with toys or games, make pictorial directions (see Figures 1.34 and 1.35). Encourage the student to use these pictorial directions to play with the toy or game.

Family Interventions

Primary, Intermediate, and Secondary Levels. Ask the parents to purchase table games and toys appropriate to their youngster's age and ability level. Tell

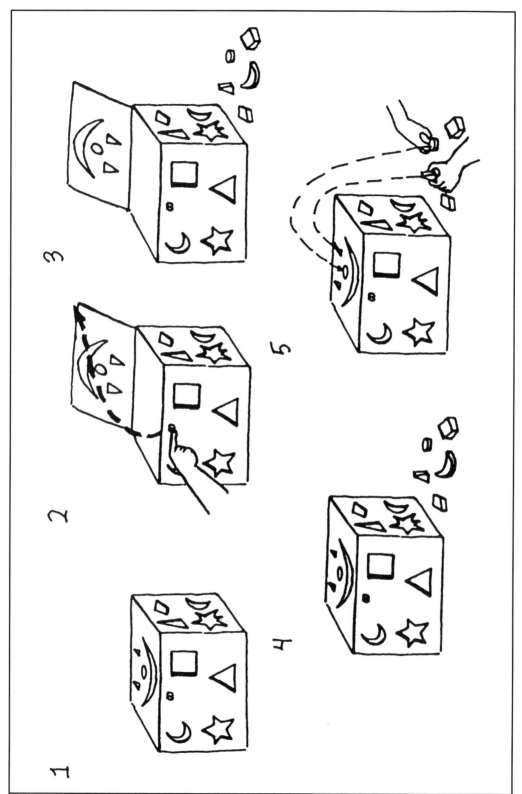

FIGURE 1.34. Pictorial directions for simple toys.

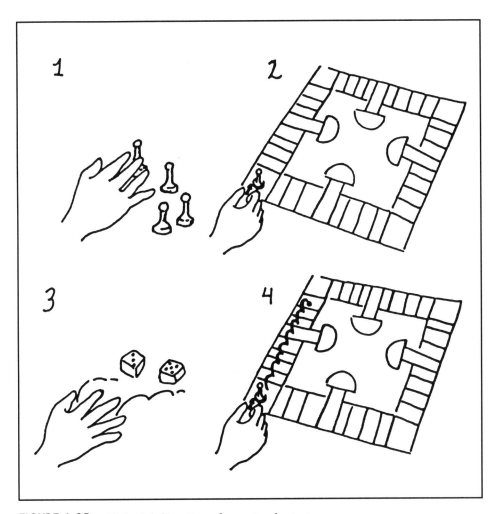

FIGURE 1.35. Pictorial directions for a simple game.

the parents to play with the games and toys as part of their family's leisure-time activities. Urge them to use games and toys as an interesting and enjoyable substitution for watching television or listening to music on the radio or stereo system.

 Specific Objective E

The student follows the directions provided with objects to be assembled.

Teacher Interventions

Intermediate and Secondary Levels.   Bring into the classroom a variety of items that need to be assembled and the printed directions found in inserts and written on boxes (e.g., balsa wood airplanes, flashlights and batteries, electric toothbrushes and batteries). Show the student the unassembled items and the directions. Choose one item, read aloud the directions, one at a time, and carry them out. Emphasize key words.

Once the object is assembled, disassemble it, and ask the student to assemble the item, using the directions. Proceed to similar objects to be assembled without providing the student with a demonstration to model.

Make flashcards of words and phrases that are frequently found in directions for assembling objects. Practice with these flashcards until the student is able to identify, explain, and perform such actions as INSERT, PLACE, JOIN, CONNECT, TWIST, and REMOVE.

For those students who are experiencing difficulty in reading the directions, it may be necessary to prepare pictorial directions (see Figure 1.36) for those items that will most likely have to be assembled (e.g., a pump bottle for window spray and other household cleaners).

Family Interventions

Intermediate and Secondary Levels.   Ask the parents to demonstrate to their youngster how to assemble various items that are used in household maintenance and repair. Encourage the parents to turn over responsibility for assembling and using these items to their youngster.

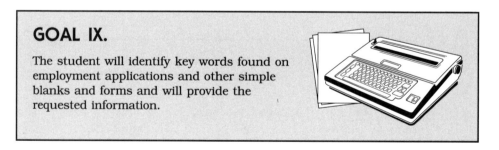

GOAL IX.

The student will identify key words found on employment applications and other simple blanks and forms and will provide the requested information.

See Unit 2, "Functional Writing," Goal II, for suggested activities.

GOAL X.

The student will locate and utilize written information found on bills, work time cards, check stubs, and store receipts.

Merchandise Receipt	
Item #1	$25.00
Item #2	40.00
Total	$65.00
Paid	$80.00
Change	$15.00

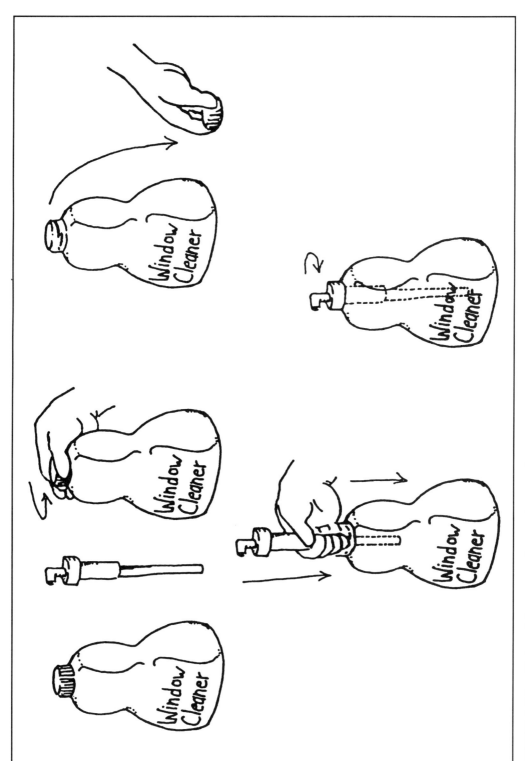

FIGURE 1.36. Pictorial directions for an object to be assembled.

149

See the Sample Lesson Plans near the end of this unit.

SPECIFIC OBJECTIVES

The student:

❏ A. Pays, by the due date, the correct amount for goods received and services obtained.

❏ B. Identifies and verifies gross pay, net pay, and deduction information found on paycheck stubs.

❏ C. Checks store receipts to verify that they are correct and that any change received is also correct.

❏ D. Verifies information found on work time cards.

SUGGESTED ACTIVITIES

 Specific Objective A

The student pays, by the due date, the correct amount for goods received and services obtained.

Teacher Interventions

Intermediate Level. Bring to the classroom a selection of bills with due dates printed on them (e.g., utility, insurance, department store, and telephone bills). Point out the information on the bills, including the amount due, the due date, and late charges. Assist the student in identifying the key information.

If needed, make flashcards of key words and phrases typically found on bills, such as AMOUNT DUE, PLEASE REMIT, PAY BY, PAYMENT DUE, KEEP THIS PART OF BILL FOR YOUR RECORDS, INCLUDE STUB WITH PAYMENT, MAKE CHECK PAYABLE TO, and MAIL TO.

Continue by asking the student to write out "mock" checks to pay the bills. Review the alternate ways of writing dates: with the written name of the month and with only numbers separated by slash marks or hyphens. Make flashcards with the three different ways, and ask the student to make matching sets.

Secondary Level. If the student gets bills of any kind, ask him or her to bring them to the classroom. (Make sure you do not invade the student's privacy.)

Ask the student to review the bills with you, identifying the key words and phrases. Assist the student, if needed, in writing checks and identifying places in the community where he or she can pay the bill in person. Ask the student to tell you how he or she would travel to these locations to pay his or her bills.

Family Interventions

Intermediate Level. Ask the parents to involve their child in the bill-paying process, including opening the bills, putting them aside for payment, and actually paying them by mail or in person.

Secondary Level. Ask the parents to give their youngster increasing responsibility for the payment of any personal bills when he or she demonstrates independence in the several sequential steps involved. Tell the parents to work for complete independence but to accept and reward partial performance.

Specific Objective B

The student identifies and verifies gross pay, net pay, and deduction information found on paycheck stubs.

Teacher Interventions

Intermediate Level. Bring a selection of paychecks (simulated, if necessary) and paycheck stubs to the classroom. Point out and explain the information on the checks and check stubs (e.g., gross pay, net pay, F.I.C.A., state tax, federal tax, medical insurance).

Ask the student to read each item aloud and to explain what it means. Provide assistance and explanations as needed, in terms of not only what each item is but also what the reason or purpose is for each one.

Secondary Level. Make a worksheet for verifying deduction information and pay amounts on the paycheck stub (see Figure 1.37). Ask the student to bring one of his or her own actual paychecks, if available, to the classroom. If the parents are willing, ask them to give the student one of their paycheck stubs to bring to the class to use in this verification activity.

Give the student a blank worksheet, and ask him or her to use a paycheck stub to fill in and to verify the deduction information by doing the necessary arithmetical computations.

Place of Employment

Identifica-tion number	Pay Period ending	Gross earnings	Annuity option	F.I.C.A.	Federal income tax withheld	State income tax withheld	Net amount after taxes
000-00-0000	2/15/74	200.00		11.75	40.22	9.70	139.53

Total earnings and taxes since January 1

Gross earnings	Annuity option	F.I.C.A.	Federal tax	State tax	Other deductions	
600.00		33.45	120.66	27.30	Med. ins.	5.50

Net amount of check   134.03

Name:

FIGURE 1.37.   Sample paycheck stub.

Family Interventions

Intermediate Level.   Ask the parents to make flashcards of the words and phrases typically found on paychecks and pay stubs. Tell the parents to use these flashcards to assist their child in the rapid recognition of these key words and phrases.

Secondary Level.   Ask the parents to involve their youngster in the budgeting process in which paychecks (and any other income) are used to determine budgetary constraints and decisions. Remind them to emphasize the verification of the information on the paycheck stub and the recording of that information for future reference as in income tax preparation and social security credits.

 ## Specific Objective C

The student checks store receipts to verify that they are correct and that any change received is also correct.

Teacher Interventions

Primary Level.   Construct a price-matching game. On a large piece of tagboard, draw squares and print a price in each square. Give the student square playing pieces with prices on them to match the prices printed on the tagboard playing card. Play the first game by asking the student to simply make the matches. Continue by calling out each price and having the student locate the correct square and place it on the playing board in its appropriate spot.

Intermediate Level.   Bring empty food and other packages to the classroom with their prices still on them. Draw up several sample store receipts that reflect the prices and total bill of different arrangements of the packages. Ask the student to verify that he or she has only been charged for the items received and that all listed prices and the total bill are correct. Encourage the student to use a calculator in carrying out the process.

Include several incorrect receipts as well as correct ones. Start off with the correct ones before introducing the concept that errors can be made. Ask the student what he or she should do upon finding an error in a store receipt. Engage the student in a role-play in which he or she returns to the store and finds the manager to demonstrate the error and to seek a refund.

Secondary Level. Plan a classroom activity such as a luncheon for parents or a holiday party. Ask the student to play a major role in carrying out the several steps in the process: making up the shopping list, estimating costs, doing the shopping, verifying store receipts, preparing the snacks and meal, decorating the room, and organizing the luncheon/party.

Introduce an additional step in the process in which the student must monitor cash register figures as an integral part of the verification process.

Family Interventions

Intermediate Level. Ask the parents to take their child to various stores and shops in which they make needed purchases. Tell the parents to demonstrate how they monitor cash register figures, check store receipts, and verify the accuracy of change received. Tell the parents to talk aloud each step so that their child has an opportunity to share their thought processes.

Secondary Level. Ask the parents to give their youngster the task of doing the weekly shopping. Tell the parents to accompany him or her and to provide as little assistance as possible. Encourage them to turn over the total assignment to their youngster whenever he or she demonstrates independent competence.

Specific Objective D

The student verifies information found on work time cards.

Teacher Interventions

Intermediate Level. Obtain sample work time cards from your school (if used) and from businesses in the community that use time cards. Identify the information on these cards, and point out the information as you read it.

Make flashcards of the information, including time notations written in numerals, the days of the week (abbreviated and written out), the months of the year (numerically and in words), and the student's name. Practice with the student until he or she is able to identify the information found on the card.

Secondary Level. If possible, arrange to have a work time clock in the classroom that the student must use to check in and check out and to time specific classroom activities. If one is not available, give the student a small pad or notebook. Ask him or her to label each page with the month, day of the week, and date. Tell the student to write down his or her arrival and departure times each day.

Also, expect the student to mark down starting and finishing times for periods of class work to assist him or her in estimating the time needed to perform certain tasks, especially when attempting to increase his or her speed of response and/or time on task.

Family Interventions

Intermediate and Secondary Levels. Ask the parents if they must punch in at work. If so, ask them to bring home sample time cards and to show them to their youngster. Tell the parents to explain the information on these cards and how they use the information to verify any notations on pay-check stubs and other work records. If they do not, describe your intermediate-level activity, provide them with a duplicate set of flashcards, and ask them to engage in the same activity at home.

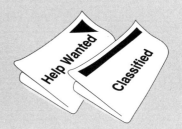

GOAL XI.

The student will locate and utilize information found in help wanted and other classified ads, printed advertisements, brochures, pamphlets, and other written materials.

SPECIFIC OBJECTIVES

The student:

❏ A. Locates information in help wanted and other classified sections of newspapers and magazines and uses the information in seeking employment and making purchases.

❏ B. Locates information of interest in printed advertisements and uses the information to purchase goods and services.

❏ C. Reviews pamphlets, brochures, and manuals and uses the information to make decisions on recreational, educational, vocational, and other activities.

SUGGESTED ACTIVITIES

Specific Objective A

The student locates information in help wanted and other classified sections of newspapers and magazines and uses the information in seeking employment and making purchases.

Teacher Interventions

Intermediate Level.   Show the student several copies of daily and Sunday newspapers and of appropriate magazines of interest to the student. Demonstrate how you use the table of contents to locate the various sections of the newspapers and magazines. Give the student additional copies, and ask him or her to locate the various sections from the table of contents.

Emphasize finding the help wanted (employment section) and other classified sections that include apartments and homes for rent/purchase as well as special purchases such as automobile sales and available services. Review the words that are commonly used in these ads along with frequently used abbreviations (see Figure 1.38). Assist the student in reading and comprehending the information in these ads. Discuss the ads that are of interest to the student now and that might be of interest as he or she gets older and, for example, looks for a job.

Secondary Level.   Give the student a variety of problems to solve in which he or she must locate information in the classified sections of newspapers and magazines. For example, ask the student to find employment opportunities that are located in specific parts of town, have specific job titles, specify desired wage and salary ranges, or indicate working hours and job duration.

Continue by asking the student to look through other classified ads to locate service companies that provide electrical work, plumbing services, and so on, as well as ads that provide information on available homes and apartments for rent/purchase.

Family Interventions

Intermediate Level.   Ask the parents to show their child how to locate the classified sections of newspapers and magazines found in the home. Tell the parents to review the information found in these ads by discussing commonly found terms and abbreviations with their child.

A.M.	= morning	sal.	= salary
P.M.	= afternoon and evening	exc.	= excellent
hrs.	= hours	comm.	= commission
Mon.	= Monday	w/	= with
Tues.	= Tuesday	w/sales	= with sales
Wed.	= Wednesday	w/stds.	= with standards
Thurs.	= Thursday	pd.	= paid
Fri.	= Friday	refs.	= references
wk.	= week	pos.	= position
wkly.	= weekly	mfr.	= manufacturer
mo.	= month	oppt.	= opportunity
eves.	= evenings	co.	= company
yr.	= year	mgr.	= manager
mgmt.	= management	exp.	= experience
ass't	= assistant	exp'd.	= experienced
thru	= through	dept.	= department
pref.	= preferred	sts.	= streets
bldgs.	= buildings	equip.	= equipment
dntwn.	= downtown	lic.	= license
transp.	= transportation	appt.	= appointment
gen.	= general	nec.	= necessary
estab.	= established	perm.	= permanent
temp.	= temporary	avail.	= available

FIGURE 1.38. Help wanted ad abbreviations.

Ask them to demonstrate the use of these sections whenever they are actually used. For example, "Andrew, I am looking for someone to repair the heating unit. I am going to check the classified section for possible furnace repair companies and individuals. Let's see if we can find any advertisements for furnace repair people together."

Secondary Level. Ask the parents to encourage their youngster to explore the jobs available in their community (either for current part-time employment or for potential future employment) by researching the employment classified ads. Tell them to do the same for major purchases of interest to the youngster and for services that he or she might need as an adult in the future.

Specific Objective B

The student locates information of interest in printed advertisements and uses the information to purchase goods and services.

Teacher Interventions

Intermediate Level. Give the student newspapers, magazines, and copies of advertising flyers. Discuss with the student the information found in these advertisements. Give the student sample shopping lists, and ask him or her to show you those advertisements that include the items that are found on the lists. Set aside an area to be used as an advertisement bulletin board.

Each day, post advertisements of interest to the student that you have cut out from newspapers and magazines. Also, post flyers obtained from supermarkets and other stores. Ask the student to tell you what is being advertised on today's bulletin board and the specific elements and details of each potential purchase.

Secondary Level. Give the student the task of locating advertisements for specific social and recreational purposes: for example, "We are planning some field trips into the community. Please find advertisements for entertainment, cultural, and sporting events that are available during the next several weeks." Ask the student to review these advertisements and make recommendations to you and to specify which events he or she might recommend to his or her parents as part of the family's recreational activities.

Continue by giving the student problems to solve such as "The electric fixture in the kitchen needs to be replaced. Please help me find a company or an individual whom we might wish to call."

Family Interventions

Intermediate Level. Ask the parents to involve their child in family decisions involving the purchasing of goods and services based on information found in newspapers and magazines and flyers that are received in the mail or left at their doorstep.

Secondary Level. Ask the parents to give their youngster the task of locating pertinent advertisements in newspapers, magazines, and flyers for specific household and family needs. Tell them to ask their youngster to make recommendations based on his or her review of the print materials.

 ## Specific Objective C

The student reviews pamphlets, brochures, and manuals and uses the information to make decisions on recreational, educational, vocational, and other activities.

Teacher Interventions

Intermediate and Secondary Levels. Obtain brochures and pamphlets such as the State Department of Motor Vehicles' driver's manual, travel brochures from travel agents, and pamphlets put out by businesses in the community for public relations purposes. Use these brochures, pamphlets, and manuals to study for the driver's test, to explore possible vacation sites, and to identify relevant information about businesses and potential jobs in the community.

Family Interventions

Intermediate and Secondary Levels. Ask the parents to share any relevant brochures, pamphlets, and manuals that are in the home with their youngster. Tell the parents to review these print materials with their youngster and to involve him or her in decisions made as a result of their review.

GOAL XII.

The student will seek the assistance of a responsible person to decode and explain, when necessary, printed and written material that he or she is unable to read.

SPECIFIC OBJECTIVES

The student:

❏ A. Identifies when he or she is experiencing difficulty in decoding and/or comprehending written materials.

❏ B. Identifies persons who are able and willing to assist him or her in decoding and interpreting written materials and seeks the assistance of these individuals at appropriate times.

SUGGESTED ACTIVITIES

 ## Specific Objective A

The student identifies when he or she is experiencing difficulty in decoding and/or comprehending written materials.

Teacher Interventions

Primary, Intermediate, and Secondary Levels. Explain to the student that there are times when everyone, including you, experiences difficulty in sounding out an individual word or understanding something that one is reading. Explain that when this occurs you may go to a dictionary for help, read more slowly, go back and reread, or ask someone for assistance.

Make it clear that a person should only go to someone else for help if he or she is not bothering the other person too much or unnecessarily and that person is willing to help.

Family Interventions

Primary, Intermediate, and Secondary Levels. Explain to the parents the strategy you are using in the classroom (see Teacher Interventions above). Emphasize to the parents that they must discourage their youngster from unnecessarily asking others for assistance while stressing independence as much as possible. Parents must be helped to understand that, while independence is usually desirable, we all are dependent on others for specific skills and tasks.

Specific Objective B

The student identifies persons who are able and willing to assist him or her in decoding and interpreting written materials and seeks the assistance of these individuals at appropriate times.

Teacher Interventions

Primary, Intermediate, and Secondary Levels. Assist the student in identifying classmates who may be able to help whenever he or she experiences difficulty in reading. If there is a team teacher, teaching assistant, volunteer, or older peer in the classroom, assist the student in identifying these individuals as potential helpers when he or she needs help in reading and in asking for assistance in a courteous way.

Family Interventions

Primary, Intermediate, and Secondary Levels. Tell the parents to assist their youngster in identifying family members and friends who can and are willing to help when he or she is experiencing difficulty with reading tasks. Ask them to set up situations in which their youngster should seek help. Remind them to discourage their youngster from asking for help when it is not needed.

Sample Lesson Plans

Sample Lesson Plan 1

Topic Area: Comprehension—Literal Level

Designed by: Charlotte Cook

Time Recommended: 30 minutes

Student Involved: Richard (Primary Special Class)

Background Information:

The student is able to identify numerals up to 999 when they are written. He is also able to identify food packages from pictures on labels. He has indicated in class discussions that one must use money to make purchases of food and other items. He has also, according to both him and his parents, made some purchases himself at a neighborhood convenience store.

General Goal *(Functional Reading X):*

The student will locate and utilize written information found on bills, work time cards, check stubs, and store receipts.

Specific Objective *(Functional Reading X-C):*

The student checks store receipts to verify that they are correct and that any change received is also correct.

Lesson Objective:

When the student is asked to play a price-matching game, he will match playing pieces with prices on them by placing them on a game board with corresponding prices. He will do so first by randomly matching them and then in response to each price as it is called out by the teacher. The student will say each price appearing on the game board when all of the squares have been filled.

Materials and Equipment:

- Tagboard with 15 squares in which various prices are marked
- Fifteen cut-out squares with matching prices as printed on tagboard game board

- Supermarket advertisement (flyer)
- Blank tagboard
- Blank game pieces

Motivating Activity:

Initiate a discussion with Richard in which he is asked to tell about trips to and purchases he has made at his local convenience store. Ask him to describe what he bought there and if he remembers approximately what each item cost. Continue by asking him to tell you what he might buy at the store if he were having a surprise birthday party for his mother and he had sufficient funds. Show him the teacher-made game board, and tell him that you and he will play a "price-matching game" at the end of the lesson.

Instructional Procedures:

Initiation—Write down the names of items the student indicated he might like to purchase for his mother's surprise birthday party. (It may be necessary for you to add items if Richard has not indicated sufficient items for the lesson or there are not enough items whose prices involve both dollar and cent notations.) Ask him what he thinks the approximate cost of each of these items is. Write the estimated prices (after a discussion of current and realistic prices) next to each of the items. Review with him how to say each of the prices in dollars and cents.

Guided Practice—Write on the chalkboard some additional prices, say each of them, and ask the student to repeat each one. Then provide the student with additional prices that he must say by himself. Provide assistance if and when needed.

Independent Practice—Give the student a flyer from a local store, and ask him to write the prices of several items on a piece of paper. Tell him to read these prices aloud to a classmate. Assign him, for homework, the task of making his own game board from the items on the flyer.

Closure—Give the student the tagboard game board and play the matching game in which he must randomly match game pieces to the board, then match them on command, and, finally, say each of the prices when the game board is complete.

Assessment Strategy:

Watch the student to see whether he matched the game pieces correctly. Listen to the student to see whether he said each of the prices on the chalkboard and on the game board correctly. Check his game board to see whether he has written the prices on his own game board correctly and if he can say the prices without error.

Follow-Up Activity or Objective:

If the student achieves the lesson objective, proceed to an activity involving the verification of store and other receipts.

Observations and Their Instructional Insights:

Sample Lesson Plan 2

Topic Area: Comprehension—Literal Level

Designed by: James Clinton

Time Recommended: 45 minutes

Student Involved: Rebecca (Intermediate Special Class)

Background Information:

The student is able to identify prices when they are written as numerals. She is also able to identify food and other products from pictures on package labels and can identify coins and paper currency. She has assisted her parents in doing the weekly shopping but has not yet paid for items purchased or verified that store receipts are correct.

General Goal (Functional Reading X):

The student will locate and utilize written information found on bills, work time cards, check stubs, and store receipts.

Specific Objective (Functional Reading X-C):

The student checks store receipts to verify that they are correct and that any change received is also correct.

Lesson Objective:

When the student is asked to review sample store receipts and to match them with items purchased to verify that she has been charged only for the purchases made and in the correct amounts, she will do so without any errors.

Materials and Equipment:

- Empty food and other packages
- Several simulated store receipts
- Pocket calculator

Motivating Activity:

Tell the student anecdotes about how on several occasions errors were made by the supermarket cashier when you did the weekly shopping. Relate how, even though you watched carefully as the cashier rang up the bill, errors were made and you were overcharged. Describe what happened when you went back to the store to get a refund. Ask Rebecca if something like that ever happened to her parents or somebody else she knew. Tell her to give you the details as she remembers them. Inform her that, at the end of the lesson, she and you will role-play seeking a refund from a store manager.

Instructional Procedures:

Initiation—Show the student empty food cans and other packages that you have brought into the classroom. Make different arrangements of the packages, and draw up simulated store receipts. Demonstrate how to use a pocket calculator to verify that the bill is correct. In the beginning, demonstrate only correct store receipts. After a while, demonstrate finding errors.

Guided Practice—Give the student some additional simulated store receipts, and ask the student to check whether each one is correct. Be sure to provide several sample store receipts that are incorrect. Provide assistance as needed.

Independent Practice—Give the student a worksheet on which there are pictures of empty grocery bags with food and other packages on a kitchen counter. (On each package, the price of the item should be marked.) To the right of each picture, show a simulated drawing of a store receipt. Ask the student to indicate which ones are correct and which ones are not.

Closure—Role-play finding errors in a store receipt and going back to the store to speak to the store manager.

Assessment Strategy:

Observe the student to see whether she used the calculator correctly and verified the simulated store receipts, identifying correctly those that were accurate and those that were not.

Follow-Up Activity or Objective:

If the student achieves the lesson objective, proceed to an activity involving the verification of change received after a purchase is made.

Observations and Their Instructional Insights:

Sample Lesson Plan 3

Topic Area: Comprehension—Literal Level

Designed by: Dewey Quayle

Time Recommended: 1 hour

Student Involved: Maureen (Secondary Special Class)

Background Information:

The student is able to identify prices when they are written as numerals. She is also able to identify coins and paper currency. She has assisted her parents in doing the weekly shopping but has not yet paid for items purchased or verified change, although she has verified whether store receipts are correct. She has not yet done any independent shopping.

General Goal *(Functional Reading X)*:

The student will locate and utilize written information found on bills, work time cards, check stubs, and store receipts.

Specific Objective *(Functional Reading X-C)*:

The student checks store receipts to verify that they are correct and that any change received is also correct.

Lesson Objective:

When the student is asked to plan a luncheon, she will make up the shopping list, carry out the shopping (in your presence), and correctly verify the accuracy of the bill and change received.

Materials and Equipment:

- Large writing pad to draw up luncheon (or party) plans
- Notepad for drawing up shopping list
- Pocket calculator
- Two pens or pencils
- Petty cash fund
- Teacher-made worksheet

Motivating Activity:

Tell the student anecdotes about how, on several occasions, you were given too little change by a supermarket cashier (or bank teller). Emphasize that if you had not checked to see whether you had received the correct change, you would have been cheated out of your money. Also relate anecdotes about when you received too much change and how you returned the extra money because it is the honest thing to do. Ask the student if she knows of similar experiences that her parents or other persons have had. Ask her to relate these incidents. Tell her that the class will be having a luncheon (or party) and that she will be acting as the "caterer."

Instructional Procedures:

Initiation—Discuss with the student that it will be necessary to reciprocate (develop the concept if necessary) for being invited to lunch by a nearby class, by inviting them to lunch in your classroom. Assist the student in making decisions about what to serve, estimating costs, and making up the required shopping list within the class budget. Demonstrate how to verify change through the addition process, that is, counting up from the cost to the amount of the payment.

Guided Practice—Play the role of the cashier, and role-play giving the student the correct change, using different costs and different amounts of payment and therefore different amounts of change. Provide assistance when needed. Begin with the correct amounts and end with some over- and some underpayments.

Independent Practice—Give the student a worksheet on which there are sample store receipts, pictures of payments made, and blanks that the student must complete with the correct amount of change that should be received, written in numerals.

Closure—Ask the student to plan the luncheon and to go on the shopping trip.

Assessment Strategy:

Observe the student to determine if she planned an appropriate luncheon, successfully made up the shopping list, carried out the shopping (in your presence), and correctly verified the accuracy of the bill and change received.

Follow-Up Activity or Objective:

If the student achieves the lesson objective, proceed to an activity involving the verification of information on bills, work time cards, and check stubs.

Observations and Their Instructional Insights:

Suggested Readings

Adams, G. L. (1984). *Normative adaptive behavior checklist.* Columbus, OH: Merrill.

Bailey, D., Jr., & Wolery, M. (1984). *Teaching infants and preschoolers with handicaps.* Columbus, OH: Merrill.

Bender, M., & Baglin, C. A. (1992). *Infants and toddlers: A resource guide for practitioners.* San Diego: Singular.

Bender, M., & Valletutti, P. J. (1982). *Teaching functional academics to adolescents and adults with learning problems.* Baltimore: University Park Press.

Berkell, D., & Brown, J. (Eds.). (1989). *Transition from school to work for persons with disabilities.* White Plains, NY: Longman.

Brighan, R., & Synder, J. (1986). *Developing application-oriented examples in language arts for students with mild handicaps.* Des Moines: Iowa State Department of Education, Bureau of Special Education.

Brolin, D. E. (1986). *Life-Centered Career Education: A competency-based approach* (rev. ed.). Reston, VA: Council for Exceptional Children.

Brolin, D. E., & Gysberg, N. C. (1989). Career education for students with disabilities. *Journal of Counseling and Development, 68,* 155–159.

Brolin, D. E., & Kokaska, C. J. (1979). *Career education for handicapped children and youth.* Columbus, OH: Merrill.

Browder, D. M., Hines, C., McCarthy, T. J., & Fees, J. (1984). A treatment package for increasing sight word recognition for use in daily living skills. *Education and Training of the Mentally Retarded, 19,* 191–200.

Brown, L. F., Branston, M. B., Hamre-Nietupski, S. M., Pumpian, L., Certo, N., & Gruenewald, L. (1979). A strategy for developing chronological-age-appropriate and functional curricular content for severely handicapped adolescents and young adults. *Journal of Special Education, 13,* 81–90.

Brown, L. F., Falvey, M., Pumpian, L., Baumgart, D., Nisbet, J., Ford, A., Schroeder, J., & Loomis, R. (Eds.). (1980). *Curricular strategies for teaching severely handicapped students functional skills in school and nonschool environments.* Madison: University of Wisconsin–Madison and Madison Metropolitan School District.

Brown, L. F., & Lehr, D. (1989). *Persons with profound disabilities.* Baltimore: Paul H. Brookes.

Bruder, M. B. (1987). Parent-to-parent teaching. *American Journal of Mental Deficiency, 91,* 435–438.

Bruininks, R., Thorlow, M., & Gilman, C. (1987). Adaptive behavior and mental retardation. *Journal of Special Eduction, 19,* 7–39.

Cavallaro, C. (1983). Language interventions in natural settings. *Teaching Exceptional Children, 16,* 65–70.

Cavallaro, C., & Poulson, C. (1987). Teaching language to handicapped children in natural settings. *Education and Treatment of Children, 8,* 1–24.

Chapman, J. E., & Heward, W. I. (1982). Improving parent-teaching communication through recorded telephone messages. *Teaching Exceptional Children, 49,* 79–82.

Chiang, B., & Ford, M. (1990). Whole language alternatives for students with learning disabilities. *LD Forum, 16,* 31–34.

Childs, R. (1979). A drastic change in curriculum for the educable mentally retarded. *Mental Retardation, 17,* 299–301.

Clark, G. M., & Knowlton, H. E. (1987). The transition from school to adult life. *Exceptional Children, 53,* 484–576.

Cohen, S. B., & Plaskon, S. P. (1980). *Language arts for the mildly handicapped.* Columbus, OH: Merrill.

Cronin, M. E., & Patton, J. R. (1993). *Life skills for students with special needs: A practical guide for developing real-life problems.* Austin, TX: PRO-ED.

Diehl, W. A., & Mikulecky, L. (1980). The nature of reading at work. *Journal of Reading, 24,* 221–227.

Drew, C. J., Logan, D. R., & Hardman, M. L. (1992). *Mental retardation: A life cycle approach* (5th ed.). New York: Merrill/Macmillan.

Dyck, N. J., Sankey, P., & Sundbye, N. W. (1983). *Survival words program.* Hindham, MA: Teaching Resources.

Falvey, M. A. (1986). *Community-based curriculum: Instructional strategies for students with severe handicaps.* Baltimore: Paul H. Brookes.

Fernald, G. M. (1983). *Remedial techniques in basic school subjects.* New York: McGraw-Hill.

Folk, M. C., & Campbell, J. (1978). Teaching functional reading to the TMR. *Education and Training of the Mentally Retarded, 13,* 322–326.

Fowler, S. A. (1988). Transition planning. *Teaching Exceptional Children, 20,* 62–63.

Garwood, S. G. (Ed.). (1983). *Educating handicapped children.* Rockville, MD: Aspen.

Gast, D. L., Ault, M. J., Wolery, M., Doyle, P. M., & Belanger, S. (1988). Comparison of constant time delay and the system of least prompts in teaching sight word reading to students with moderate retardation. *Education and Training in Mental Retardation, 23,* 117–128.

Glascoe, L. G., Miller, L. S., & Kokaska, C. J. (1986). *Life-Centered Career Education: Activity book one.* Reston, VA: Council for Exceptional Children.

Goldstein, H. (1975). *The social learning curriculum.* Columbus, OH: Merrill.

Goodman, K. S., & Goodman, Y. M. (1983). Reading and writing relationships: Pragmatic functions. *Language Arts, 60,* 590–599.

Gregory, G. P. (1979). Using the newspaper in the mainstreamed classroom. *Social Education, 43,* 140–143.

Grenot-Scheyer, M., & Falvey, M. A. (1986). Functional academic skills. In M. A. Falvey (Ed.), *Community-based curriculum: Instructional strategies for students with severe handicaps* (pp. 187–215). Baltimore: Paul H. Brookes.

Guess, D., Horner, R. D., Utley, B., Holvoet, J., Maxon, D., Tucker, D., & Warren, S. (1978). A functional curriculum sequencing model for teaching the severely handicapped. *AAESPH Review, 3,* 202–215.

Guthrie, J. T. (1981). Acquisition of newspaper readership. *The Reading Teacher, 34,* 616–618.

Guthrie, J. T., & Seifert, M. (1983). Profiles of reading activity in a community. *Journal of Reading, 26,* 498–508.

Hammill, D. D., & Bartel, N. E. (Eds.). (1990). *Teaching children with learning and behavioral problems* (5th ed.). Boston: Allyn & Bacon.

Hargis, C. H. (1982). Word recognition development. *Focus on Exceptional Children, 14,* 1–8.

Harry, B. (1992). *Cultural diversity, families, and the special education system: Communication and empowerment.* Colchester, VT: Teachers College Press.

Horner, R. H., Jones, D. N., & Williams, J. A. (1985). A functional approach to teaching generalized street crossing. *Journal of the Association for Persons with Severe Handicaps, 10,* 71–78.

Horner, R. H., Sprague, J., & Wilcox, B. (1982). Constructing general care programs for community activities. In B. Wilcox & G. T. Bellamy (Eds.), *Design of high school programs for severely handicapped students* (pp. 61–98). Baltimore: Paul H. Brookes.

Ianacone, R., & Stodden, R. (Eds.). (1987). *Transitional issues and directions for individuals who are mentally retarded.* Reston, VA: Council for Exceptional Children.

Johnson, D. W., & Johnson, R. T. (1986). Mainstreaming and cooperative learning strategies. *Exceptional Children, 52,* 553–561.

Johnston, E. B., Weinrich, B. D., & Johnson, A. R. (1984). *A sourcebook of pragmatic activities.* Tucson: Communication Skill Builders.

Jordan, J., Gallagher, J., Hutinger, P., & Karnes, M. (Eds.). (1992). *Early childhood special education: Birth to three.* Baltimore: Paul H. Brookes.

Junge, D. A., Daniels, M. H., & Karmis, J. S. (1984). Personnel managers' perceptions of requisite basic skills. *Vocational Guidance Quarterly, 33* (20), 138–146.

Kaiser, A. P., Alport, C. L., & Warren, S. (1987). Teaching functional language: Strategies for language intervention. In M. E. Snell (Ed.), *Systematic instruction for persons with severe handicaps* (pp. 247–272). Columbus, OH: Merrill.

Kirk, S. A., & Monroe, M. (1940). *Teaching reading to slow learning children.* Boston: Houghton Mifflin.

Kozol, J. (1986). *Illiterate America.* New York: Doubleday.

Kroth, R. L., & Otten, H. (1988). *Communicating with parents of exceptional children.* Denver: Love.

Marion, R. L. (1981). *Educators, parents, and exceptional children.* Rockville, MD: Aspen.

McClennen, S. E. (1991). *Cognitive skills for community living.* Austin, TX: PRO-ED.

McConachie, H., & Mitchell, D. R. (1985). Parents teaching their young mentally handicapped children. *Journal of Child Psychology and Psychiatry and Allied Disciplines, 26,* 389–405.

McDonnell, J., & Hardman, M. C. (1989). Employment preparation for high school students with severe handicaps. *Mental Retardation, 27,* 396–404.

McMullen, D. (1975). Teaching protection words. *Teaching Exceptional Children, 7,* 74–77.

Mercer, C. D., & Mercer, A. R. (1993). *Teaching students with learning problems* (4th ed.). New York: Merrill/Macmillan.

Mikulecky, L. (1984). Preparing students for workplace literacy demands. *Journal of Reading, 28,* 253–257.

Miller, L. S., Glascoe, L. G., & Kokaska, C. J. (1986). *Life-Centered Career Education: Activity book two.* Reston, VA: Council for Exceptional Children.

Miller, T. L., & Davis, E. E. (Eds.). (1982). *The mildly handicapped student.* New York: Grune & Stratton.

Mithaug, D. E., Martin, J. E., & Agran, M. (1987). Adaptability instruction: The goal of transitional programming. *Exceptional Children, 53,* 500–505.

Montieth, M. K. (1981). The magazine habit. *Language Arts, 58,* 965–969.

Nesselroad, M. L., & Nesselroad, E. M. (Eds.). (1984). *Working with parents of handicapped children: A book of readings for school personnel.* Lanham, MD: University Press of America.

Patton, J. R., Beirne-Smith, M., & Payne, J. S. (1990). *Mental retardation* (3rd ed.). Columbus, OH: Merrill.

Phelps, L. A. (Ed.). (1986). *School to work transition for handicapped youth: Perspectives on education and training.* Champaign, IL: University of Illinois Press.

Polloway, E. A., & Patton, J. R. (1993). *Strategies for teaching learners with special needs* (5th ed.). New York: Merrill/Macmillan.

Polloway, E. A., & Polloway, C. H. (1981). Survival words for disabled readers. *Academic Therapy, 16,* 443–448.

Polloway, E. A., & Smith, T.E.C. (1992). *Language instruction for students with disabilities* (2nd ed.). Denver: Love.

Robbins, F., Dunlap, G., & Plienis, A. (1991). Family characteristics, family training and the progress of young children with autism. *Journal of Early Intervention, 15,* 173–184.

Robinson, G. (1986). *Essential vocabulary: Words and phrases found in community settings.* Des Moines: Iowa State Department of Education.

Sarber, R. E., Halasz, M. M., Messmer, M. C., Bickett, A. D., & Lutzker, J. K. (1983). Teaching menu planning and grocery shopping skills to the mentally retarded mother. *Mental Retardation, 21,* 101–106.

Sawyer, H. W., & Sawyer, S. H. (1981). A teacher-parent communication training approach. *Exceptional Children, 47,* 305–306.

Schilit, J., & Caldwell, M. L. (1980). A word list of essential career/vocational words for mentally retarded students. *Education and Training of the Mentally Retarded, 15,* 113–117.

Schniedewind, N., & Salend, S. (1987). Cooperative learning works. *Teaching Exceptional Children, 19,* 22–25.

Simms, R. B., & Falcon, S. C. (1987). Teaching sight words. *Teaching Exceptional Children, 20,* 30–33.

Simpson, R. L. (1990). *Conferencing parents of exceptional children* (2nd ed.). Austin, TX: PRO-ED.

Smith, M., & Meyers, A. (1979). Telephone skills training for retarded adults: Group and individual demonstrations with and without verbal instruction. *American Journal of Mental Deficiency, 83,* 581–587.

Snell, M. E., & Browder, D. M. (1987). Domestic and community skills. In M. E. Snell (Ed.), *Systematic instruction for persons with severe handicaps* (pp. 334–389). Columbus, OH: Merrill.

Valletutti, P. J., & Bender, M. (1982). *Teaching interpersonal and community living skills: A curriculum model for handicapped adolescents and adults.* Baltimore: University Park Press.

Valletutti, P. J., & Dummett, L. (1992). *Cognitive development: A functional approach.* San Diego, CA: Singular.

Vukelich, C. (1984). Parents' role in the reading process: A review of practical suggestions and ways to communicate with parents. *The Reading Teacher, 37,* 472–477.

Wallace, G., Cohen, S. B., & Polloway, E. A. (1987). *Language arts: Teaching exceptional students.* Austin, TX: PRO-ED.

Watson, D. (Ed.). (1987). *Ideas and insights: Language arts in the elementary school.* Urbana, IL: National Council of Teachers of English.

Webster, E. J., & Ward, L. M. (1992). *Working with parents of young children with disabilities.* San Diego, CA: Singular.

Wehman, P., Renzaglia, A., & Bates, P. (1985). *Functional living skills for moderately and severely handicapped individuals.* Austin, TX: PRO-ED.

Welch, J., Nietupski, J., & Hamre-Nietupski, S. (1985). Teaching public transportation problem-solving skills to young adults with moderate handicaps. *Education and Training of the Mentally Retarded, 20,* 287–295.

Winton, P. J. (1986). Effective strategies for involving families in intervention efforts. *Focus on Exceptional Children, 19,* 1–10.

Winton, P. J. (1988). Effective communication between parents and professionals. In D. B. Bailey & R. J. Simeonsson (Eds.), *Family assessment in early intervention* (pp. 207–228). Columbus, OH: Merrill.

Selected Materials/Resources

GENERAL

Bender, M., & Valletutti, P. J. (1981). *Teaching functional academics: A curriculum guide for adolescents and adults with learning problems.* Baltimore: University Park Press.

Bogojaviensky, A. R., Grossman, D. R., Topham, C. S., & Meyer III, S. M. (1977). *The great learning book.* Menlo Park, CA: Addison-Wesley.

Brigance, A. (1992). *Vocabulary victory. Levels A–D.* East Moline, IL: Linguisystems.

Brolin, D. E. (1991). *Life-Centered Career Education: A competency based approach* (3rd ed.). Reston, VA: Council for Exceptional Children.

Dever, R. B. (1988). *A taxonomy of community living skills.* Washington, DC: American Association on Mental Retardation.

Doyle, E. (1980). *Skills for Daily Living series.* Baltimore: Media Materials.

Dupont, H., & Dupo, C. (1979). *Transition: A program to help students through the difficult passage from childhood through middle adolescence.* Circle Pines, MN: American Guidance Service.

Falvey, M. (1989). *Community-based curriculum: Instructional strategies for students with severe handicaps.* Baltimore: Paul H. Brookes.

Ferguson, D. L., & Wilcox, B. (1987). *The elementary/secondary system: Supportive education for students with severe handicaps. Module 1: The activity-based IEP.* Eugene: Specialized Training Program, University of Oregon.

Glascoe, L. G., Miller, L. S., & Kokaska, C. J. (1991). *Life-Centered Career Education: Activity book two.* Reston, VA: Council for Exceptional Children.

Hannon, K. E., & Thompson, M. A. (1992). *Life skills workshop: An active program for real-life problem solving.* East Moline, IL: Linguisystems.

McGraw, D., & Turnbow, G. N. (1991). *On my own in the community.* East Moline, IL: Linguisystems.

McGraw, D., & Turnbow, G. N. (1992). *On my own at home.* East Moline, IL: Linguisystems.

Miller, L. S., Glascoe, L. G., & Kokaska, C. J. (1989). *Life-Centered Career Education: Activity book one.* Reston, VA: Council for Exceptional Children.

Parmenter, T. R. (1980). *Vocational training for independent living.* New York: World Rehabilitation Fund.

Ritter, J. (1993). *The world is a wild place: When you share life experiences.* North Billerica, MA: Curriculum Associates.

Stiefel, B. (1987). *On my own with language.* East Moline, IL: Linguisystems.

Wehman, P., Renzaglia, A., & Bates, P. (1985). *Functional living skills for moderately and severely handicapped individuals.* Austin, TX: PRO-ED.

Wilcox, B., & Bellamy, G. T. (1987). *A comprehensive guide to the Activities Catalog: An alternative curriculum for youth and adults with severe disabilities.* Baltimore: Paul H. Brookes.

Zachman, L., Barrett, M., Huisingh, R., Orman, J., & Blagden, C. (1992). *Tasks of problem solving: A real life approach to thinking and reasoning. Adolescent.* East Moline, IL: Linguisystems.

READING

Ainsworth, B. (1980). *Functional Reading Filmstrip Series.* Baltimore: Media Materials.

Ainsworth, B., & Trautman, D. (1980). *Survival Reading at Home Series.* Baltimore: Media Materials.

Aukerman, R. C., & Aukerman, L. R. (1981). *How do I teach reading?* New York: Wiley.

Boning, R. A. (1990). *Specific Skills Series* (4th ed.). Baldwin, NY: Barnell Loft.

Brigance, A. H. (1993). *VICTORY: Reading success for intermediate, secondary-level students, ESL, and adult learners.* North Billerica, MA: Curriculum Associates.

Buchanan, C. D. (1966). *Programmed reading.* New York: McGraw-Hill, Sullivan Associates.

Dyck, N. J., Sankey, P., & Sundbye, N. W. (1983). *Survival words program.* Hingham, MA: Teaching Resources.

Engelmann, S., Becker, W., Hanner, S., & Johnson, G. (1989). *Corrective reading-decoding.* Chicago: Science Research Associates.

Engelmann, S., & Bruner, E. C. (1988). *Reading mastery: DISTAR reading.* Chicago: Science Research Associates.

Farnette, C., Forte, I., & Loss, B. (1969). *Kid's stuff: Reading and writing readiness.* Nashville: Incentive.

Harris, T., Creekmore, M., & Greenman, M. (1967). *Phonetic keys to reading.* Oklahoma City: Economy.

Kirk, S. A., Kirk, W. D., & Minskoff, E. (1985). *Phonic remedial reading drills.* Novato, CA: Academic Therapy.

Lenz, B. K., Schumaker, J. B., Deshler, D. D., & Beals, V. L. (1984). *Learning strategies curriculum: The word identification strategy.* Lawrence, KS: University of Kansas Institute for Research in Learning Disabilities.

May, F. B. (1990). *Reading as communication: An interactive approach* (3rd ed.). New York: Macmillan.

Polloway, E. A., & Polloway, C. H. (1981). Survival words for disabled readers. *Academic Therapy, 16,* 443–448.

Richey, J. (1978). *Drugstore language: A survival vocabulary.* Hayward, CA: Janus.

Richey, J. (1979). *Clothing language: A survival vocabulary.* Hayward, CA: Janus.

Richey, J. (1980). *Banking language: A survival vocabulary.* Hayward, CA: Janus.

Richey, J. (1980). *Credit language: A survival vocabulary.* Hayward, CA: Janus.

Richey, J. (1980). *Job application language: A survival vocabulary.* Hayward, CA: Janus.

Richey, J. (1980). *Restaurant language: A survival vocabulary.* Hayward, CA: Janus.

Richey, J. (1980). *Supermarket language: A survival vocabulary.* Hayward, CA: Janus.

Robinson, G. A. (1986). *Essential vocabulary: Words and phrases found in community settings.* Des Moines: Iowa Department of Education.

Roderman, W. H. (1978). *Reading and following directions: A Janus Survival Guide.* Hayward, CA: Janus.

Schoolfield, L. D., & Timberlake, J. B. (1974). *The phonovisual method* (rev. ed.). Rockville, MD: Phonovisual Products.

Spache, E. B. (1976). *Reading activities for child involvement.* Boston: Allyn & Bacon.

Stauffer, R. S. (1970). *The language experience approach to the teaching of reading.* New York: HarperCollins.

Sternberg, L. (1977). *Essential math and language skills.* Northbrook, IL: Hubbard.

Sullivan, M. W. (1966). *Sullivan Reading Program.* Palo Alto, CA: Behavioral Research Laboratories.

Sundbye, N. W., Dyck, N. J., & Wyatt, F. R. (1980). *Essential Sight Words Program.* Allen, TX: DLM.

Tavzel, C. S. (1987). *Blooming recipes.* East Moline, IL: Linguisystems.

Woodcock, R. W., Clark, C. R., & Davies, C. O. (1979). *Peabody Rebus Reading Program.* Circle Pines, MN: American Guidance Service, Longman.

Functional Writing

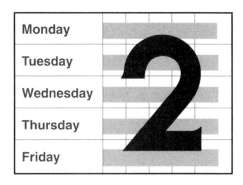

Monday	
Tuesday	
Wednesday	
Thursday	
Friday	

The implementation of a functional writing curriculum requires both the identification of the *specific content* of the writing program and the *instructional strategy* to be employed.

The *specific content* consists of those numerals, words, phrases, sentences, and abbreviations a person wishes to or is expected by others to put in writing as he or she interacts with others in diverse communicative contexts including the following:

- in response to the written inquiries of others (for example, when completing application and mail-order forms)

- when wishing to communicate one's needs, desires, thoughts, and feelings to others when speech is not feasible or possible (personal notes and correspondence)

- when used as an organizing and memory strategy (shopping and packing lists)

- when a permanent record is necessary or desired (business letters and tax forms)

The *instructional strategy* refers to the method to be used in teaching students with disabilities to translate their thoughts and oral language into written messages. The functional approach to teaching writing requires teachers and other trainers to provide their students with real and simulated experiences that vivify those functional life situations in which written communication is necessary for the optimal life functioning of the individual.

This is true whether the written communication is designed to provide personal and other data to others, to record pertinent information for future use, or to communicate one's thoughts and feelings to others on either a formal or an informal basis.

When implementing a functional writing curriculum, attention also has to be paid to the mechanical aspects involved in translating thought and oral communication units into their written counterparts. Legibility of production (shape, position, size, and space utilization) supplants speech intelligibility requirements. Punctuation, capitalization, and spelling, while of lesser functional importance than legibility, becomes significant whenever errors or significant deviations interfere with communication.

The goals and their specific instructional objectives that have been included in this functional writing curriculum were identified by the authors from their

- review of relevant professional literature and pertinent instructional materials and resources;

- observations of children, youth, and adults with disabilities as these individuals functioned on a daily basis in school and the community;

- consultations with parents and other caregivers;

- conferences with students with disabilities, especially those former students who, now as adults, were functioning successfully in the community; and

- analysis of the daily writing requirements of their own lives.

Throughout the process of identifying the sequence and scope of a functional writing curriculum, attention was directed to the various life settings in which individuals function on a daily basis and as they fulfill their various social roles: as a member of a family unit, a household, a community; as a learner; as a participant in leisure activities; and as a consumer of goods and services; as a worker; and as a traveler.

Teachers, other professionals, parents, and other caregivers who implement this section of the curriculum need to engage in their own exploration of additional pertinent functional instructional goals and objectives. This task, perhaps, is best accomplished if one records the various writing requirements and expectations of diverse life experiences as soon as possible after one experiences them oneself. Toward this end, a functional curriculum and its successful implementation could be enhanced if one were to record in a notepad the written information one is expected to provide others in business, legal, and other structured and formal interactions.

It could also prove beneficial to record the vocabulary one has needed in less structured and less formal situations of a personal nature, such as writing thank-you notes and friendly letters. Not only might this exploration activity suggest other relevant life experiences and/or emphases; it is also likely to lead to a more fully realized appreciation of the many life occasions when there is the need to communicate in writing.

Putting something in writing might then be viewed as a key functional skill, whether it is to communicate with others or to communicate with oneself as in developing a shopping or packing list or making appointment or things-to-be-done notations on a wall calendar. Curriculum exploration, development, and enhancement activities such as these should vividly demonstrate the many life problems that are likely to be experienced by individuals with deficits in written communication.

General Goals of This Unit

I. The student will acquire those perceptual motor skills that will facilitate effective written communication.

II. The student will write his or her personal data, needs, and thoughts with such clarity that they are communicated readily to readers.

GOAL I.

The student will acquire those perceptual motor skills that will facilitate effective written communication.

SPECIFIC OBJECTIVES

The student:

☐ A. Picks up and holds pens and pencils correctly and makes marks with them on paper.

☐ B. Positions his or her body in a suitable and comfortable position for writing and positions a sheet of paper so that he or she writes comfortably, efficiently, and legibly.

☐ C. Reproduces straight and curved lines, circles, and semicircles.

☐ D. Reproduces simple geometric shapes, upper- and lowercase letters, and numerals.

SUGGESTED ACTIVITIES

 ### Specific Objective A

The student picks up and hold pens and pencils correctly and makes marks with them on paper.

Teacher Interventions

Primary Level. Place a pencil or ballpoint pen and a sheet of white paper in front of the student. Tell the student that a pen or pencil is used to make marks on paper, to sketch and draw, and, most important of all, to communicate to other people. (You may wish to start with crayons because the various colors can be more motivating and stimulating and the thickness of crayons may be easier for the beginner to hold and manipulate than a pen or pencil.)

Holding a pen or pencil (or crayon) in your hand, demonstrate how to hold it so that one can easily make marks on the paper.

Place a pen or pencil (or crayon) in the student's preferred hand so that it rests on the upper portion of the third finger. Assist him or her in holding the pen or pencil (or crayon) in place with the thumb held in opposition to the index finger. After the pen or pencil (or crayon) is positioned properly, hold the student's hand, and guide it so that marks are made on the paper. Show delight in these marks, and explain that the movements of the student's hand and arm helped the pen or pencil (or crayon) to make the marks.

Remove your hand, and encourage the student to scribble, doodle, or make marks on his or her own. Join the student in doodling on your own sheet of paper while commenting on how you move your hand in specific ways to make specific marks and that you watch the marks carefully as they "flow out" of your pen or pencil. Be sure to comment on the fact that the student must also watch the marks he or she makes as they "flow out" of the pen or pencil (or crayon) to see how the pattern of marks is like the pattern of movements made by his or her hand.

Intermediate and Secondary Levels. Monitor the student frequently during all activities in which some writing is required. Make sure that the student is holding the pen or pencil correctly. Remember, evaluating the legibility of the final written product is not sufficient. One must monitor the writing process as well as the finished product to make certain that the motor process is carried out properly.

Family Interventions

Primary Level. Ask the parents to engage their child in leisure-time activities in which he or she is expected to make marks on white paper with different-colored crayons and marking pens and with soft-lead pencils and different-colored pens.

Show the parents the proper hand position for holding a writing implement, and impress upon them that they should allow their child to hold his or her hand only in this position (unless a physical reason exists that makes their child unable to do so), because it is part of the total writing process, which should be designed for maximum comfort, speed of response, and legibility.

Specific Objective B

The student positions his or her body in a suitable and comfortable position for writing and positions a sheet of paper so that he or she writes comfortably, efficiently, and legibly.

Teacher Interventions

Primary Level. Repeat the activity described in Objective A above. Observe how the student aligns and positions his or her body. (Remember that an awkward position will interfere later with comfort, legibility, and speed of writing; therefore, do not allow the student to write while using a body or paper position that is likely to create problems later on.) If the student aligns and positions his or her body properly and positions the paper correctly, praise him or her, and explain that he or she is sitting and holding the paper in the proper position for writing.

Explain that writing is an action that requires a series of bodily movements and that for all activities that require movement, such as walking, throwing and catching a ball, or riding a bicycle, it is important to align our bodies in a proper way. If the student does not align and position his or her body or position the paper correctly, make corrections as needed. (Of course, modifications in alignment and positioning of the body may be necessary in the presence of a physical disability that requires such modification. Check with a physical therapist or physician for verification that a modification is necessary and for programming suggestions.)

Use verbal clues whenever they can be comprehended by the student, and, if needed, sit alongside the student at a similar desk and demonstrate how you align and position your body and position the paper for writing.

Follow up by asking the student to make marks on his or her sheet of paper. Reward the student for monitoring the marks made as they "flow out" of the writing implement. Remember to slant the student's paper in the opposite direction of his or her preferred hand, that is, if the student is left-handed, slant the paper to the right. If the student is experiencing difficulty, use masking tape to create an outline for the sheet of paper on the desk. Use this model only as long as it is needed by the student.

Intermediate and Secondary Levels. Monitor the student frequently during writing activities. It is insufficient to merely check the written product; the student's process during the writing must be monitored as well. Correct any faulty alignment or positioning of the body during written activities, such as writing with one's legs tucked underneath the body or writing with the head resting on the shoulder of the side opposite the preferred hand.

Remind the student that if he or she did not ride a bicycle with the right alignment and positioning of the body, he or she would probably fall off and that if he or she did not align and position the body properly for swimming, he or she would at best swim poorly and at worst drown. Also correct any faulty positioning of paper.

Family Interventions

Primary Level. Show the parents the proper body alignment and position for writing and for holding a sheet of paper, and impress upon them that they should only allow their child to write when his or her body is aligned and positioned properly and the paper is positioned correctly (unless a physical reason exists that makes their child unable to do so), because it is part of the total writing process, which should be designed for maximum comfort, speed of response, and legibility.

Tell the parents to stop their child when he or she is not in the correct position for writing and to assist him or her to align the body and position the paper properly.

Intermediate and Secondary Levels. Ask the parents to engage their child in household duties (such as making up a shopping list and putting notes on a wall calendar), leisure-time activities (such as keeping score during a board or card game), and social activities (writing a get-well card to a sick relative or friend) in which he or she is expected to write. Remind the parents to stop their youngster if he or she is not aligning and positioning the body or the paper properly.

 ## Specific Objective C

The student reproduces straight and curved lines, circles, and semicircles.

Teacher Interventions

Primary Level. Create horizontal, vertical, and diagonal lines in sand using the index finger of your hand (use the same hand as the student would). Take the student's preferred hand, and assist him or her in tracing over these straight lines.

Continue by cutting out 1-inch straight lines from sandpaper and pasting them in vertical, horizontal, and diagonal patterns on a sheet of paper. Then, using your index finger as above, trace over the lines, going from left to right for the horizontal lines and from top to bottom for the vertical and diagonal lines. Engage the student in this tracing activity.

Proceed to using a felt pen to make vertical, then horizontal, and, finally, diagonal lines. Say, "When I move the pen straight down from top to bottom [or starting at the top and going straight down] like this, I make a line that starts at the top and goes straight down." "When I move the pen from left to right like this, I make a line that goes from left to right." "When I move the pen from top to bottom but do not go straight down but go like this [demonstrating the right-to-left and then the left-to-right-diagonals], then I make a line that looks like this [pointing to each of the diagonals]." After each type of line is drawn, ask the student to trace the line you just drew, first with the index finger of his or her preferred hand and then with a felt pen.

Assist the student in making the several straight lines from memory (i.e., after a model of each of the several straight lines has been removed) with a variety of pens and pencils. Proceed in a similar manner to reproducing the circles, semicircles, and curved lines from which the manuscript letters and numerals are formed (see Figure 2.1): starting with tracing with the index finger of the preferred hand, to tracing with pens

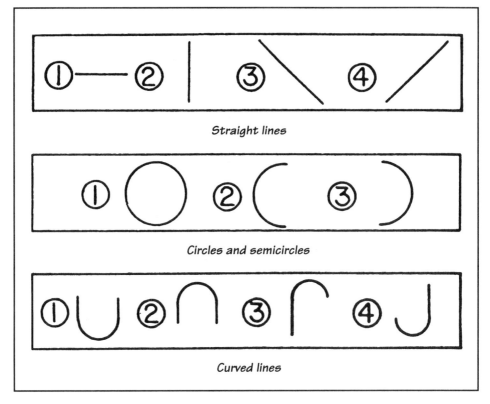

FIGURE 2.1. Straight lines, circles, and semicircles found in numerals and manuscript letters.

and pencils, and, finally, to reproducing the circles and semicircles from models shown to the student and then removed.

Avoid copying, as writing requires revisualization (seeing the words again in one's mind) and reproducing. Copying activities discourage revisualization and, thus, reproduction in functional situations when models are not present.

Family Interventions

Primary Level. Review with the parents the various straight lines, circles, semicircles, and curved lines from which manuscript letters and numerals are formed. Ask the parents to assist their child in reproducing these lines, circles, semicircles, and curved lines. Impress upon the parents the need to discourage copying activities.

 ## Specific Objective D

The student reproduces simple geometric shapes, upper- and lowercase letters, and numerals.

Teacher Interventions

Primary Level. Add the square, rectangle, triangle, and diamond to the student's tracing and reproduction activities as described in Special Objective C above (the circle has already been reproduced in Special Objective C). Then proceed to the manuscript letters (upper- and lowercase) and numerals that are formed with the straight lines (see Figure 2.2). Next,

CAPITAL   A E F H I K L M N T V W X Y Z

SMALL   i k l r t v w x y z

NUMERALS   1 4 7

FIGURE 2.2.   Letters and numbers made from straight lines.

continue with the manuscript letters (both upper- and lowercase) and numerals that are formed by connecting straight lines with circles, semicircles, and curved lines (see Figure 2.3).

Family Interventions

Primary Level. Review the simple two-dimensional shapes with the parents: the circle, square, rectangle, triangle, and diamond. Tell the parents to assist their child in reproducing these shapes and in reproducing the manuscript letters (upper- and lowercase) and numerals that are formed with straight lines and the manuscript letters (both upper- and lowercase) and numerals that are formed by connecting straight lines with circles, semicircles, and curved lines.

Give the parents charts of Figures 2.2 and 2.3 and ask them to use these charts as a guide in assisting their child to reproduce letters and numerals. Impress upon the parents the need to shun copying activities and to encourage memory for the various letter and numeral shapes.

GOAL II.

The student will write his or her personal data, needs, and thoughts with such clarity that they are communicated readily to readers.

See the Sample Lesson Plans near the end of this unit.

CAPITAL	B C D G J O P Q R S U
SMALL	b c d e f g h j m n o p q s u
NUMERALS	2 3 5 6 8 9

FIGURE 2.3. Letters and numerals made from straight and curved lines and circular shapes.

SPECIFIC OBJECTIVES

The student:

    ❒ A. Prints his or her name and writes his or her signature.

    ❒ B. Writes his or her parents' names in manuscript.

    ❒ C. Writes the date in its various forms.

    ❒ D. Writes his or her address in manuscript.

    ❒ E. Writes his or her age and birth date, using numerals, abbreviations, and words.

    ❒ F. Correctly addresses envelopes, postcards, and packages to be mailed.

    ❒ G. Writes shopping and other lists in manuscript.

    ❒ H. Writes notes and other simple correspondence in manuscript.

    ❒ I. Identifies key words, abbreviations, and symbols (FIRST NAME, LAST NAME, MAIDEN NAME, M.I.; ADDRESS; DATE; HOME TELEPHONE #, WORK TELEPHONE #; BIRTHDATE; SOCIAL SECURITY #; SEX—M OR F; MARITAL STATUS—M, S, W, OR D; PREVIOUS EMPLOYMENT RECORD; PARENTS' NAMES; REFERENCES; ACCOUNT NUMBER, DEPOSIT, WITHDRAWAL, CASH; etc.) found on employment applications, deposit and withdrawal slips, checks, mail-order forms, and other simple blanks and forms and provides the requested information.

SUGGESTED ACTIVITIES

 ## Specific Objective A

The student prints his or her name and writes his or her signature.

Teacher Interventions

Primary Level. Once the student is able to reproduce each of the upper- and lowercase letters that are in his or her full name when asked to do so (see Specific Objective D), print the student's first name in bold letters on a large flashcard. (If the student is referred to by parents and others by a nickname, make certain to clarify the difference between the real name and nickname.)

Ask the student to trace the flashcard with his or her index finger and then with a pen or pencil. Tell the student to look at his or her name and to try to take a picture of it with his or her eyes. Indicate that the student should study the name and then close his or her eyes and try to see it again in his or her head.

If needed, show the student the first letter of the first name, and ask him or her to reproduce it. If the student is successful, add one additional letter at a time until he or she produces the entire first name correctly and consistently. Proceed in the same way with the student's last name until he or she is able to reproduce consistently and correctly the full name when asked to do so.

Intermediate Level.   Once the student is able to reproduce his or her full name in manuscript, demonstrate the visual relationship of the cursive letters to the manuscript letters in the name. You may wish to demonstrate this relationship by converting the manuscript form of the name into the cursive form (see Figure 2.4) as an intermediate step before expecting the student to reproduce the cursive form.

Continue by clarifying when the student should sign his or her name as opposed to printing it. Develop the concepts underlying the words (common on forms) PRINT and SIGNATURE and the expressions DON'T FORGET TO SIGN YOUR NAME, HAVE YOU REMEMBERED TO SIGN YOUR NAME (or CHECK)?, PRINT YOUR NAME LEGIBLY, and BE SURE TO PRESS DOWN HARD ON YOUR PEN!

Provide simple forms such as a bank deposit slip for the student to sign and a simple mail-order form on which the student must both print and sign his or her name.

Secondary Level.   Provide the student with experiences such as signing greeting cards and simple notes and with forms on which he or she must print and/or sign his or her name.

Family Interventions

Primary Level.   Ask the parents to place cards with their child's first name printed on them on his or her furniture and other belongings. Tell the parents to make sure their child differentiates the written form of his or her name from other written material in the home. (Make sure that if the child has a nickname, you inform the parents of the need to clarify with their child the difference between a real name and a nickname.)

If possible, show the parents how to play a visual memory game in which they show their child a card on which his or her first name is printed, then remove the card, and next give him or her several cards with different

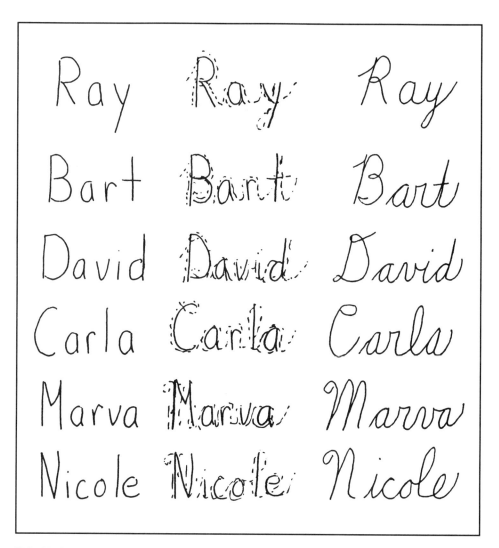

FIGURE 2.4.   From manuscript to cursive.

words printed on them from which the student is to select the card that matches the card that had been previously shown to him or her. Tell the parents to play this game with individual letters if their child is unable to match whole words from memory. Finally, ask the parents to assist the student in reproducing his or her first and then last name from memory.

Intermediate and Secondary Levels.   Ask the parents to practice with their youngster until he or she can reproduce his or her full name in both manuscript and cursive. Tell the parents to share with their youngster the various forms on which they must print and/or sign their names. Tell the parents to obtain duplicates of these forms so that their youngster can model their behavior while signing and/or printing his or her own name.

 ## Specific Objective B

The student writes his or her parents' names in manuscript.

Teacher Interventions

Intermediate and Secondary Levels. Explain to the student that there will be occasions in life when he or she will need to write his or her parents' names. Provide the student with concrete examples, such as job application forms that require him or her to supply the parents' names.

At this point, it may be necessary to acquaint the student with the concept of a maiden name and with the written expression MOTHER'S MAIDEN NAME, since many forms, especially those that require an identification code (such as credit cards and safe-deposit boxes), require individuals to supply this information. Make certain that the student is able to say the correct (legal) name of each of his or her parents.

It may be necessary to take some time to assist the student in understanding that the relationship names that he or she uses for his or her parents are not their real names.

Ask the parents to send in envelopes on which their names have been typed or printed. Assist the student in visual memory activities in which the student is shown a card with his or her name or the name of each family member (including the parents) and he or she is expected to select from a duplicate set of cards the one that matches the card that he or she has just been shown.

Continue by giving the student copies of forms that request the names of his or her parents, including the mother's maiden name. Assist the student in supplying this information until he or she is able to do so independently.

Family Interventions

Primary Level. Ask the parents to assist their child in understanding that just as he or she has a name, they have names as well. Tell the parents to review their names with their child until he or she is able to respond with these names when asked to respond to the questions "What is your father's name?" and "What is your mother's name?"

Intermediate and Secondary Levels. Ask the parents to show their youngster the written form (manuscript) of their names by showing him or her their names on correspondence and important documents. Tell the parents to make cards on which their names are written and to encourage their youngster to study the written form, then remove it, and encourage him or her to reproduce it from memory.

Remind them that it is necessary to acquaint their youngster with the concept of the term MOTHER'S MAIDEN NAME and its written counterpart, as this information is required on some forms. Ask them to locate forms that require their youngster to write their names and to use these forms for practice and review sessions.

 ## Specific Objective C

The student writes the date in its various forms.

Teacher Interventions

Primary Level. Show the student store and other receipts, bills, and postmarks to demonstrate the different ways that dates are written. Then, once the student is able to find the date by using a calendar (see Unit 1, "Functional Reading," Goal VI, Specific Objective A), show him or her how to use the information from the calendar to write the date.

Underline the month and the year on top of each page. At the end of the day, cross out the date on the calendar so that the student can more easily find the correct date the next day. Demonstrate how to use the calendar, and ask the student to model your behavior. As the student gains proficiency, assign him or her the task of writing the day's date on the chalkboard each morning for a week each month. Require the student to write the date on his or her written and creative work, including drawings and paintings.

Intermediate and Secondary Levels. Collect representative forms on which the student will be expected to write the date (checks, withdrawal and deposit slips, order forms, etc.), ask him or her to find the place on the form that instructs him or her to write the date, and assist the student until he or she is able to write the date in its several different patterns (e.g., in words and numerals, with slashes in between numerals, and with dashes in between numerals).

Review the various ways to determine the date, such as from calendars, radio and television broadcasts, or newspaper notations and by asking someone.

Family Interventions

Primary Level. Ask the parents to show their child the date on a home calendar and to announce the date as part of the family's morning routine. Tell the parents to comment on the date when it is announced on radio and television and to refer to the date on appropriate occasions: for example, "Today is February 3rd. It is Uncle Tony's birthday. We mustn't forget to call him to wish him 'Happy Birthday'!" and "Today is April 15th. Don't forget to mail the income tax forms!"

Intermediate and Secondary Levels. Ask the parents to show their youngster applications and other forms on which they have written the date (withdrawal and deposit slips, loan applications, library card applications, etc.). Tell them to provide their youngster with similar forms and to assist him or her in finding the place on the form that requires him or her to write the date and to assist their youngster until he or she is able to write the date in its several different patterns (e.g., in words and numerals, with slashes between numerals, and with dashes between numerals).

 ## Specific Objective D

The student writes his or her address in manuscript.

Teacher Interventions

Primary Level. Once the student successfully identifies his or her address (see Unit 1, "Functional Reading," Goal I, Specific Objective B), assist him or her in printing the number part of the address. Begin by using a template, and encourage the student to use the index finger of his or her preferred hand to trace the outline of each number. Proceed to asking the student to trace the outline of each number with a crayon, pen, or pencil.

Next, give the student a card with the number written on it, and put a piece of tracing paper over the card. Tell the student to trace the numbers of his or her address and to use the tracing paper to print the address on a second card.

Follow up by giving the student plastic or metal numbers and asking him or her to put together the numbers just as they look on his or her house, on the mailbox outside his or her apartment, and so on. (Check with the parents to determine where the house numbers are displayed on or near the house.) Conclude by asking the student to try to get a picture of the house number in his or her head, close his or her eyes, and then reproduce it on a piece of paper that has the words CURRENT ADDRESS written on it.

Proceed by assisting the student in adding the street name (using street signs), the town or city name (using names of businesses with the city or town name in their name and a map), the name of the state (using names of businesses with the state name in their name and a map), and the zip code (using envelopes addressed to his or her home).

At this stage, ask the parents to give you copies of envelopes addressed to their home so that the student can practice tracing and then reproducing his or her entire address.

Intermediate and Secondary Levels. Collect copies of various forms that the student is likely to encounter in life and that require him or her to indicate his or her address. Help the student to develop the concept of CURRENT ADDRESS, TEMPORARY ADDRESS, and PERMANENT ADDRESS. Assist the student in completing these forms until he or she can do so independently.

Also, engage the student in letter writing (friendly and business) and other correspondence activities (greeting cards and postcards) in which the student must write his or her return address on cards and letters.

Family Interventions

Primary Level. Ask the parents to show their child the house numbers appearing on their home and/or on mailboxes. Tell the parents to explain that the numbers are part of the house's "name" and that they help mail carriers, visitors, and even emergency vehicles to find their house. Encourage the parents to show their child the name of their street on street signs.

Tell them to explain to their child that the name of their street is also part of the "name" of their house. Ask them to show their child the name of the house as it appears on mail received at their home. Review with the parents the steps they should follow in assisting their child in reproducing his or her entire address, from tracing to reproducing it.

Intermediate and Secondary Levels. Ask the parents to show their youngster forms that they have completed on which they have written their address. Tell them to tell their youngster, when appropriate, that since they all live in the same house, their address is the same as his or hers.

Encourage them to then give their youngster a duplicate form on which he or she must reproduce the address (from memory) after studying the model on their form. Finally, ask the parents to monitor the youngster's correspondence to make certain he or she has written a correct return address.

Specific Objective E

The student writes his or her age and birth date, using numerals, abbreviations, and words.

Teacher Interventions

Primary Level.   If the student's birthday occurs on a school day, arrange for a party or special treat, and ask the student to tell you his or her *new* age. (If the birthday does not occur on a school day, ask the student to tell you his or her *new* age the first time you see him or her after the birthday.)

Remind the student that he or she will have this *new* age for a long time. Also point out that when the next birthday comes he or she will have a *different* age, one that is one number higher.

Sing "Happy Birthday" and "How Old Are You Now?" After the student has consistently answered the questions "How old are you?" and "When is your birthday?" show him or her how to write his or her age and birth date in numerals and in their several forms (e.g., September 23, 1988; 9/23/88; or 9-23-88). Practice with the student until he or she can reproduce his or her age in numerals, abbreviations, and words without assistance.

Intermediate and Secondary Levels.   Collect various forms on which the student is asked to indicate his or her birth date and/or age. Assist the student in identifying the words BIRTH DATE, DATE OF BIRTH, and AGE. Provide the student with models of the several possible response patterns, and practice together at reproducing each pattern on a variety of forms that he or she is likely to encounter in life (job applications, voter registration, driver's license, etc.).

Family Interventions

Primary Level.   Ask the parents to celebrate their child's birthday and to make certain that he or she indicates the age. Tell the parents to put a numeral candle holder on their child's birthday cake and to write, for example, "Happy 9th Birthday" on his or her birthday card.

Urge the parents to ask their child to draw a picture of his or her birthday cake with the numeral candle holder (see Figure 2.5) and to ask the child to write his or her age on a piece of paper. Tell the parents to show their child a copy of his or her birth certificate and to show him or her forms on which they have written their own birth dates and forms (such as medical insurance applications) on which they have had to indicate the

FIGURE 2.5.   Number birthday candle.

child's birth date. Encourage the parents to practice with their child until he or she can write his or her birth date in its various patterns.

Intermediate and Secondary Levels. Ask the parents to collect various forms on which their youngster is asked to indicate his or her birth date and/or age. Tell the parents to assist their youngster in identifying the notations BIRTH DATE, DATE OF BIRTH, and AGE. Tell them to provide their youngster with models of the several possible response patterns and to practice with the youngster until he or she is able to reproduce each pattern on a variety of forms that he or she is likely to encounter in life (social security number, insurance, job applications, etc.).

 Specific Objective F

The student correctly addresses envelopes, postcards, and packages to be mailed.

Teacher Interventions

Primary Level.   Assist the student (with the aid of the parents) in compiling a personal telephone directory in which he or she has written the names and addresses of relatives and close friends.

Then set up a mock card store or card section of a larger store, and assist the student in identifying greeting cards (birthday cake = birthday card; a person with a cast in a hospital bed = get-well card; and winter scenes, religious figures, and Santa Claus = Christmas cards).

Next, give the student sample envelopes that he or she will address to persons who are listed in his or her directory on "pretend" occasions. (Note: This is one of the few life situations in which copying written information is appropriate.)

Intermediate and Secondary Levels.   Engage the student in a role-play in which he or she is on vacation and addresses postcards to friends and relatives. Use postcards if available in your community or make a mock postcard for various locations suggested by the student(s). Assist the student in addressing these real or mock cards and in writing a simple note such as "Having a wonderful time here in ___. Miss you, and can't wait to tell you all about it when I get home."

Continue by setting up a mock mailroom in which the student practices wrapping different-sized packages and addresses them to friends and relatives. Follow up with an activity in which you supply the student with letters from local businesses, and he or she must address envelopes being mailed to these business firms by copying their address as it appears on their stationery.

Family Interventions

Primary Level.   Ask the parents to involve their child in family activities in which postcards, letters, and packages are mailed. Tell the parents to show their child how they locate the addresses of friends and relatives from a personal directory and the names of business firms from their personal directory and from the firm's stationery or bill.

Intermediate and Secondary Levels.   Ask the parents to give their youngster increasing responsibility in addressing correspondence and packages to friends and relatives and to business firms. Urge the parents to provide their youngster with diverse experiences such as sending postcards when on vacation, sending thank-you notes for gifts received, returning packages with faulty goods to business firms, sending letters of complaint to business firms, and sending a variety of greeting cards on both happy and sad occasions.

Specific Objective G

The student writes shopping and other lists in manuscript.

Teacher Interventions

Primary Level. Explain to the student that there will be many times in his or her life when he or she will need to make lists that will help organize his or her actions and behavior. Explain and practice making and using shopping lists to purchase food, paper goods, and decorations for a class luncheon or party; a packing list for a class camping trip (see Figure 2.6); and a "Things to Do" list for class projects, such as the sequence of activities involved in putting on a play. Follow up by using the words used in these lists on spelling tests.

Intermediate and Secondary Levels. Assign the student the task of drawing up shopping, packing, and other lists as they are needed in class projects. Try to vary the items listed to expand the student's written vocabulary and to improve his or her functional spelling skills.

Family Interventions

Primary Level. Ask the parents to show their child any lists that they write to help organize their life. Tell the parents to model the process they use in writing the list as well as the finished product.

For example, in making up a shopping list, ask the parents to say the process aloud: "I plan to make the following meals this week: ___, ___, ___, ___, and ___. According to the recipes, I need the following items to make these meals: ___, ___, ___, ___, and ___. Let me check the freezer, the refrigerator, and the kitchen closet to see what we have on hand and don't need to buy. We don't have any ___ and we don't have enough ___, ___, and ___. I'd better put these items on the shopping list."

Intermediate and Secondary Levels. Ask the parents to give their youngster increasing responsibility in drawing up lists needed by the family. Tell the parents to accept, in the beginning, any misspellings that are easily understood but to expect, when feasible, improved and correct spelling as their youngster becomes increasingly competent.

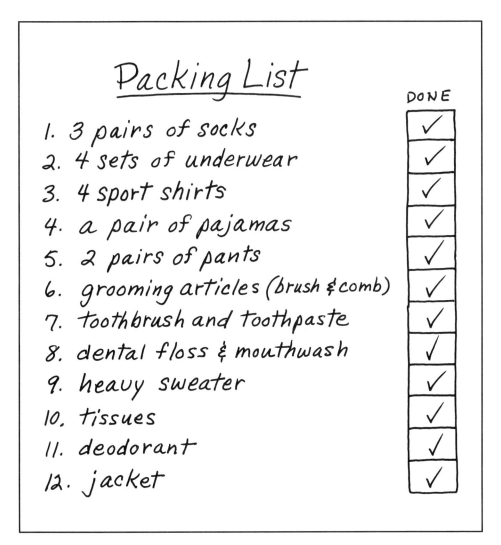

FIGURE 2.6.   Packing list.

   ## Specific Objective H

The student writes notes and other simple correspondence in manuscript.

See the Sample Lesson Plans near the end of this unit.

Teacher Interventions

Primary Level. Show the student how to write the relationship designations and/or the names of close relatives and family members (e.g., Mommy, Daddy, the names of siblings, Grandma, Grandpa, Aunt ___, and Uncle ___). Make a list of the first names and/or relationship designations of family members and of the first names of friends.

Ask the parents to send in a photograph album with photographs of these individuals with their relationship designations and/or first names as captions written below each picture. Use this album to assist the student in writing the name of each of the persons in a simple note in which he or she leaves instructions or directions to others (see Unit 1, "Functional Reading," Goal V, for some sample notes) or makes simple requests such as the following:

Dear Daddy,

I know that you said that I could not go fishing with you on Saturday because I didn't clean my room. I spent last night cleaning my room, and I promise never to skip cleaning my room again. Will you please change your mind and take me along on the fishing trip? Thank you!

Your sorry son,
Robert

Intermediate and Secondary Levels. Assist the student in writing a variety of letters, both friendly and business. Begin by role-playing situations in which the student is unable to reach someone by telephone and must write a message or note to that friend or relative.

Proceed to writing other friendly letters and to writing business letters in which information or material is sought, complaints or commendations are being made, purchases are being made, and so on.

In the beginning emphasize effective communication, not spelling or syntactical accuracy. As the student develops skill in writing, seek improved spelling and standard syntax and word usage.

Family Interventions

Primary Level. Ask the parents to write simple notes to their child (see Unit 1, "Functional Reading," Goal V). Tell the parents to set up role-playing situations in which their child should leave them a note.

For instance, the parents may write, "If you go out to a friend's house before I get home, leave me a note to tell me where you have gone and when you expect to be home" and the child may write, "I forgot to tell you before you left for work that I must stay after school for a Scout meeting. Grandma is picking me up. We should be home in time for supper."

Intermediate and Secondary Levels. Ask the parents to show their youngster copies of letters they have written to friends and relatives (if privacy is not a concern) and letters sent to business firms for a variety of reasons. Tell the parents to review these letters in terms of their purpose and content.

Encourage the parents to follow up by identifying occasions when their youngster may need to write letters to relatives, friends, and businesses and to assist him or her in communicating the necessary content in the appropriate style and format. Remind them to provide assistance and monitoring only as long as they are needed.

 ## Specific Objective I

The student identifies key words, abbreviations, and symbols (FIRST NAME, LAST NAME, MAIDEN NAME, M.I.; ADDRESS; DATE; HOME TELEPHONE #, WORK TELEPHONE #; BIRTHDATE; SOCIAL SECURITY #; SEX—M OR F; MARITAL STATUS—M, S, W, OR D; PREVIOUS EMPLOYMENT RECORD; PARENTS' NAMES; REFERENCES; ACCOUNT NUMBER, DEPOSIT, WITHDRAWAL, CASH; etc.) found on employment applications, deposit and withdrawal slips, checks, mail-order forms, and other simple blanks and forms and provides the requested information.

Teacher Interventions

Intermediate and Secondary Levels. Review the activities for Specific Objectives A through E. Collect all the blanks and simple forms that the student will likely need to fill out throughout his or her life.

Assist the student in developing the concept and in identifying and then responding correctly to any unfamiliar terms and abbreviations such as MAIDEN NAME, M.I., MARITAL STATUS, SINGLE, MARRIED, DIVORCED, SEPARATED, WIDOWED, PREVIOUS EMPLOYMENT RECORD, REFERENCES, and SOCIAL SECURITY #.

Practice with a wide variety of forms, including those involved in diverse banking transactions; job applications; purchases of goods and services; tax, insurance, medical, investment, and other financial transactions; and other forms required by local, state, and federal governmental agencies.

Family Interventions

Intermediate and Secondary Levels. Ask the parents to involve their youngster in their own form-completion activities and to review with him or her the completed forms as well. Tell the parents to require their youngster to fill out forms that directly relate to his or her own life. Remind the parents to provide guidance and assistance and to encourage independence as soon as their youngster has the requisite skills.

Sample Lesson Plan 1

Topic Area: Written Expression

Designed by: Lionel Roosevelt

Time Recommended: 30 minutes

Student Involved: Paul (Primary Special Class)

Background Information:

The student identifies the members of his family by their relationships and/or first names. He lives with his mother, father, a brother, Mark, and a sister, Mary Lou, and is very close to his grandmother and Uncle George.

General Goal *(Functional Writing II):*

The student will write his personal data, needs, and thoughts with such clarity that they are communicated readily to readers.

Specific Objective *(Functional Writing II-H):*

The student writes notes and other simple correspondence in manuscript.

Lesson Objective:

When the student is asked to write a simple note to selected family members, he will correctly address the intended reader and will independently write a simple note that will be readily understood by the reader.

Materials and Equipment:

- Photographs of the student's mother, father, brother, sister, maternal grandmother, and Uncle George
- Photograph album
- Marking pen
- Writing paper or stationery and pen
- Duplicating machine
- Teacher-made worksheet

Motivating Activity:

Tell the student that his parents have sent in photographs of some of his family members and an empty photograph album and that you need his help in identifying the people and in putting together his very own photograph album. Tell him that, at the end of the lesson, he will be writing some notes to several of his favorite people.

Instructional Procedures:

Initiation—Ask the student to name each of the people in the photographs. After he has named each one, give him a model of their relationship designation and/or first name. Tell him to trace several of the names with his index finger, then trace them with his pen, and then reproduce them on a piece of paper.

Guided Practice—Ask the student to paste the photographs in the album and to print each person's name under the photograph. Provide assistance as needed.

Independent Practice—Make a worksheet on which duplicated copies of the family photographs are presented. Ask the student to write the name of each person under his or her picture.

Closure—After the student has successfully written the relationship designations and/or the first names of selected family members, assist the student in writing simple notes to them. Make certain that the student has the responsibility of writing the salutation with little or no assistance provided.

Assessment Strategy:

Check to see whether the student has written the salutation on the sample notes without any errors.

Follow-Up Activity or Objective:

If the student achieves the lesson objective, proceed to an activity in which the student writes simple notes without assistance or with only minimal assistance.

Observations and Their Instructional Insights:

Sample Lesson Plan 2

Topic Area: Written Expression

Designed by: Estrella Rodriguez

Time Recommended: 45 minutes

Student Involved: Martha (Intermediate Special Class)

Background Information:

The student identifies the members of her family by their relationships and/or first names, and she is able to write their names in manuscript. She is also able to write simple notes, using the correct format and organization. She lives with her mother, her stepfather, her brothers, José and Antonio, her sister, María, and her Aunt Teresa.

General Goal *(Functional Writing II)*:

The student will write her personal data, needs, and thoughts with such clarity that they are communicated readily to readers.

Specific Objective *(Functional Writing II-H)*:

The student writes notes and other simple correspondence in manuscript.

Lesson Objective:

When the student is asked to write a simple note to selected family members, she will correctly address the intended reader and will independently write a simple note that will be readily understood by the reader.

Materials and Equipment:

- Models of sample notes
- Writing paper or stationery and pen
- Envelopes
- Teacher-made worksheet

Motivating Activity:

Show the student a simulated note you found on the kitchen table (from a family member who was not at home at the time) when you got home from work on the previous day. Ask her to read the note and to explain the message in the note.

Ask the student whether she has ever received notes like that from family members and if she has ever written such notes. Ask her to describe these situations. Tell her that at the end of the lesson she will practice writing some notes to several family members.

Instructional Procedures:

Initiation—Review with the student those situations in which she may need to write simple notes or messages to family members. Be sure to cover the situations in which (a) directions are given to the reader and (b) the note simply provides the reader with information as to the writer's whereabouts and subsequent plans. Provide the student with models of these two types of notes as they might be written from her point of view. Review and discuss.

Guided Practice—Ask the student to select two family members and to pretend that she is confronted with situations when she might need to write them notes. After the student has specified orally the desired contents of these notes, assist her, as needed, in writing the notes. Be sure to practice writing each type of note: one whose message is giving directions to the reader and the other whose message is providing information to the reader.

Independent Practice—Make a worksheet on which there are two new situations that the student must read independently and about which she must then write two simple notes.

Closure—After the student has successfully written the simple notes, ask her to write a note home to her parents informing them of a class activity to which they are invited.

Assessment Strategy:

Check to see whether the student has written simple notes with the correct format and that are easily understood by readers in terms of both legibility and clarity of content.

Follow-Up Activity or Objective:

If the student achieves the lesson objective, proceed to an activity in which the student writes business letters without assistance or with only minimal assistance.

Observations and Their Instructional Insights:

Sample Lesson Plan 3

Topic Area: Written Expression

Designed by: Ruth Feingold

Time Recommended: 45 minutes

Student Involved: Cynthia (Secondary Special Class)

Background Information:

The student is able to write simple notes and friendly letters, using the correct format and organization. She, as of yet, has had no direct experience in writing business letters. She has known, according to her parents, that they have had to write business letters in the past and has witnessed their discussions involving the situations that necessitated writing these letters.

General Goal *(Functional Writing II):*

The student will write her personal data, needs, and thoughts with such clarity that they are communicated readily to readers.

Specific Objective *(Functional Writing II-H):*

The student writes notes and other simple correspondence in manuscript.

Lesson Objective:

When the student is asked to write a business letter of complaint about defective merchandise, she will do so independently and with acceptable spelling, punctuation, word usage, and syntax.

Materials and Equipment:

- Appliance that is broken or not working
- Sample business letter of complaint
- Business-sized envelopes
- Teacher-made worksheet

Motivating Activity:

Show the student an appliance that is not working. Tell the student that you are pretending that you just bought the item, and ask her what you should do. After the discussion, show the student a sample business letter of complaint that you had written on a previous occasion to complain about an article of clothing that was torn and shabby when you received it through mail order.

Ask the student to describe any situations in which her family had bought appliances or other items that were defective and had to write letters of complaint. Tell the student that she will write her own letter of complaint at the end of the lesson.

Instructional Procedures:

Initiation—Review with the student those situations in which she may need to write business letters: requests for information and free materials, complaints, commendations, and purchases. Discuss the kinds of things you would write in such letters.

Show the student, once again, the sample business letter that you had previously written, and review the correct format and the content. Be sure to point out that you clearly stated what was wrong and what action you expected the reader to take. Remind the student that you need to write a new letter of complaint about the defective merchandise you just received. Demonstrate by talking aloud your thought processes and then put these thoughts into writing.

Guided Practice—Give the student a hypothetical situation in which she might need to write a business letter of complaint. Assist her, as needed, in talking out the necessary contents and then in putting her ideas down in a business letter.

Independent Practice—Prepare a worksheet on which you have described several different situations that require the student to write letters of complaint.

Closure—After the student has successfully written these business letters, ask her to read them aloud to you to make certain that she has made clear to the reader exactly what is wrong and what action she expects the reader to take.

Assessment Strategy:

Check to see whether the student has successfully written business letters complaining of defective merchandise, identified the problem as well as the action she wishes the reader to take, used the correct format, and written letters that are easily understood in terms of legibility and clarity of content.

Follow-Up Activity or Objective:

If the student achieves the lesson objective, proceed to an activity where the student writes business letters in which she seeks information and/or free materials.

Observations and Their Instructional Insights:

Suggested Readings

Adams, G. L. (1984). *Normative adaptive behavior checklist.* Columbus, OH: Merrill.

Bailey, D., Jr., & Wolery, M. (1984). *Teaching infants and preschoolers with handicaps.* Columbus, OH: Merrill.

Barbe, W. B., Lucas, V. H., Wasylyk, T. M., Hackney, C. S., & Braun, L. (1987). *Handwriting: Basic skills and application.* Columbus, OH: Zaner-Blouser.

Barbe, W. B., Milone, M. N., & Wasylyk, T. M. (1983). Manuscript is the "write" start. *Academic Therapy, 18,* 397–405.

Barenbaum, E. M. (1983). Writing in the special class. *Topics in Learning and Learning Disabilities, 3,* 12–20.

Bender, M., & Baglin, C. A. (1992). *Infants and toddlers: A resource guide for practitioners.* San Diego: Singular Publishing Group.

Bender, M., & Valletutti, P. J. (1982). *Teaching functional academics to adolescents and adults with learning problems.* Baltimore: University Park Press.

Berkell, D., & Brown, J. (Eds.). (1989). *Transition from school to work for persons with disabilities.* White Plains, NY: Longman.

Brighan, R., & Snyder, J. (1986). *Developing application-oriented examples in language arts for students with mild handicaps.* Des Moines: Iowa State Department of Education, Bureau of Special Education.

Brolin, D. E. (1986). *Life-Centered Career Education: A competency-based approach* (rev. ed.). Reston, VA: Council for Exceptional Children.

Brolin, D. E., & Gysberg, N. C. (1989). Career education for students with disabilities. *Journal of Counseling and Development, 68,* 155–159.

Brolin, D. E., & Kokaska, C. J. (1979). *Career education for handicapped children and youth.* Columbus, OH: Merrill.

Brown, L. F., Branston, M. B., Hamre-Nietupski, S. M., Pumpian, L., Certo, N., & Gruenewald, L. (1979). A strategy for developing chronological-age-appropriate and functional curricular content for severely handicapped adolescents and young adults. *Journal of Special Education, 13,* 81–90.

Brown, L., Falvey, M., Pumpian, L., Baumgart, D., Nisbet, J., Ford, A., Schroeder, J., & Loomis, R. (Eds.). (1980). *Curricular strategies for teaching severely handicapped students functional skills in school and nonschool environments.* Madison: University of Wisconsin–Madison and Madison Metropolitan School District.

Brown, L. F., & Lehr, D. (1989). *Persons with profound disabilities.* Baltimore: Paul H. Brookes.

Bruder, M. B. (1987). Parent-to-parent teaching. *American Journal of Mental Deficiency, 91,* 435–438.

Bruininks, R., Thorlow, M., & Gilman, C. (1987). Adaptive behavior and mental retardation. *Journal of Special Education, 19*, 7–39.

Chapman, J. E., & Heward, W. I. (1982). Improving parent-teacher communication through recorded telephone messages. *Teaching Exceptional Children, 49*, 79–82.

Childs, R. (1979). A drastic change in curriculum for the educable mentally retarded. *Mental Retardation, 17*, 299–301.

Clark, G. M., & Knowlton, H. E. (1987). The transition from school to adult life. *Exceptional Children, 53*, 484–576.

Cronin, M. E., & Patton, J. R. (1993). *Life skills for students with special needs: A practical guide for developing real-life programs.* Austin, TX: PRO-ED.

Drew, C. J., Logan, D. R., & Hardman, M. L. (1992). *Mental retardation: A life cycle approach* (5th ed.). New York: Merrill/Macmillan.

Falvey, M. A. (1986). *Community-based curriculum: Instructional strategies for students with severe handicaps.* Baltimore: Paul H. Brookes.

Fernald, G. M. (1943). *Remedial techniques in basic school subjects.* New York: McGraw-Hill.

Fowler, S. A. (1988). Transition planning. *Teaching Exceptional Children, 20*, 62–63.

Garwood, S. G. (Ed.). (1983). *Educating handicapped children.* Rockville, MD: Aspen.

Glascoe, L. G., Miller, L. S., & Kokaska, C. J. (1986). *Life-Centered Career Education: Activity book one.* Reston, VA: Council for Exceptional Children.

Goldstein, H. (1975). *The social learning curriculum.* Columbus, OH: Merrill.

Goodman, K. S., & Goodman, Y. M. (1983). Reading and writing relationships: Pragmatic functions. *Language Arts, 60*, 590–599.

Grenot-Scheyer, M., & Falvey, M. A. (1986). Functional academic skills. In M. A. Falvey (Ed.), *Community-based curriculum: Instructional strategies for students with severe handicaps* (pp. 187–215). Baltimore: Paul H. Brookes.

Guess, D., Horner, R. D., Utley, B., Holvoet, J., Maxon, D., Tucker, D., & Warren, S. (1978). A functional curriculum sequencing model for teaching the severely handicapped. *AAESPH Review, 3*, 202–215.

Gunderson, L., & Shapiro, J. (1988). Whole language instruction: Writing in first grade. *The Reading Teacher, 41*, 430–440.

Hammill, D. D., & Bartel, N. E. (Eds.). (1990). *Teaching children with learning and behavioral problems* (5th ed.). Boston: Allyn & Bacon.

Harry, B. (1992). *Cultural diversity, families, and the special education system: Communication and empowerment.* Colchester, VT: Teachers College Press.

Ianacone, R., & Stodden, R. (Eds.). (1987). *Transitional issues and directions for individuals who are mentally retarded.* Reston, VA: Council for Exceptional Children.

Isaacson, S. L. (1987). Effective instruction in written language. *Focus on Exceptional Children, 19*, 1–12.

Johnson, D. W., & Johnson, R. T. (1986). Mainstreaming and cooperative learning strategies. *Exceptional Children, 52*, 553–561.

Johnston, E. B., Weinrich, B. D., & Johnson, A. R. (1984). *A sourcebook of pragmatic activities.* Tucson: Communication Skill Builders.

Jordan, J., Gallagher, J., Hutinger, P., & Karnes, M. (Eds.). (1992). *Early childhood special education: Birth to three.* Baltimore: Paul H. Brookes.

Junge, D. A., Daniels, M. H., & Karmis, J. A. (1984). Personnel managers' perceptions for requisite basic skills. *Vocational Guidance Quarterly, 33* (20), 138–146.

Kroth, R. L., & Otten, H. (1988). *Communicating with parents of exceptional children.* Denver: Love.

Marion, R. L. (1981). *Educators, parents, and exceptional children.* Rockville, MD: Aspen.

McClennen, S. E. (1991). *Cognitive skills for community living.* Austin, TX: PRO-ED.

McConachie, H., & Mitchell, D. R. (1985). Parents teaching their young mentally handicapped children. *Journal of Child Psychology and Psychiatry and Allied Disciplines, 26,* 389–405.

McDonnell, J., & Hardman, M. C. (1989). Employment preparation for high school students with severe handicaps. *Mental Retardation, 27,* 396–404.

McWhirter, A. M. (1990). Whole language in the middle school. *The Reading Teacher, 43,* 562–567.

Mercer, C. D., & Mercer, A. R. (1993). *Teaching students with learning problems* (4th ed.). New York: Merrill/Macmillan.

Miller, L. S., Glascoe, L. G., & Kokaska, C. J. (1986). *Life-Centered Career Education: Activity book two.* Reston, VA: Council for Exceptional Children.

Miller, T. L., & Davis, E. E. (Eds.). (1982). *The mildly handicapped student.* New York: Grune & Stratton.

Mithaug, D. E., Martin, J. E., & Agran, M. (1987). Adaptability instruction: The goal of transitional programming. *Exceptional Children, 53,* 500–505.

Nesselroad, M. L., & Nesselroad, E. M. (Eds.). (1984). *Working with parents of handicapped children: A book of readings for school personnel.* Lanham, MD: University Press of America.

Norris, J. A. (1989). Facilitating developmental changes in spelling. *Academic Therapy, 25,* 97–107.

Patton, J. R., Beirne-Smith, M., & Payne, J. S. (1990). *Mental retardation* (3rd ed.). Columbus, OH: Merrill.

Phelps, L. A. (Ed.). (1986). *School to work transition for handicapped youth: Perspectives on education and training.* Champaign: University of Illinois Press.

Polloway, E. A., & Patton, J. R. (1993). *Strategies for teaching learners with special needs* (5th ed.). New York: Merrill/Macmillan.

Polloway, E. A., Patton, J. R., & Cohen, S. B. (1981). Written language for the mildly handicapped. *Focus on Exceptional Children, 14,* 1–16.

Polloway, E. A., & Smith, T.E.C. (1992). *Language instruction for students with disabilities* (2nd ed.). Denver: Love.

Robbins, F., Dunlap, G., & Plienis, A. (1991). Family characteristics, family training, and the progress of young children with autism. *Journal of Early Intervention, 15,* 173–184.

Rose, K. (1982). *Teaching language arts to children.* New York: Harcourt Brace Jovanovich.

Sawyer, H. W., & Sawyer, S. H. (1981). A teacher-parent communication training approach. *Exceptional Children, 47,* 305–306.

Schniedewind, N., & Salend, S. (1987). Cooperative learning works. *Teaching Exceptional Children, 19,* 22–25.

Simpson, R. L. (1990). *Conferencing parents of exceptional children* (2nd ed.). Austin, TX: PRO-ED.

Snell, M. E., & Browder, D. M. (1987). Domestic and community skills. In M. E. Snell (Ed.), *Systematic instruction for persons with severe handicaps* (pp. 334–389). Columbus, OH: Merrill.

Valletutti, P. J., & Bender, M. (1982). *Teaching interpersonal and community living skills: A curriculum model for handicapped adolescents and adults.* Baltimore: University Park Press.

Wallace, G., Cohen, S. B., & Polloway, E. A. (1987). *Language arts: Teaching exceptional students.* Austin, TX: PRO-ED.

Webster, E. J., & Ward, L. M. (1992). *Working with parents of young children with disabilities.* San Diego: Singular.

Wehman, P., Renzaglia, A., & Bates, P. (1985). *Functional living skills for moderately and severely handicapped individuals.* Austin, TX: PRO-ED.

Winton, P. J. (1986). Effective strategies for involving families in intervention efforts. *Focus on Exceptional Children, 19,* 1–10.

Winton, P. J. (1988). Effective communication between parents and professionals. In D. B. Bailey & R. J. Simeonsson (Eds.), *Family assessment in early intervention* (pp. 207–228). Columbus, OH: Merrill.

Selected Materials/Resources

GENERAL

Bender, M., & Valletutti, P. J. (1981). *Teaching functional academics: A curriculum guide for adolescents and adults with learning problems.* Baltimore: University Park Press.

Bogojaviensky, A. R., Grossman, D. R., Topham, C. S., & Meyer III, S. M. (1977). *The great learning book.* Menlo Park, CA: Addison-Wesley.

Brigance, A. (1992). *Vocabulary victory: Levels A–D.* East Moline, IL: Linguisystems.

Brolin, D. E. (1991). *Life-Centered Career Education: A competency-based approach* (3rd ed.). Reston, VA: Council for Exceptional Children.

Dever, R. B. (1988). *A taxonomy of community living skills.* Washington, DC: American Association on Mental Retardation.

Doyle, E. (1980). *Skills for Daily Living Series.* Baltimore: Media Materials.

Dupont, H., & Dupo, C. (1979). *Transition: A program to help students through the difficult passage from childhood through middle adolescence.* Circle Pines, MN: American Guidance Service.

Falvey, M. (1989). *Community-based curriculum: Instructional strategies for students with severe handicaps.* Baltimore: Paul H. Brookes.

Ferguson, D. L., & Wilcox, B. (1987). *The elementary/secondary system: Supportive education for students with severe handicaps. Module 1: The activity-based IEP.* Eugene: Specialized Training Program, University of Oregon.

Glascoe, L. G., Miller, L. S., & Kokaska, C. J. (1991). *Life-Centered Career Education: Activity book two.* Reston, VA: Council for Exceptional Children.

Hannon, K. E., & Thompson, M. A. (1992). *Life skills workshop: An active program for real-life problem solving.* East Moline, IL: Linguisystems.

McGraw, D., & Turnbow, G. N. (1991). *On my own in the community.* East Moline, IL: Linguisystems.

McGraw, D., & Turnbow, G. N. (1992). *On my own at home.* East Moline, IL: Linguisystems.

Miller, L. S., Glascoe, L. G., & Kokaska, C. J. (1989). *Life-Centered Career Education: Activity book one.* Reston, VA: Council for Exceptional Children.

Parmenter, T. R. (1980). *Vocational training for independent living.* New York: World Rehabilitation Fund.

Ritter, J. (1993). *The world is a wild place: When you share life experiences.* North Billerica, MA: Curriculum Associates.

Stiefel, B. (1987). *On my own with language.* East Moline, IL: Linguisystems.

Wehman, P., Renzaglia, A., & Bates, P. (1985). *Functional living skills for moderately and severely handicapped individuals.* Austin, TX: PRO-ED.

Wilcox, B., & Bellamy, G. T. (1987). *A comprehensive guide to the Activities Catalog: An alternative curriculum for youth and adults with severe disabilities.* Baltimore: Paul H. Brookes.

Zachman, L., Barrett, M., Huisingh, R., Orman, J., & Blagden, C. (1992). *Tasks of problem solving: A real life approach to thinking and reasoning. Adolescent.* East Moline, IL: Linguisystems.

WRITING

Alfred, L. (1992). *The quick-word handbook for beginning writers.* North Billerica, MA: Curriculum Associates.

Barbe, W. B., Lucas, V. H., Wasylyk, T., Hackney, C. S., & Braun, L. A. (1987). *Zaner-Bloser handwriting: Basic skills and application book I.* Columbus, OH: Zaner-Bloser.

Bender, M., & Valletutti, P. J. (1981). *Teaching functional academics: A curriculum guide for adolescents and adults with learning problems.* Baltimore: University Park Press.

Curriculum Associates. (1993). *Handbook for practical writing.* North Billerica, MA: Author.

Farnette, C., Forte, I., & Loss, B. (1969). *Kid's stuff: Reading and writing readiness.* Nashville: Incentive.

Gould, B. W. (1991). Curricular strategies for written expression. In A. M. Bain, L. L. Bailet, & L. C. Moats (Eds.), *Written language disorders: Theory into practice* (pp. 129–164). Austin, TX: PRO-ED.

Hodges, R. (1981). *Learning to spell: Theory and research into practice.* Urbana, IL: National Council of Teachers of English.

Media Materials. (1980). *Developing Writing Skills.* Baltimore: Author.

Moore, G. N., Talbot, R. A., & Woodruff, G. W. (1988). *Spellex: Word finder.* North Billerica, MA: Curriculum Associates.

Phelps-Teraski, D., & Phelps-Gunn, T. (1988). *Teaching competence in written language: A systematic program for developing writing skills.* Austin, TX: PRO-ED.

Scott, Foresman. (1987). *D'Nealian Handwriting Program.* Glenview, IL: Author.

Tompkins, G. E. (1990). *Teaching writing: Balancing process and product.* New York: Macmillan.

Functional Mathematics

Monday	
Tuesday	
Wednesday	**3**
Thursday	
Friday	

Mathematics may be considered the most functionally relevant academic subject. If one studies the evolution of mathematical systems and concepts, it is patently clear that solutions to everyday problems were the early and appropriate focus of this academic area.

Mathematics, for all persons in a society who are not university bound, must have as its essential thrust and ultimate goal the application of mathematical concepts and skills to daily life. Unfortunately, for many students with and without disabilities, this historical truth has been overlooked, perhaps as a result of an inordinate and elitist emphasis on mathematical applications of limited personal value, except for those few individuals who seek careers, such as engineering, in which higher-order mathematical systems must be applied.

The application of mathematical understandings is especially pertinent when one reviews the critical importance of relevant knowledge and skills as they apply to the management of *money, measurement,* and *time.* These three crucial personal-environmental interactions strongly suggest that mathematical competency should be assigned high priority in a functional curriculum. Moreover, because of the nature of these three areas of human endeavor, the application of requisite skills is invariably highly motivating to students, particularly when the students are provided with instruction in the handling of money and monetary transactions.

An emphasis on money, measurement, and time in a functional curriculum also provides teachers, other trainers, and family members with extraordinary opportunities to design and implement instructional plans that rely heavily on "hands-on" materials and experiences. The use of actual currency and coins in teaching/learning experiences brings not only relevance but also a degree of "magic" to these experiences. The use of rulers, yardsticks, measuring cups and spoons, and other instruments of measurement helps students meet their life needs in completing household tasks such as cooking, decorating, and maintaining a home; in leisure-time pursuits, especially in arts and crafts projects; and in numerous vocational applications.

Mathematics, as an *applied* symbol system, within the context of a life skills curriculum, must receive major attention. As the long-range goal of a functional curriculum is the *ultimate successful functioning* of the individual as an adult member of society, the role of mathematics is crucial to that ultimate success.

General Goals of This Unit

I.   The student will acquire those basic arithmetic skills that facilitate independence in functional situations.

II. The student will acquire those skills necessary for participating successfully and independently in cash transactions.

III. The student will acquire functional measurement skills that facilitate independence in various measurement activities.

IV. The student will acquire those functional time measurement skills that facilitate time management.

GOAL I.

The student will acquire those basic arithmetic skills that facilitate independence in functional situations.

SPECIFIC OBJECTIVES

The student:

☐ A. Matches objects to objects (one-to-one correspondence).

☐ B. Counts with meaning.

☐ C. Identifies and matches numerals.

☐ D. Matches objects that occur in pairs.

☐ E. Identifies the basic shapes of a circle, triangle, square, and rectangle when they have functional relevance.

☐ F. Discriminates between left and right.

☐ G. Uses a number line.

☐ H. Identifies the ordinal positions of people and objects.

❏ I. Follows oral directions involving a sequence of steps described in their ordinal sequence.

❏ J. Identifies numerals of personal importance (such as birth date, age, address, telephone number, and social security number) when this information appears in written materials and documents.

❏ K. Writes numerals when supplying personal data on various forms and documents.

❏ L. Identifies the written expression for simple numerals when it appears in written materials.

❏ M. Writes the written expression for numerals when requested to do so in check writing, deposit and withdrawal slips, and other financial transactions.

❏ N. Identifies the fractions ½, ⅓, and ¼ when they occur alone and when they are part of simple mixed numbers.

❏ O. Correctly computes simple addition problems when presented with various terms for adding: *plus, more, add,* and *sum.*

❏ P. Correctly computes simple subtraction problems when presented with various terms for subtracting: *take away, minus,* and *subtract.*

❏ Q. Uses the process signs (–) and (+) in addition and subtraction when given simple arithmetic problems.

❏ R. Identifies and uses numbers appearing on common equipment, appliances, and materials.

SUGGESTED ACTIVITIES

 ## Specific Objective A

The student matches objects to objects (one-to-one correspondence).

Teacher Interventions

Infant and Toddler/Preschool.　Place a pile of small toy blocks in front of the student and ask the student to watch the game you are playing. Take one block from the pile, and place it on the floor or table directly in front of the student, telling the student it is his or her block.

Ask the student to watch as you find another block just like the one in front of him or her. As you place this new block next to the first block, tell the student that it is your block and now he or she has one block and you have one just like it, too.

Repeat this activity with other concrete objects found in the student's environment, including plates and eating utensils, having the student select one object to place in front of you and one to place in front of him- or herself.

Primary Level. Place a pile of small blocks in front of the student and a second pile in front of yourself, asking the student to watch what you are doing because you both are going to play a game. Point out that you are taking two blocks from in front of yourself. Have the student do the same with his or her pile of blocks.

Reinforce if the student performs this activity correctly. Repeat this activity in functional situations: for example, in setting a table and in passing out supplies for an arts and crafts project.

Intermediate Level. Place a pile of assorted nuts and bolts in front of the student. Explain that he or she might find these materials in his or her home because they are needed for simple household repairs. Ask him or her to watch you match a bolt to the appropriate size of nut. Have the student imitate what you have done and finish assembling the nuts and bolts.

Secondary Level. Place a number of familiar objects such as pencils or crayons in front of the student. With the index finger of your preferred hand, touch each item. (Depending on the student's level of functioning, you may want to count along as you point to each object.)

Encourage the student to imitate your actions. When the student imitates you, make sure that he or she does not skip an object or touch it more than once. Assist the student if necessary. If the student is experiencing difficulty, use different objects and repeat the activity. (Note: This pointing activity should help facilitate counting with meaning.)

Family Interventions

Infant and Toddler/Preschool. Ask the parents to engage in the infant and toddler/preschool activity specified in the Teacher Interventions for this objective.

Primary Level. Ask the parents to request that their child assist them in matching paired articles of clothing (socks) after removing them from the dryer.

(This activity can also be carried out when the child is dressing and getting ready to go outside.) Suggest that the family member hold one of the child's mittens, gloves, or socks in front of him or her and ask the child to select the one that matches it from a pile of clothing.

Intermediate Level.   Ask the parents to set one place at the table, using a place mat, a napkin, dishes, a glass, and silverware. Suggest that the parents take the child to the other side of the table and give him or her the necessary utensils and materials to duplicate the place setting, supporting with verbal directions, if necessary.

Secondary Level.   After the dishes have been dried or removed from the dishwasher, the parents can assist the youngster in placing the silverware into the silverware tray. Ask them to model how to put the knives, forks, and spoons in the correct section of the silverware tray. If the family has separate silverware for special occasions, ask the parents to assist their youngster in sorting by the different patterns.

 ## Specific Objective B

The student counts with meaning.

Teacher Interventions

Infant and Toddler/Preschool.   Ask the student to sit cross-legged on the floor facing you to sing a song. Tell the student that the song you are going to sing is a counting song and has lots of fun hand movements.

Begin singing the song "The Ants Go Marching." Each time you sing a number, hold up the correct number of fingers. The first time through the song, tell the student to do exactly what you do with your fingers. Begin to sing:

> "The ants go marching one by one, hurrah, hurrah! The ants go marching one by one, hurrah, hurrah! The ants go marching one by one, and the last one stops to suck his thumb, and they all go marching down into the ground to get out of the rain, BOOM! BOOM! BOOM! The ants go marching two by two, hurrah, hurrah! The ants go marching two by two, hurrah, hurrah! The ants go marching two by two, the last one stops to pick up a shoe, and they all go marching down into the ground to get out of the rain, BOOM! BOOM! BOOM!"

Continue singing until the ants go marching ten by ten. Remember that the activities performed by the ants must rhyme with the corresponding number. The next time through the song, ask the student to sing the numbers and to hold up his or her fingers with you. This activity can be done with any counting song (e.g., "One, Two, Buckle My Shoe").

Primary Level. When it is time for a snack, ask the student to be the snack helper for the day. Have the student go to the area of the room where you keep the snacks. Tell him or her to get two cookies and one napkin for each of the students.

Tell the student that he or she should give each student a napkin and to count out loud as he or she places "one" napkin in front of each student. (Initially, you may want to model this for the student by saying, "Watch me and then do what I do.")

As you place a napkin in front of the first student, say, "One napkin for you." Ask the student to count "One for you!" as he or she gives each of the other students a napkin. After the student has given each student a napkin, tell the student to count out "two" cookies for each student. Follow the same procedure as for the napkin. If there are more than eight students, you may assign more than one student helper.

Intermediate Level. Tell the student that you want him or her to help you find out how many students there are in the classroom. At first, you may wish to model how to count each student without missing anyone. (The best way to do this is to stand next to each student as he or she calls out the number.)

Write the numbers in order on the board and tell the student that he or she may look at them if he or she forgets what number comes next.

Have the student watch you and ask him or her to do exactly as you do. Stand next to a student, say, "One," and then move to the next student and say, "Two." Tell the student it is his or her turn. Ask the student to join you as you stand next to the first student and also join you in counting out loud with the first student. Next, encourage the student to proceed by him- or herself.

Secondary Level. Request that the student go to the school or class store to purchase a desired item. Remind the student that he or she must remember to count the number of pennies he or she will need to buy a specific item (e.g., 10 cents for a pencil and 5 cents for an eraser) once he or she knows the price.

Tell the student to go to the classroom bank and bring the money drawer to the table. Model getting money from the bank to buy a pencil for yourself. Ask the student to help you find out how much the pencil costs (10 cents) by looking at the price list. The student should watch you count 10 pennies and say the number with you. When you finish, tell the student to make his or her purchase in the same way.

Family Interventions

Infant and Toddler/Preschool. Ask the parents to engage in the activity outlined for the infant and toddler/preschool level as described under the Teacher Interventions.

Primary Level. Encourage the parents to incorporate counting activities into many household chores or activities (engaging in this activity during meal-times is often a good way to begin). Request that the parents assign the child the role of "snack helper," which requires him or her to pass out a set number of snacks and the appropriate number of dishes and utensils.

Other counting tasks you may ask the parent to require of the child might include counting the number of pillowcases needed to change the bed linen and checking the number of a clothing item (undershirts) that went into the washer against the number that came out.

Intermediate Level. Encourage the parents to take their child for a walk in the community. Tell them to point out objects as they pass them. Tell the parents to take a piece of paper (on a clipboard) and marking pens with them and to make a chart with column headings for each new item they see (perhaps four or five items).

Tell them to require the child to place a mark in the appropriate column each time he or she sees a sample of the item. Tell the parents to continue this activity until the child has marked about 6 to 10 items in each column. Tell the parents to wait until they get home to sit down and count the number of items they saw. For example, if the first column is cars, ask them to say, "Let's count the number of cars that we saw."

Secondary Level. Ask the parents to take the child to a supermarket or grocery store. Encourage the parents to tell the youngster to make a purchase at the store in which he or she must count a specified number of an item and a specified number of coins (e.g., "Buy three cans of peas and pay for them with four quarters).

Specific Objective C

The student identifies and matches numerals.

Teacher Interventions

Primary Level.   Set up a flannelboard with flannel numbers 1 to 10 placed on it. Place a stack of corresponding flannel numbers in front of the student and another in front of yourself. (Make sure that the numbers are in the correct sequential order.) Take the number 1 from your stack, and place it first on top of the number 1 on the flannelboard that is already on the board. Point out the exact match to the student. Tell the student that these two numbers are the same and place the second number next to its mate.

Ask the student to find number 1 in his or her pile and place it next to the one it matches on the flannelboard. Continue until the student has matched all the numbers. Reward the student for his or her successes and help him or her to self-correct, if necessary. Follow up by repeating the activity without modeling and later by placing the numbers in random order.

Intermediate Level.   Prepare two sets of flashcards upon which you have written numerals pertinent to the student's life, such as his or her bus number, house number, and telephone number. Tell the student that he or she is going to play a matching game with you. Hold up a card with a number on it, and he or she will make a match by finding the correct flashcard from his or her set. As you hold up each card, say, "Find the number that looks just like this."

Secondary Level.   Obtain several table games that use spinners or number cards that indicate the number of spaces a player is to move. If you cannot find a game, construct one of your own. If you construct your own game board, name the game using a current popular theme, for example, "SEGA Jumper" or "Mario Blaster."

The object of your game might be to get to the top of the mountain. Tell the student to spin the pointer, say the number on which it stops, and move his or her game piece to the number (or the number of spaces) that matches the number on the spinner.

Family Interventions

Primary Level.   Ask the parents to schedule a "Game Time" with their child. One of the best games to help children with numbers is Bingo. Urge the parents to buy Bingo or a similar game or assist them in constructing their own number recognition game.

Intermediate and Secondary Levels.   Encourage the parents to take their youngster for trips into the community in which they identify numerals found there, such as house numbers, bus lines, aisles in supermarkets, and office numbers on office directories.

Specific Objective D

The student matches objects that occur in pairs.

Teacher Interventions

Infant and Toddler/Preschool.   Have the student sit on the floor, and join him or her in singing the "Sesame Street" song "I Got Two." As you sing the song, point to things that go together.

> "I got two eyes, one [point to one eye], two [point to the other eye], and they're both the same. They are called a pair."

Continue to sing, listing each of the pairs of body parts: "I got two [ears, hands, feet, and arms]."

Primary Level.   Describe to the student that you are going to do an activity that involves something we call *pairs.* Ask the student if he or she has ever heard the word *pair* before. (If the student confuses it with the word *pear,* explain the difference.)

Show the student that there are pairs of things all around us. For example, you have two eyes (a pair of eyes). Ask the student, at this level, to tell you other pairs found on his or her body such as elbows, wrists, shoulders, and eyebrows. You may continue by asking the student to sing the song "I Got Two" at this level and to name pairs of objects commonly found in his or her environment.

Intermediate Level.   Hide clothing "pairs" around the classroom and then tell the student that he or she is going to go on a treasure hunt or be a detective on a mystery case and will be trying to find the mystery pairs. Show him or her a pair of gloves, and tell him or her that he or she will be searching for several clothing pairs. Before the hunt begins, ask the student to name other clothing pairs that may be hidden.

Divide the students in teams of two (pairs), and tell them to place all the pairs they find on the table in front of the room in a basket on which the team names have been written. (The team with the most pairs discovered in a 10-minute period will be the winners. The winners should receive a certificate stating that they are the mystery detectives of the year or famous treasure hunters.)

Secondary Level.   Select several vocational activities that require using objects in pairs (e.g., two screws to attach a small hinge, two nails to attach a piece of wood, and two nut-and-bolt sets to attach two parts of an object that is to be assembled). Place these items in separate containers. Demonstrate the specific task, and ask the student to engage in each of the required tasks. Reward the student for selecting the paired items needed to accomplish the task.

Family Interventions

Infant and Toddler/Preschool. If necessary, teach the parents the "Sesame Street" song "I Got Two." (If needed, the parents can obtain the "Sesame Street" tape from a public library.) Suggest that the parents sing and act out the song with their child.

Primary Level. Ask the parents to assist their child in matching socks after taking laundry from the dryer. Tell them to also show the student clean pairs and to point out that each of the pairs is put together like that because the socks are *exactly* alike. If possible, also encourage them to use an unopened pair that is still in the original wrapper.

Remind the parents to place all the socks in a basket and to say to the child, "Each sock has one that looks *exactly* like it, and when the two are placed together, they are called a pair." Ask the parents to assign the child the task of picking out the pairs and putting them together.

During the winter months, suggest that the parents repeat this activity, this time, however, with gloves and mittens.

Intermediate and Secondary Levels. Ask the parents to continue with the matching activity. At these levels, however, tell them to make the task more challenging by matching pairs of shoes, sheets, pillowcases, curtains, and items that are pairs but are *not* exactly alike: for example, boy and girl figurines and paired pictures of the same size and with the same frame but with different scenes (e.g, two winter scenes).

 ## Specific Objective E

The student identifies the basic shapes of a circle, triangle, square, and rectangle when they have functional relevance.

Teacher Interventions

Primary Level. During several arts and crafts activities, refer to the basic shapes of materials being used: for example, the round or circular shapes of both the jar of paste and its top and the rectangular shapes of the crayon box, box of old buttons, and tissue box.

During winter (if in an area where there is snow), join the student in making a snowman. If snow is not available, show the student a piece of construction paper and comment that it is the shape of a rectangle while you trace the four sides of its perimeter.

Draw two circles on the paper to make the snowman's body and head. Ask the student to find a round object to trace the snowman. Use the round bottom of the paste jar to draw your circles. Involve the student by placing his or her hand over yours as you trace the circles. When finished, ask the student to look at the round shapes you have drawn. Encourage the student to watch as you take off the "round" top of the paste jar. Ask the student to assist you in placing paste in the drawn circles.

Remove the tissue from the box that is shaped like a rectangle. Trace the shape of the tissue box with your index finger. Have the student make the snowman's body by crumpling up the tissue and placing it on the pasted areas of the snowman's body. Tell the student to use small, round buttons to make the snowman's eyes, nose, and mouth. This activity can be done for any season of the year. Instead of a snowman, the circle shapes can be made into a rabbit.

Intermediate Level. Make or draw safety signs, such as the yield sign, railroad crossing sign, and other danger signs. Tell the student you are going to play the safety game. In this game the student must identify the sign by its shape alone. Show the student each sign, and ask him or her to tell you what it means and to name its shape. Place several signs facedown on a table, and ask the student to find each one based on its shape.

Secondary Level. Take the student for a walk in the school's neighborhood and note all the signs you see and their shapes. Develop this information into a checklist for the student to use. (See Figure 3.1.) During a walk in the neighborhood, have the student make a note of the safety signs and their shapes that he or she finds there.

Signs			Shapes
Speed Limit	Yield	Caution	△ ◇ ▢
Speed Limit	Yield	Caution	△ ◇ ▢
Speed Limit	Yield	Caution	△ ◇ ▢
Speed Limit	Yield	Caution	△ ◇ ▢

FIGURE 3.1. Checklist for parents: shapes and signs.

As you walk in the neighborhood with the student, point out the first sign you see. Indicate the name of the sign and its shape. For example, the first sign you might see could be a speed limit sign. Show the student how to find the speed limit sign on his or her checklist, and also say its shape. Continue this activity until the student has identified four or five different signs and placed the data on his or her checklist.

Family Interventions

Infant and Toddler/Preschool.   Have the parents involve their child in the household task of putting away the dishes. This activity is an appropriate one for introducing the concept of a round shape or something whose shape makes a circle. Encourage the parents to involve the child in identifying all the round things found in the home, such as a round pillow (or a pillow in the shape of a circle), a round mirror, and a round picture.

Primary Level.   Suggest that the parents, at this level, introduce the square and rectangular shapes as these shapes are found in the home, for example, a square box of tissues versus a rectangular one and a square baking pan versus a rectangular one. The parents can point out various household objects and ask the child to tell what shapes they are. For example, tell the parents to point to a picture on the wall and ask the child what shape it is.

The parents can carry a piece of construction paper with models of the basic shapes pasted on it as a reference for the child.

Intermediate and Secondary Levels.   Encourage the parents to take their youngster with them as they do their errands and as they drive or walk through the community. Remind them to point out the various signs seen there. Tell the parents to say such things as, "Look, there is a yield sign. It is shaped like a triangle. It tells us, if we are walking or in a car, to be careful since a car coming from the other direction has the right to go before us."

Tell the parents to then say, "The next time we come to a yield sign, I am going to ask you if you know what sign it is and what it is telling us to do." The parents need to make sure that the route they are taking has several yield signs on it. Once the youngster can identify the yield sign, the parents may proceed to other safety signs and their meaning in terms of indicating safe or cautious behavior.

 ## Specific Objective F

The student discriminates between left and right.

Teacher Interventions

Infant and Toddler/Preschool. During dressing activities, tell the student that you are going to help him or her put on his or her left shoe. (Note: It is recommended that you start with the left shoe to avoid, in the initial stage, the confusion between the two basic meanings of right, i.e., *correct* as well as the direction.)

Assist the student in picking up his or her left shoe, and tap his or her left foot as a cue to the student. Show the shoe to the student and match its shape with the shape of the foot. Also, show the mismatch with his or her right foot. As you help the student put on the shoe, say, "We are putting your left shoe on your left foot."

If helpful, place a green strip of tape on the toe area of the left shoe, and tell the student that the tape will be a temporary help to assist him or her in putting on his or her left shoe. Once the student has identified his or her left foot, proceed to identify the left leg, arm, and hand.

Primary Level. Continue by introducing the student to the word that describes the other side of his or her body. Begin by asking the student to point to the left parts of his or her body that were introduced earlier. Then show him or her the corresponding parts on the other side, and say, "This is not your left foot. It is on the other side of your body. The parts on this side of your body have a different name. This is your right foot." Begin again with the student's shoes, this time using a strip of red tape on the toe area of the right shoe. Proceed with the student identifying both the left and right parts of his or her body along with his or her right and left shoes and gloves.

Intermediate Level. Play the game Simon Says. Give the student a series of instructions (e.g., "Hop on your right leg," "Hop on your left leg," "Raise your right hand," "Raise your left hand," and "Place your left hand on your head").

Secondary Level. Practice with the student following left and right directions by preparing some small, hand-held, plastic-covered mazes (see Figure 3.2). Tell the student that knowing left from right can help him or her avoid getting lost and can also help with reading maps (e.g., a hand-drawn map giving directions to a friend's house).

Give the student one maze and a transparency marker, and ask the student to mark the maze according to your directions. Say, "First, I want you to go straight until I tell you to stop, and then I want you to go to the right until you come to a dead end."

Continue with this until the student has completed the maze. Be sure that the student will be blocked inside the maze if he or she does not follow your left and right directions correctly.

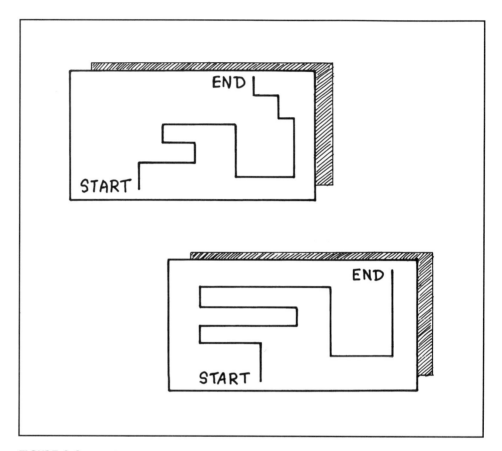

FIGURE 3.2. Left and right directions: maze cards.

Family Interventions

Infant and Toddler/Preschool. Suggest that, as the parents are dressing the child, they refer to the child's left and right sides of the body. For example, as they are putting on the child's right sock, they might say, "We are putting the sock on your right foot." Encourage the parents to carry out this activity throughout the dressing sequence. For example, tell the parents to name the child's left and right arms when putting on shirts or dresses. Tell the parents that during these activities the child should be expected to identify his or her left and right. Tell the parents that all that is expected of the child at this level is to assist in getting dressed and to listen to them as they indicate left and right.

Primary Level. At this level, the child should be expected to assist in the dressing process by moving the left or right body parts when they are named by the parents. For example, tell the parents that, when they say, "OK, let's put on your right sock; give me your right foot," the child should lift up his or her right foot.

Intermediate and Secondary Levels.   The parents (unless there are restrictions based on religious beliefs) can assist their youngster in learning and saying the "Pledge of Allegiance." At the secondary level, concentrate on following directions in moving about the community, that is, turning right means turning in the direction of the right side of the body. Tell the parents to show their youngster how to move his or her hand imperceptibly as a method of guiding his or her movements in space.

Since youngsters at this level are likely to be interested in driving, ask the parents to play the "automobile game," in which they set up chairs so that they are seated behind the youngster and ask him or her to "make a left-hand turn" or "make a right-hand turn." Tell them to teach the youngster the appropriate hand signals so they can verify that he or she is following the instructions correctly.

Specific Objective G

The student uses a number line.

Teacher Interventions

Primary Level.   Lay a long piece of white paper (12′ × 12″) on the floor. Construct an oversized number line large enough for the student to walk on (see Figure 3.3). Prepare a deck of index cards with single-digit addition and subtraction problems. Tell the student that you are going to show him or her how to add numbers by using the number line.

Have the student pick a card from the deck. The student can read the top number (if the problem is vertically presented) or the first number (if the problem is horizontally presented) out loud. Then tell him or her to go to that number on the number line.

Next, tell the student to read the bottom (or second) number, count out the number, and move the amount on the number line. For example, if the student picks the problem "2 + 2," tell the student to go and stand on the number "2," and then ask him or her to read and tell you the second number. After he or she reads the number, ask the student to count out loud and move to the next number.

After the student has counted out the numbers, ask him or her to look down on the number line and tell you what number he or she is standing on. Then ask the student, "What does 2 + 2 equal?" Repeat this activity throughout the week, until you are sure he or she can do it without your verbal prompts.

Intermediate and Secondary Levels.   Engage the student in a card game called Pitty Pat. Tell the student that the object of the game is to match like cards

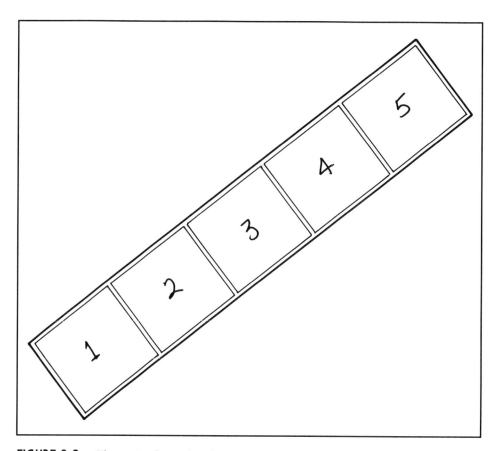

FIGURE 3.3. Floor-sized number line.

(i.e., like numbers and like face cards) in pairs and that he or she will be
the scorekeeper and will do so by using the number line. Tell the student
to give each player five cards from the deck. (The game is best with two
to four players.)

After all the players have five cards, tell the student to place the
remaining cards in a pile facedown on the table. (Each player checks his
or her cards for pairs. If the player has pairs, they are to be placed
together faceup on the table.) The person on the dealer's left begins the
play by taking a card from the stack. Tell the student to ask each player
if he or she needs the card drawn. If the player does not need the card,
the card is then placed in a second pile, the discard pile. The game continues until one player no longer has any cards left.

Have the student count the number of pairs that each player has at
the end of each game in a set and then record that information on the
score sheet you give him or her. The play continues until someone gets
15 matched pairs. Remind the student to use the number line to record
the score after each game.

Family Interventions

Primary Level.   Discuss with the parents that you want them to assist you in developing their child's skill in using a number line. Give the parents a chart that has a number line for each participant in at-home leisure activities involving table or card games. For example, they can play a simple card game like Go Fish. Tell the parents to model using each player's number line to chart everyone's score.

Intermediate and Secondary Levels.   Encourage the parents to have their youngster use a number line for certain household activities. For example, the child could assist the parents in composing the weekly shopping list by keeping an updated inventory of the number of specific food and other household items (which he or she has been given the responsibility of keeping track of) that are on hand (e.g., cans of tomato sauce, tomato paste, and whole tomatoes needed for periodic pasta dishes).

Tell the parents to assist the youngster in using number lines for those items for which he or she has been given responsibility.

 ## Specific Objective H

The student identifies the ordinal positions of people and objects.

Teacher Interventions

Infant and Toddler/Preschool.   Begin by identifying events in the student's environment in their ordinal position. For example, tell the student that it is time for lunch and that he or she will soon eat lunch; however, *first* he or she must wash his or her hands. The concept of *first* should be developed by using this approach throughout the school day, for example, "First we put away all our papers before we can go out to play!" and "First we eat our sandwich before we have dessert."

Primary Level.   Discuss with the students that you are going to do an activity to help them understand what *first, second,* and *third* mean. Place three students in a line, and then refer to each student by saying, "Peter is the *first* in line, Paul is the *second* in line, and Mary is the *third* in line." As you announce each one, touch the student on his or her shoulder.

After sufficient repetition, ask the student to be the first one in line because you are taking him or her out to the school playground. Praise the student if he or she stands in the first place in the line or makes an attempt to be first. Tell the student to direct a classmate you have named to the second place in line. Direct the student to direct another classmate to the third place in line. Repeat as necessary.

Intermediate Level. During leisure-time activities, tell the student and his or her classmates that you are going to conduct races for which there are first, second, and third prizes. Clarify for the students what prize each position will receive, and also post this information on a chart. After the race, ask the student to identify the order of finish. Vary this activity to have a slow race in which the first place goes to the person who is the slowest.

Secondary Level. Announce that today is prize-ribbon day and that the first student to finish his or her work or project, at the performance level required, will be given (to wear or place on his or her progress chart) the blue prize ribbon that reads "First"; the student who finishes second will be given the red prize ribbon that reads "Second"; and the student who finishes third will be given the yellow prize ribbon that reads "Third."

When the first person comes to you, give him or her the blue ribbon and say, "I am giving you the ribbon that reads 'First,' because you have done your work well and finished first." As each of the first three students is called, announce his or her ordinal position.

Family Interventions

Infant and Toddler/Preschool. Have the parents identify the usual or customary events in their child's life by their ordinal position. For example, encourage them to say to the child that it is time for breakfast, but *first* he or she must wash his or her hands.

Tell the parents to talk about other typical activities that involve a sequence of steps or activities: for example, "We must *first* take the top off of the toothpaste before we squeeze it" and "It is bedtime, but *first* you must brush your teeth." It is not expected that the student will necessarily understand the concept. The emphasis, at this level, is introducing the word in context.

Primary and Intermediate Levels. Encourage the parents to introduce the concepts of *second* and *third* (and *fourth*) at this level. Again, tell them to use these words in demonstrating the steps in a typical household task in which they engage: for example, "First, I put on the bottom fitted sheet; second, I put on the top sheet; and third, I put on the comforter," and "First, I preheat the oven; second, I mix the ingredients; third, I put it in a baking pan; and fourth, I put it in the oven."

Tell them to do another multistep task and to ask the student to describe the steps after he or she has observed the total sequence.

Secondary Level. If their youngster is able to give another person the directions for a multipart task, the parents should ask him or her to use the ordinal numbers when giving another person, including a younger sibling, the directions to follow. Perhaps the youngster can tell a younger family member how to tie a tie, make a knot, or play a game.

 ## Specific Objective I

The student follows oral directions involving a sequence of steps described in their ordinal sequence.

Teacher Interventions

Primary Level. Tell the student that you are going to play a listening game. Have the student listen very closely to your instructions. Tell the student he or she must follow your instructions exactly as you say them and wait for the next instruction. For example, say, "First, clear the dishes from the table. Second, rinse them. Third, put them in the dishwasher."

Reward the student for following the directions correctly. If the student does not do so, model the steps and then repeat them to the student for him or her to carry out.

Intermediate Level. At this level, give the student multipart commands that he or she must perform immediately after all the directions have been given.

Secondary Level. At this level, give the student multipart directions that he or she must perform at a later time or date. Check to determine whether the task was done correctly and in the proper sequence.

Family Interventions

Primary Level. Suggest that the parents involve their child in following directions. The parents can give the child several two-step directions. For example, encourage the parents to tell the child to brush his or her teeth and then wash his or her face. Tell the parents to observe to see whether the child followed the directions in the designated sequence.

If the child is unsuccessful, tell the parents to repeat the directions by asking, "What will you do first? Then what will you do second?" When the parents believe that the child can do two-step directions, tell them to add a third step to the directions.

Intermediate and Secondary Levels. Ask the parents to tape a set of after-school instructions for their child. Tell the parents that these steps should be sequential. An example of the taped directions might provide the sequence of steps for throwing out household trash, as follows:

1. Go into the kitchen.

2. Check the counter and floor for trash.

3. Place any trash in the garbage can.

4. Go to the bathrooms and get the wastebaskets from those areas.

5. Add bathroom trash to the kitchen trash.

6. Properly secure the trash.

7. Open the back door.

8. Take the trash out to the backyard trash receptacle.

9. Place the trash in the receptacle.

Parents can change these steps any way that best matches their situation.

Specific Objective J

The student identifies numerals of personal importance (such as birth date, age, address, telephone number, and social security number) when this information appears in written materials and documents.

Teacher Interventions

Primary Level. If the student's birthday occurs on a school day, arrange for a party or special treat, and ask him or her to tell you his or her *new* age (see Unit 2, "Functional Writing," Goal II, Specific Objective E). Sing "Happy Birthday," including the verse, "How old are you now?"

After the student has consistently answered the questions, "How old are you?" and "When is your birthday?" show him or her a card with his or her age and birth date in numerals and its several forms (e.g., September 23, 1988; 9/23/88; or 9-23-88). Practice with the student until he or she can correctly identify his or her age and birth date in numerals without assistance.

Intermediate and Secondary Levels.   Collect various forms on which the student is asked to identify his or her birth date and/or age. Assist the student in identifying the words BIRTH DATE, DATE OF BIRTH, and AGE. Provide him or her with models of the several possible response patterns (see Unit 2, "Functional Writing," Goal II, Specific Objective E).

Family Interventions

Primary Level.   Suggest that the parents take the child to Baskin Robbins or some other local store or business that gives young children a free food item on their birthdays. The parents can involve the child in the process of completing the required birthday card, which usually asks for the child's name, address, age, birth date, and telephone number. As the parents fill out the card, they should show the card to the child and explain that on his or her birthday, the store will give him or her free ___.

Intermediate Level.   Encourage the parents to take their child to the public library to fill out an application for a library card. Tell the parents to bring with them a set of flashcards with the pertinent information printed on them. Tell the parents to ask the child to pick the correct card for the specific information that the application requests.

   Tell the parents that if the card requests the child's address, they should give the child three cards and ask him or her to pick out the card on which his or her address is printed. The parents can continue until the application has been completed. Encourage the parents, after the application has been answered, to ask the child to identify the information on the card.

Secondary Level.   The parents can repeat the suggested activity recommended for the intermediate level with a number of different application forms, including employment forms.

 ## Specific Objective K

The student writes numerals when supplying personal data on various forms and documents.

Teacher and Family Interventions

Primary Level.   See Unit 2, "Functional Writing," Goal II, Specific Objective E.

Intermediate and Secondary Levels.   See Unit 2, "Functional Writing," Goal II, Specific Objective E.

Specific Objective L

The student identifies the written expression for simple numerals when it appears in written materials.

Teacher Interventions

Primary Level. Take the student on a walking tour of the neighborhood. As you walk point out any numbers on houses that are written as words. (As you see these numbers, write them down to be used when you return to the classroom.) For example, the address 71 Cedar Street may be written as "Seventy-One Cedar Street."

When you return to the classroom, make language strips with the numerals in their written expression and index cards with the matching numerals. Place the language strips on the board. Remind the student that they are the addresses that you saw on the walk, and ask him or her to find the matching house number in the pile of index cards. Tell the student, "I want you to find the number 71 in your pile." Tell the student that "seventy-one" and "71" are the same number; they are just written in a different fashion.

Intermediate and Secondary Levels. Provide the student with several prepared 3″ × 5″ index cards with the student's age, birth date (month only), and address written in words, and on the back of these cards write the numerals.

Ask the student to read each of the cards, first from the side with numerals only and then from the side written with both numerals and words. Especially at the secondary level, show the student samples of checks, deposit slips, and withdrawal slips on which the numerals for the designated amount have been omitted.

Give the student a chart of numerals from which he or she must select the correct amount to be recorded on the check to match the amount written there in words. Follow up by leaving out the amount written in words that he or she must find on a chart of numbers written in words.

Family Interventions

Primary Level. The parents should be encouraged to take their child for a walk to the neighborhood park and on the way point out to the child any house numbers and business addresses that are written in numeral expressions. Tell the parents to write the numbers down to be used for instructional purposes when they return home.

Intermediate and Secondary Levels. The parents can involve their youngster as they write checks, deposit slips, and withdrawal slips, using both the numerical and the written expression forms of numbers on these forms. Encourage the parents to emphasize that both forms indicate the same amount.

 ## Specific Objective M

The student writes the written expression for numerals when requested to do so in check writing, deposit and withdrawal slips, and other financial transactions.

Teacher Interventions

Intermediate and Secondary Levels. Review the activities in Unit 2, "Functional Writing," Goal II, Specific Objectives A through E. Collect representative blank checks and deposit and withdrawal slips the student might need to fill out in life.

Assist him or her in developing the concept and the requisite skills and in identifying and then responding correctly to forms requiring him or her to supply amounts in either their numerical or written form.

Depending on his or her functioning level, economic factors, and personal status, introduce forms for insurance and other financial transactions that may require the student to provide amounts invested or submitted, written in words as well as numerals.

Family Interventions

Intermediate and Secondary Levels. Review the activities in Unit 2, "Functional Writing," Goal II, Specific Objectives A through E. Parents should be encouraged to take their youngster with them when going to the bank and assign him or her the task of filling out the blank deposit or withdrawal forms. The parents should check the forms to see if they were filled out correctly. If the youngster has made a mistake, the parent can point out the error and assist the youngster in completing the form correctly.

Specific Objective N

The student identifies the fractions ½, ⅓, and ¼ when they occur alone and when they are part of simple mixed numbers.

Teacher Interventions

Infant and Toddler/Preschool. During snack time, explain that the snack will be graham crackers and peanut butter. Tell the student that you will use a knife to spread the peanut butter on a graham cracker and that you will give him or her one-half of the cracker.

Divide the cracker and give the student one-half. As you give the student one-half, say, "I am giving you one half, and I'm going to give [student's name] the other half." Repeat this activity until all students have half a graham cracker with peanut butter.

Primary Level. Provide the student with the directions for making quick and easy microwave cupcakes or some other simple recipe that requires the use of fractions. Make sure you have all the ingredients and materials (including measuring spoons and a measuring cup).

Place all the ingredients and materials on the table in front of the student. Show the student those ingredients that are written as fractions, tell him or her the name of the fraction, and assist the student in locating the fractional part on a measuring spoon or measuring cup as appropriate. Follow through by making the food item and then eating it for a snack.

Give the student a sewing or construction task that involves the reading of fractions or simple mixed numbers. Use flashcards to demonstrate identifying these numbers as correctly and rapidly as possible. Engage the student in the rapid identification of simple fractions and simple mixed numbers.

Intermediate and Secondary Levels. Determine whether the student and his or her family members wear clothing sizes that are mixed numbers, for example, shoe and shirt sizes. (Do not invade the privacy of the student or family members. Be sensitive to people who do not wish to share clothing sizes with others.) Set up a classroom store in which he or she must select the right size of a clothing item for him- or herself or as a gift for a family member.

Family Interventions

Infant and Toddler/Preschool.   During mealtimes or snack times, the parents should point out to the child when they are using halves. For example, ask the parents to tell the child that they are going to make a sandwich for a snack. The parents can cut the sandwich in half and give the child a half.

Tell the parents to say, "I have a half of the sandwich and you have a half of the sandwich." Tell the parents to repeat this activity each time they have a snack or lunch item that has been cut or separated in halves.

Primary Level.   The parents can involve their child in cooking or baking and provide the child with the directions for making quick and easy cupcakes, cornbread, or some other easy-to-prepare box mix. Tell the parents to make sure they have all the ingredients and materials (including measuring spoons and a cup) and to point out the fractions to the child as they carry out the recipe.

Intermediate and Secondary Levels.   Encourage the parents to take the child on a trip to a department store clothing section. When they arrive at the store, the parents should ask the youngster what size shirt or shoes should be purchased (if he or she wears a clothing size that is a mixed number).

If the youngster does not wear any clothing items that are of a mixed size, tell them to identify a family member who does wear a mixed-size garment and to ask the youngster to help them shop for a gift for that individual. Also, ask the parents to show the youngster items to be assembled or made that call for the use of hardware and other materials of different sizes.

Specific Objective O

The student correctly computes simple addition problems when presented with various terms for adding: *plus, more, add,* and *sum.*

Teacher Interventions

Primary Level.   During an arts and crafts activity, put several pieces of construction paper on the table. Ask the student to count the number of pieces. Then, tell the student you will need two *more* sheets of construction paper for the project.

Ask the student to go to the art supply cabinet to bring you two *more* sheets of paper. Thank the student, and say you asked for *more* because you wanted to *add* to the amount you started with. Say, "Let's count how many pieces of construction paper we now have since we added to what we started with." Repeat this activity with a variety of classroom materials, such as boxes of crayons, books, and pencils.

Intermediate Level. Repeat the activity described in the primary level. At this level, after the student has successfully done the mental arithmetic, ask the student to put his or her computation on paper.

Secondary Level. Take the student to a department store that has clothing displayed on racks. Point out the price tags on the clothing. Tell the student that if he or she wants to buy any of these items, the price would be the cost of the item *plus* state tax.

Show the student a sweater that has a clearly marked price tag. Ask the student to tell you what the price of the sweater is. Then tell the student that the state tax he or she would have to pay is ___. The student, now that he or she knows the price of the item and the *added* tax, should figure out the *total* cost of the item.

Remind him or her, if necessary, that the total cost of the sweater is the price on the tag *plus* the tax. To assist the student with this task, provide the student with paper and pencil or a calculator.

Family Interventions

Primary Level. Ask the parents to take their child for a trip into the community. Tell them to make purchases and then change their mind about the amount as they really need *more* of the item (e.g., at the bakery: "May I have three rolls? Excuse me. I really need two *more* rolls. Please add that to my order").

Intermediate Level. Ask the parents to follow up their "mental arithmetic" trips in the community by asking the child, when they return home, to convert the mental arithmetic done at the primary level into its written counterpart, for example, "Remember, I bought two pounds of apples and then I changed my mind because I needed *more* to make enough applesauce and bought another pound. Show me how many pounds of apples I bought *all together*."

Secondary Level. Encourage the parents to take their youngster shopping for groceries. Tell the parents to assist the youngster in preparing a short grocery list. Tell the parents to assist the child in selecting the items on his or her list and placing them in the shopping cart. Tell them to assist the youngster in estimating the total cost of the items. Tell the parents to review the cash register receipt with the student to see if it *adds* up correctly.

Specific Objective P

The student correctly computes simple subtraction problems when presented with various terms for subtracting: *take away, minus*, and *subtract*.

Teacher Interventions

Infant and Toddler/Preschool. This activity is to assist the young student in developing the concept of *take away*. While sitting on the floor, facing the student, place several toys near him or her. Tell the student you are going to join him or her in singing a new song called "Where Is ___?" (This song is sung to the tune of "Where Is Thumpkin?" and acted out in the same way.)

   Explain to the student that in this song you will be taking away some of the toys, but they will be returned after the song is over. Place a couple of the student's toys behind your back and begin singing and acting out the song.

Primary Level. During snack time, place the cookie container on the table. Take out four cookies and place them on a plate. Tell the student it is time for a snack, and he or she may have two cookies. After the student has eaten two cookies, say, "There were four cookies and you ate two of them. Look, how many cookies are left?" If the student answers correctly, say, "That's right. Four cookies minus two cookies leaves only two cookies."

   Repeat this activity with other items being eliminated or subtracted from an original amount by a variety of processes, such as eating or consuming a food item, throwing away a spoiled piece of fruit, giving away a crayon, and taking away a distracting toy from a classmate.

Intermediate Level. Repeat the activity recommended for the primary level. At this level, follow up the mental arithmetic by requiring the student to write the problem and its solution on a piece of paper.

Secondary Level. Show the student sale advertisements from local newspapers, from mailed promotions, and from flyers distributed in the community. Demonstrate how to subtract the percentage of discount from the original price. (Note: It will probably be necessary to figure the amount of discount for the student, who will then do the subtraction.) Ask the student to figure out the final cost of sample discount items—mentally, on paper, or with a calculator.

Family Interventions

Infant and Toddler/Preschool.   Encourage the parents to help establish the concept of *take away*. They should use this term when they have to discipline the child by *taking away* a favorite toy for inappropriate behavior. Tell them to say, for example, "You were playing with *one* of your toy cars, but you were playing too rough with it and were breaking it, so I had to *take it away*. Now you have *no* toys. One toy car, *take away* the toy car, and [child's name] has *no* toy cars to play with."

Primary Level.   The parents can collect bottles that can be returned to the store for a return deposit. Suggest that the parents take the child to the store and ask the child to purchase a new bottle of the beverage, and have the parents tell him or her to subtract the amount of the deposit.

Ask the parents to tell the child to take the beverage to the cash register and to pay for the beverage *minus* what he or she should receive for the deposit. This same type of activity can be done with any other items for which a refund or deposit is given.

Intermediate and Secondary Level.   Children can assist parents in cutting out coupons for specific items they are going to buy when they go grocery shopping. Tell the parents to take pencil and paper with them to the grocery store and to ask the child to find the articles for which they have coupons.

Ask the parents to tell the youngster to subtract the amount of the coupon from the price that is marked on the article. Tell the parents to take the item to the cash register and ask the youngster to watch to see if each coupon's amount was correctly subtracted.

 ## Specific Objective Q

The student uses the process signs (–) and (+) in addition and subtraction when given simple arithmetic problems.

Teacher Interventions

Primary Level.   Obtain some computer software that provides drill and practice with basic addition and subtraction problems. Set the software for the difficulty level appropriate to the student. The computer software will provide the process sign prompts and will also provide feedback to the student.

Intermediate and Secondary Levels. Assign the student the task of being the class banker in a classroom role-play. Tell the student that he or she must make sure the bank has the correct amount of money at the end of banking hours. Tell the student that after each classmate makes a withdrawal transaction, he or she must set up a subtraction problem.

Tell him or her that after each student makes a deposit, he or she must set up an addition problem. Also demonstrate and require the student to do checking account deposits and withdrawals and checking account reconciliations.

Family Interventions

Primary Level. Ask the parents to develop an inventory checklist of food and household supplies. Tell them to involve their child in adding and subtracting amounts as appropriate.

Intermediate and Secondary Levels. Ask the parents to help the youngster work out a personal budget in which he or she must add each of the various estimated expenditures in arriving at weekly and monthly budgets and do subtractions from the budget as these expenditures occur.

Specific Objective R

The student identifies and uses numbers appearing on common equipment, appliances, and materials.

Teacher Interventions

Infant and Toddler/Preschool. During snack time or lunchtime, take the student to the kitchen area, and tell him or her that you are going to heat the water for hot cocoa. Tell the student you are going to put the water in the microwave cup, press the clear button, and then turn the dial to 3 minutes.

Tell the student that the microwave will make a beeping sound when the time is up. This activity can be done with any microwave item you wish to prepare.

Primary Level.   Ask the student to set the time on the microwave to prepare several food items (e.g., soup or hot cereal). Tell the student that the microwave should be set for ___ minutes. Give the student an index card with the corresponding digital time written on it. The student can use the index card to set the microwave to the correct number of minutes.

Intermediate and Secondary Levels.   Give the student various telephone numbers to call as part of a role-play while using an unconnected telephone, preferably his or her home telephone and the numbers of friends or relatives. (Check with the parents beforehand for these numbers.) Demonstrate how to dial each number, and ask the student to imitate what you have done.

After sufficient practice, arrange for the student to actually make some of these calls. (It is advisable to call in advance to make sure that the person called will be there to receive it. In this way, you will be sure to provide the reinforcement that is a necessary part of the activity.)

Family Interventions

Infant and Toddler/Preschool.   The parents can take a piece of construction paper and write the channels and times of their child's favorite television shows and then, next to the time and channel, paste a picture that represents that show.

Assist the parents in finding the pictures in magazines, newspapers, or *TV Guide.* For example, if the child likes to watch "Sesame Street," find pictures of Big Bird, Ernie, and other characters and paste them next to the specific channel number and time.

At the appropriate time, tell the parents to let their child join them in looking at the chart to determine the channel that will show the program "Sesame Street." Tell the parents to then demonstrate the use of the numbers on the remote control to select the appropriate channel.

Primary Level.   The parents should show their child the numbers on any household equipment and appliances, such as washing machines, dryers, dishwashers, mixers, stoves, and refrigerator dials. Encourage the parents to explain these numbers and why they selected a particular setting when they use the appliance.

Intermediate Level.   Suggest that the parents demonstrate the use of the various household appliances that are found in their household. Tell them that once their child is able to, they should supervise him or her as he or she uses these appliances.

FIGURE 3.4.   Microwave time setting and matching index card.

Encourage them to discontinue this supervision once the youngster is able to do the task independently. For example, once their youngster is able to use the microwave without adult supervision, tell the parents to assign the youngster the task of making several snacks, parts of meals, and meals for the family unit (see Figure 3.4).

Secondary Level.   Tell the parents to show the youngster the heating system's thermostat. Then encourage the parents to explain that the thermostat controls the heat (and perhaps the air conditioning) in the house, that it is not a toy, and that he or she should not use it without adult supervision, permission, or as part of an assigned household chore (depending on the youngster's performance level). Instruct the parents, on a day when the system is not needed, to turn the system off and to demonstrate turning the thermostat to various temperature settings.

GOAL II.

The student will acquire those skills necessary for participating successfully and independently in cash transactions.

SPECIFIC OBJECTIVES

The student:

- ❐ A. Identifies and names coins: penny, nickel, dime, quarter, and half-dollar.
- ❐ B. Identifies the money symbols: cent sign, dollar sign, and decimal point.
- ❐ C. Converts one denomination of coins into another denomination (e.g., five pennies equal one nickel).
- ❐ D. When making purchases, determines that coins received as change are the correct amount.
- ❐ E. Identifies and names 1-, 5-, and 10-dollar bills.
- ❐ F. Uses currency when making purchases.
- ❐ G. Uses a combination of coins and currency when making purchases and verifies any change received.

SUGGESTED ACTIVITIES

 ## Specific Objective A

The student identifies and names coins: penny, nickel, dime, quarter, and half-dollar.

Teacher Interventions

Infant and Toddler/Preschool. Bring in a large gum ball machine filled with sugar-free M&Ms. Show the student the gum ball machine, and ask him or her if he or she would like to have some M&Ms. Tell the student you will show him or her how to get the M&Ms from the machine.

Place a penny on a table in front of the student. Point to the penny, and say, "This is a penny." Give the student the penny, and tell him or her to look at it closely and to feel it. Show him or her how to put the penny in the machine, turn the knob, and hold his or her hand to catch the M&Ms.

Put a penny and a quarter in front of the student, and ask him or her to pick the coin needed to get the M&Ms. If the student fails to pick up the penny, pick it up, and say, "This is the penny." At this point, if the student is able to, ask him or her to say its name. When he or she says the name, even if it is only in imitation, assist the student in putting the penny in the machine and successfully catching the M&Ms.

Primary Level.   Bring to school a large toy bank. Tell the student that this is a very special bank, and for today the bank will only accept pennies. Place assorted coins in a large bowl. Pick up one of the pennies, and say and demonstrate that the penny looks different in color and size from all the other coins.

Ask the student to note the picture of Abraham Lincoln on the front and the leaf design on the back of the penny and to make two piles of coins, one for pennies and the other for all those coins that are not pennies. Tell the student to pick up all the pennies and place them in the bank. Repeat this activity for all the other coins.

Intermediate Level.   Take the student on a trip to the museum, supermarket, or airport. Park the school vehicle at a parking meter. Tell him or her that in order to park there, the person who is parking a car must insert coins in the parking meter. Inform the student that the meter will accept pennies, nickels, dimes, and/or quarters. Provide the student with a small amount of change, and tell him or her to pick out the coins you requested and to insert them into the parking meter.

Secondary Level.   Take the student to a coin-operated laundromat, and tell him or her to wash the bag of dirty clothes that he or she brought from home. Say that the washing machine only accepts quarters and that you have a bag of mixed change (quarters, nickels, and dimes), and you will put some coins on the counter and he or she is to find the quarters.

Family Interventions

Infant and Toddler/Preschool.   Encourage the parents to take their child for trips into the community where there are gum ball machines or other machines that dispense little toys or trinkets and require a penny, nickel, or dime. Tell the parents to reward the child for behaving appropriately and to give him or her the correct coin for the machine.

Remind them to describe the coin and to say its name. Suggest that the parents ask the child to assist them in putting the coin in the machine, turning any knobs, and obtaining the desired item. Have the parents repeat the activity and ask the child to do as much as he or she can without assistance.

Primary Level. Encourage the parents to get the child a toy bank of his or her own. Tell the parents to empty their pockets or purses of any change at the end of the day and to place this change in a large container. Tell the parents to expect the child to sort the coins into piles of pennies, nickels, dimes, quarters, and half-dollars. Tell the parents to tell the child that he or she can only have the pennies and nickels to put into the bank.

Intermediate Level. Ask the parents to demonstrate the use of vending machines found in the community. Announce the coins needed when coin combinations can be used and when exact change must be used. Have the parents name each coin needed and request that the youngster select it from coins in their hands.

Secondary Level. Explain the laundromat activity listed under Teacher Interventions for them to engage in with the youngster. Tell the parents that they may want to take the student to a video arcade as well. Again, they should require the youngster to sort the quarters from a container of other coins. Encourage the parents to tell the youngster the number of quarters the video game requires and to ask him or her to count that number of quarters.

 ## Specific Objective B

The student identifies the money symbols: cent sign, dollar sign, and decimal point.

Teacher Interventions

Primary Level. Make price tags, put them on various objects in the classroom, and role-play "Going Shopping." Also bring in some toys and articles of clothing. Ask the student if he or she has ever gone shopping and if he or she can show or tell you how to find out how much things cost.

The student might respond that the items have prices on them. If so, tell the student that he or she is correct and that the items are all marked with price tags. Tell and show the student that price tags come in many different sizes and shapes.

Tell him or her that you have made some price tags and that today he or she will point to various things besides numbers that are found on price tags.

Write the symbol for dollar on the chalkboard. Explain to the student that this symbol may be easy for him or her to write, because it looks just like a large S with two lines drawn down through it. Write various dollar amounts on the board without the decimal point, and ask the student to point to the dollar sign and not to the numerals.

Provide prompts if the student needs assistance with this. Then tell the student you want him or her to walk around the room with a partner and circle all the dollar signs that they find on the price tags. Introduce the cent sign and decimal point in the same way.

Intermediate and Secondary Levels. Take the student to a gas station, and point out the gasoline pumps. Tell the student to look at the several gauges on the pump. Show him or her the gauges (regular, super, and premium) that indicate the prices of the several types of gasoline. Ask the student to identify the dollar symbol and the decimal points that are found on the pumps. After you finish pumping your gas, ask the student how much you owe the cashier (if he or she is able to read the pump).

Family Interventions

Primary Level. Suggest that the parents take their child with them when they go shopping. Tell the parents to point out to the child the price tags on articles of clothing and other merchandise. Encourage the parents to show the child the dollar symbol and explain what the symbol means.

Tell the parents, after pointing out several dollar signs to the child, to point out a price tag and ask the child to point to the dollar sign. Urge the parents to repeat this activity throughout the time that you are working on money symbols in the classroom.

Intermediate and Secondary Levels. Encourage the parents to take their youngster to a gas station and to a supermarket. When they take the youngster to a gas station, tell the parents to point out the money symbols on the gasoline pumps. When they take the youngster to a supermarket, encourage them to point out money symbols on packages and on store shelves and signs.

Specific Objective C

The student converts one denomination of coins into another denomination (e.g., five pennies equal one nickel).

Teacher Interventions

Primary Level.   Bring in a penny vending machine such as a Mickey Mouse gum ball machine with sugar-free M&Ms. Give the student a nickel with which to buy a midmorning snack. Explain that today, for a snack, he or she will have sugar-free M&Ms. Tell the student that there is a problem, however, because the vending machine will work only with pennies and he or she only has a nickel.

Ask the student if he or she can solve this problem. If the student does not suggest changing the nickel for pennies, ask the student whether a nickel has another name.

First, tell the student that almost all our coins (except for the dollar coin) have two names and that a penny is often called "1 cent." Next, tell the student that the other name for a nickel is "5 cents" and that "5 cents" is the same as "5 pennies." Therefore, "a nickel is the same as 5 pennies."

Give the student 10 pennies, and ask him or her to count out 5 cents. Tell him or her that the 5 pennies may look like they are more than just 1 nickel, but actually they are the same amount of money since a nickel *is* the same as 5 pennies. Tell the student that you will exchange 5 pennies for his or her nickel. Then, tell him or her to use the 5 pennies to get his or her snack.

Intermediate and Secondary Levels.   Take the student to a vending machine in the community that only takes quarters. Remind him or her that almost all coins have two names and that the other name for a quarter is 25 cents. Give the student the correct amount of change that, when added together, equals a quarter, but do not give him or her a quarter.

Ask the student how he or she thinks the item can be gotten since he or she does not have a quarter. If the student does not suggest exchanging the change for a quarter, show the student how to count the various possible combinations of dimes and nickels that equal a quarter.

Begin with using the other names of the coins, for example, "Ten cents, another 10 cents, and 5 cents more make 25 cents." If the student does this correctly, ask him or her to repeat the equation using the coin's basic name: "A dime, another dime, and a nickel make a quarter."

Do this for each of the possible combinations of coins, including pennies. Continue, especially at the secondary level, in the same fashion with the half-dollar and, finally, with making change for a dollar bill.

Family Interventions

Primary Level. The parents can request that their child take out a toy bank that has pennies in it. Tell the parents that they should help the child exchange his or her pennies for other coins. Review the other names for the coins as specified in the Teacher Interventions, and tell them to ask the child to count out 5 cents using only pennies.

Tell the parents that each time the child counts out 5 pennies they should give the child a nickel in exchange and explain that his or her nickel has the same value as the 5 pennies have. Encourage the parents to do the reverse exchange as well, in which the child receives 5 pennies for his or her nickel.

Tell the parents that once the child has counted out and exchanged enough pennies for 6 nickels, they should then assist the child in exchanging the nickels for dimes. Tell the parents to say, "These 2 nickels are the same amount of money as 1 dime. That's right, 5 cents and 5 cents does equal 10 cents. Therefore, if you give me 2 nickels, I will exchange them for 1 dime."

Encourage the parents to practice exchanging all the nickels for dimes. This home activity should be used as a follow-up to the in-class activities for this objective.

Intermediate and Secondary Levels. Encourage the parents to take the youngster for trips into the community where he or she can use vending machines to make purchases of snacks or beverages. Tell the parents to find vending machines that only take quarters. Ask them to practice with the youngster in the same fashion suggested in the Teacher Interventions.

 ## Specific Objective D

The student, when making purchases, determines that coins received as change are the correct amount.

Teacher Intervention

Primary Level. Take the student shopping for an item (or items) that costs less than a dollar. Give the student four quarters or a dollar bill. Tell the student you will accompany him or her to the cashier. Tell the student to make sure that the correct amount is being rung up on the register and to verify that he or she has received the correct change.

Tell the student to hold the change in the palm of his or her hand. Demonstrate counting up from the cost of the item(s) to arrive at the amount given for payment. (Note: Change should be verified through addition rather than subtraction when done orally or mentally.) After several demonstrations, encourage the student to verify change received without assistance. Check to determine whether the student is doing the task correctly.

Intermediate and Secondary Levels.   Take the student to the post office to purchase two or three stamps. Give the student a dollar bill or four quarters, and remind him or her to pay the postal clerk and to count the change received. After the student has made the purchase, ask him or her how much change was received. Provide minimal assistance, since at these levels the goal is for the student to be independent in verifying change.

At these levels you may wish to introduce purchases in which the student verifies change received when given a 5-dollar bill and the items purchased total more than 4 dollars and also when given a 10-dollar bill and the purchases cost more than 9 dollars.

Family Interventions

Primary Level.   Encourage the parents to take their child shopping with them and to demonstrate how they verify change received through the addition method. Explain this method, if necessary. Urge the parents to impress upon their child the need to verify change since there are people who try to *cheat* people out of their money and since cheating people out of their money is like *stealing*.

Help the parents develop the concept underlying the word *cheat*. Encourage them to give the child the opportunity to verify change received when the change is solely in coins.

Intermediate and Secondary Levels.   At these levels ask the parents to monitor their youngster's purchases to make certain that he or she verifies the amounts on the cash register, market receipts, and change received when paying with different denominations of currency and when the change received is solely in coins.

Remind the parents that, if the youngster is able to translate the mental arithmetic involved in verifying change into a written algorithm, they should ask the youngster to check his or her mental arithmetic with paper and pencil.

Specific Objective E

The student identifies and names 1-, 5-, and 10-dollar bills.

Teacher Interventions

Primary Level. Place two stacks of 1- and 5-dollar bills on the student's desk. (Note: Do not use play money!) Hold up a 1-dollar bill, and say, "This is a 1-dollar bill. See the number 1 on it. Show me all the places where the number 1 appears." Then ask the student to locate another 1-dollar bill. Repeat this until you are sure that the student is able to identify 1-dollar bills, distinguishing them from 5-dollar bills.

As the student picks up each 1-dollar bill, ask him or her to say its name. Repeat this procedure for the 5-dollar bills.

Intermediate Level. Place a number of 1-, 5-, and 10-dollar bills in a cash box. Take a 1-dollar bill out of the cash box and place it on the student's desk. Do the same with a 5-dollar bill and a 10-dollar bill.

Point out to the student the number indicators on each of the bills. Give the student the cash box and tell him or her to sort the bills into three different piles by matching them to the bills already on the desk. If the student is successful, ask him or her to name the bills in each pile, and give him or her one of the dollar bills to use in making a purchase in the school store or when on a field trip in the community.

Secondary Level. Take the student to a bank, and give him or her a 10-dollar bill to change. Arrange with the teller beforehand to give the student the change with two 5-dollar bills. When he or she is given the change, ask the student whether he or she received the right amount of money.

Repeat this activity with different bills exchanged and with the student cashing checks, such as a paycheck received for part-time work or for a gift. Also, show the student how to use change-making machines, such as those at the airport, when change currency is necessary to pay the parking meter, as well as those found at subway or metro stations when change is needed to purchase tickets from a ticket machine that only accepts coins.

Family Interventions

Primary Level. Encourage the parents to take their child to the post office to buy some stamps from a stamp-vending machine that accepts only

1-dollar bills. Ask them to demonstrate how they go through their currency to find the 1-dollar bills needed.

The parents can hold up each dollar bill and say, "Look at all the number 1s on this bill. It is a 1-dollar bill. I can use this bill in this machine." Tell them to hold up a 5- (or 10-) dollar bill and say, "Look at all the 5s (or 10s) on this bill. It is a 5- (or 10-) dollar bill. I can't use this bill in this machine."

Urge the parents to give the child the responsibility of putting the correct number of 1-dollar bills into the stamp-vending machine.

Intermediate and Secondary Levels.   Suggest that the parents take their youngster to the bank with them. Ask the parents to give the youngster a 10- (or 20-) dollar bill to get changed while in the bank. Tell the parents to tell the youngster to take the bill to the teller and ask for change in a previously established way, for example, one 5-dollar bill and five singles.

(Note: It may be necessary, at this point, to explain to the youngster that the word *single*, when referring to money, is another name for a 1-dollar bill.)

Urge the parents to remind the youngster to count the money received. Also, ask the parents to give the youngster checks to be cashed. (Note: If they give the youngster money as an allowance, as a gift, or to make needed purchases, tell them to write a check on occasion, instead of always giving him or her cash, so that the youngster can have this additional money-related experience.)

 ## Specific Objective F

The student uses currency when making purchases.

Teacher Interventions

Primary Level.   Plan a class luncheon or other special event that requires the expenditure of substantial sums of money, for example, to buy decorations, food, beverages, and supplies such as paper plates, napkins, and plastic eating utensils. Involve the student in making up the shopping list. Visit the supermarket as a first step in estimating the costs involved.

Tell the student the approximate cost, and ask him or her to tell you how much money will be needed for the event and to specify how much currency will be needed and in what possible combination of bills.

Then ask the student on the day of the actual shopping trip to tell you the amount of money to be taken and the denomination of bills he or she would like to take. Finally, accompany the student on the actual shopping trip, and monitor his or her paying of the bill.

Intermediate and Secondary Levels.   At these levels give the student greater responsibility in creating a budget for large purchases (e.g., for his or her clothing, grooming supplies and materials, leisure activities, gift giving, and hypothetical work-related expenses). Ask the student to specify the approximate amount of money and the possible denominations of currency needed. Role-play making these purchases, using real money, if feasible. Reward the student for correctly selecting different combinations of currency in repetitions of the role-play.

Family Interventions

Primary Level.   Encourage the parents to take their child on shopping trips. Tell them to demonstrate their use of currency in making purchases, starting with small purchases that involve the expenditure of several dollars and gradually escalating the costs so that the child is exposed to the use of larger denominations and various combinations of currency in making needed household purchases.

Intermediate and Secondary Levels.   At these levels, tell the parents to give their youngster increased responsibility for making purchases that involve the selection of various denominations of currency both for family shopping and for personal shopping. At the intermediate level, encourage them to accompany the youngster on the trip with the eventual goal (perhaps at the secondary level) of checking him or her only upon his or her return from the shopping trip or refraining from checking because the youngster has mastered the skill.

***

 ## Specific Objective G

The student uses a combination of coins and currency when making purchases and verifies any change received.

***

Teacher Interventions

Primary Level.   When appropriate, give the student a combination of coins and currency that is greater than the actual cost of the school lunch. Demonstrate how to select the best combination of currency and coins to pay for lunch and how to verify change received. Demonstrate in this way for several days before asking the student to do it by him- or herself. When you believe he or she is ready, tell the student to pay for his or her own lunch in the school cafeteria.

Monitor the student's use of currency and coins and verification of change. When the student demonstrates sufficient skill, arrange for the cafeteria cashier to make a mistake in the change. Reward the student for requesting the correct amount courteously when he or she has been shortchanged and for being honest when receiving too much change.

Intermediate and Secondary Levels. At these levels arrange for the student to make purchases for the class in the school store (or in the community if there is no school store). Give him or her a lot of coins along with sufficient currency. Urge him or her to use as many coins as possible because the coins are becoming too heavy to carry and are taking up too much room in your change purse.

At first, demonstrate your use of a combination of coins and currency to make purchases, and, in subsequent shopping trips, assign the student the responsibility for paying the bill, using both coins and currency. Remind the student to verify any change received.

Family Interventions

Primary Level. Encourage the parents to take their child with them on shopping trips. Tell them to demonstrate using both coins and currency to pay the cashier or salesperson. At this level ask the parents to give the child responsibility for paying for small purchases involving the use of both coins and currency.

Intermediate and Secondary Levels. At these levels ask the parents to give their youngster increasing responsibility for doing the family shopping. Tell them to gradually increase the amount of the expenditures so that the youngster is provided with experiences involving larger and larger amounts of money and higher denominations of currency.

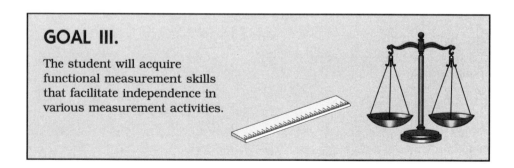

GOAL III.

The student will acquire functional measurement skills that facilitate independence in various measurement activities.

SPECIFIC OBJECTIVES

See the Sample Lesson Plans near the end of this unit.

The student:

❐ A. Discriminates between large and small and big and little items.

❐ B. Discriminates between short and tall and short and long.

❐ C. Discriminates between full and empty.

❐ D. Uses a ruler to measure the dimensions of objects and things.

❐ E. Uses measuring cups and spoons in cooking and other functional activities.

❐ F. Uses a scale to measure his or her weight and a food scale to measure in food preparation activities.

❐ G. Uses a yardstick and a measuring tape to measure length, width, depth, and height.

❐ H. Measures objects and recipe items using whole numbers, fractions (½, ⅓, and ¼), and mixed numbers.

❐ I. Estimates size, distance, and quantity.

SUGGESTED ACTIVITIES

 ## Specific Objective A

The student discriminates between large and small and big and little items.

Teacher Interventions

Infant and Toddler/Preschool. Show the student a dressing doll that is wearing a buttoning vest with big and little buttons. Tell the student to watch as you button the vest. Tell the student you will first button the big buttons. Say, "Watch, [student's name], as I button this big button."

After you finish the big buttons, tell the student to watch as you button the ones that are *not big*. Explain that another way of saying that the buttons are *not big* is to say they are *little*. Then tell the student that the dressing doll (give it a name) is tired (move it to show the eyelids closing) and must take a nap.

Tell the student that because it is nap time, we must now remove the vest so that (doll's name) will be able to have a comfortable nap, and ask the student to watch as you unbutton the big buttons. Say, "Look, [student's name], I am unbuttoning the big buttons. First I am unbuttoning the big top button, then the next big button, and I have one more big button to unbutton. Now I will unbutton the little buttons."

Tell the student you are now going to put (doll's name) in the crib or doll carriage. (Note: If the student is able to do some of the unbuttoning and buttoning, ask him or her to assist you.) Repeat this activity on subsequent days, and use the terms *large* and *small* instead.

Primary Level.   Ask the student to assist you during a classroom decoration activity to plant some flowers. Place large and small flowerpots on a table. Provide the potting soil and the miniature gardening tools that the student will need to plant the seeds.

Tell the student that you want him or her to plant a small seed in the small pot and a large seed in the large pot. Show the student a large seed, and say, "This is a large seed. This is the seed you should put in the large pot."

Instruct the student to prepare the soil for the large pot. Have the student put the large seed in the pot. After the student finishes this task, say, "Now I want you to plant the small seed in the small pot. This time I want to see how much you can do without my help."

If the student plants the small seed without your assistance, provide him or her with the appropriate reinforcers. Tell the student you will take photographs of the flowers when they bloom.

Intermediate and Secondary Levels.   Obtain some pot-weary plants from a local greenhouse or the horticulture department in your high school or bring some from home. Tell the student to look at what you have brought in for the class today. Ask the student to tell you what he or she sees. If the student says, "Plants," ask if he or she notices anything special about these plants.

If the student does not respond correctly, tell him or her that the plants are getting too big for the pots they are in. In fact, the pots are now too "small" for the plants, and it is time to move the plants into a "large" flowerpot. Give the student the directions for transplanting the plants from one pot to the other.

Family Interventions

Primary Level.   Ask the parents to arrange for their child to engage in a painting project in an appropriate area of the home. Encourage them to give the child an oversized painting shirt to wear that has both large and small buttons. Tell the parents to point out the buttons on the shirt. Tell the parents to say, "See, this button is a large button, and this button is a small one."

Tell the parents to ask the child to button all the large buttons and to stop the child if he or she starts to button a small button, explaining that it is not a large button. Tell them to repeat the directions, this time dealing with the small buttons, and to then engage the child in the painting activity.

Intermediate and Secondary Levels. Encourage the parents to involve the youngster in assisting them in a variety of household tasks that require him or her to differentiate between big and little (and large and small) objects in order to complete household chores (e.g., "Please get me the large pot to heat the pasta and the small pot to make the gravy for the turkey" or "I need the big can of tuna, because we are having guests for lunch, and the small jar of black olives to decorate the platter of tuna salad."

 ## Specific Objective B

The student discriminates between short and tall and short and long.

Teacher Interventions

Infant and Toddler/Preschool. For snack time, prepare some celery and carrot sticks by cutting them into both short and long pieces. Pick up a long piece of one of the vegetables and a short one. Demonstrate the difference in length with the index fingers of both hands, and say, "I will use the long pieces for finger food and the short pieces for a salad." Tell the student to watch as you prepare the salad with the short pieces.

Primary Level. Draw two lines on the chalkboard of different heights. Point to the shorter of the two, and say, "This is a short line." Point to the taller line, and say, "This line is not short; it is tall." Explain to the student that some people are short and others are tall. (Note: Do not engage in this next suggested activity if it might be embarrassing to the student or his or her classmates who might be sensitive about their height.) Say, "Today we will find out who is short and who is tall in this classroom."

Ask the student to stand next to one of his or her taller peers. Explain that standing next to a person is not the best way to tell who is taller. Then, go to the place where you have already posted some long roll paper. Ask the student to stand with his or her back against the paper and the classmate to mark the paper. Then ask the student to mark the paper to show the height of his or her classmate.

Ask the student to say which mark shows who is short and which one shows who is tall. You may wish to save these markings to demonstrate any growth that has taken place during the school year.

Intermediate and Secondary Levels. Give the student items of different lengths that he or she must put into appropriate-sized containers. For example, say, "Please, put the long nails in the long container and the short ones in the short container and put them in the toolbox," or "Please, put the long [new] pencils in the long container and the short [used] pencils in the short container and put them in the supply closet." Also give the student the task of stacking books by their size.

Family Interventions

Infant and Toddler/Preschool. Have the parents involve their child in meal and snack preparations that involve preparing foods of different lengths. Tell the parents, for example, to implement their plan for preparing raw vegetables for finger food and a dip by saying, "We want long slices for finger food, so I am going to cut this [name of vegetable] into long pieces. Now we want to prepare some short pieces for a dip, so I am going to cut the [name of vegetable] into short pieces."

Primary Level. Parents can get a height-measuring poster or a large sheet of white paper or just measure their child against a closet door. The parents can measure each other and say such things as "I have stopped growing taller, but I still need to check how tall I am because I often have to fill out forms that want to know how tall I am." Then tell them to measure the child and to say, "You are not as tall as we are because you are still growing" (see Figure 3.5).

Intermediate and Secondary Levels. Parents can videotape a sporting event on television (e.g., basketball), replay it, and comment on the players who are tall and the ones who are short. Encourage the parents to ask their youngster to point out those players who are tall and those who are short.

 ## Specific Objective C

The student discriminates between full and empty.

Width and Height Chart												
WIDTH									HEIGHT			
1.	27	28	30	31	32	34	35	36	45	55	64	74
2.	27	28	30	31	32	34	35	36	45	55	64	74
3.	27	28	30	31	32	34	35	36	45	55	64	74
4.	27	28	30	31	32	34	35	36	45	55	64	74
5.	27	28	30	31	32	34	35	36	45	55	64	74

Have child circle the correct measurement for width and height. If necessary, write in the correct measurement.

FIGURE 3.5. Width and height chart for parents.

Teacher Interventions

Infant and Toddler/Preschool. Make popcorn with the student as a reward for his or her appropriate behavior. Once the corn is popped, place it in a bowl. Say to the student that the bowl is now full of popcorn. Give the student the popcorn to eat. If the student does not finish the popcorn, empty the bowl so that it has nothing in it.

Show the student the empty bowl and say, "Look, [student's name], all the popcorn is gone; the bowl is now empty." At this point, take your hand and swirl it around the inside of the bowl (without touching the sides of the bowl). Repeat this activity using different foods and beverages (full and empty glasses and cups) at snack time.

Primary Level. At snack time, place several small boxes of raisins (some empty and some full) in front of the student. Tell the student that some boxes have raisins in them and others are empty. Open a box and show the student that it has raisins in it and tell him or her that the box is full. Then pick up any empty box and open it to show that it is empty. Tell the student that the box is empty and that you want him or her to place all of the full boxes on the snack table and to throw away the empty boxes.

Next, assign the student the job of "snack assistant," asking him or her to pass out the boxes to his or her classmates. Ask all the other students to make sure they have received a full box of raisins. If a classmate receives an empty box, tell that student to show it to the "snack assistant." Explain that a classmate received an empty box and that he or she must go to the snack shelf to get a full box.

Intermediate and Secondary Levels. At the beginning of the school day, ask the student to check the classroom wastebasket to see whether it is empty. At the end of the day, ask him or her to check the wastebasket again to see whether it is now full and should be emptied. Also, make the student the inventory monitor who lets you know when boxes, jars, and bottles of class supplies are almost empty and a supply order must be made.

Family Interventions

Infant and Toddler/Preschool. During meal and snack times, parents can comment on whether glasses, cups, and plates are full or empty. For example, when they fill their child's cup with milk or juice, tell them to say, "[Child's name], your cup is full of juice." When the liquid has been drunk, encourage the parents to say, "All gone! [Child's name], your cup is empty; do you want some more juice?"

Primary Level. Encourage the parents to permit their child to fill his or her own glass during meal and snack times. Tell the parents to note when the glass is empty and to say, "[Child's name], your glass is empty. Would you like some more? If so, you may fill your glass." Tell the parents to comment when the glass is full. Also, urge the parents not to allow the student to have seconds until his or her plate is empty.

Intermediate and Secondary Levels. Ask the parents to give the youngster the responsibility for taking inventory of household supplies (e.g., "When the bottle of window cleaner with the spray top is empty, remember to fill it with the window cleaner fluid from the large bottle" or "When your tube of toothpaste is almost empty, remind me to put 'a tube of toothpaste' on the shopping list").

 ## Specific Objective D

The student uses a ruler to measure the dimensions of objects and things.

Teacher Interventions

See the Sample Lesson Plans near the end of this unit.

Primary Level. Start an indoor or, when possible, an outdoor garden. Plant seeds that produce quick-growing plants. Examples might be green beans, radishes, dill, and chives. Tell the student that he or she will keep a record of the rate of growth of the plants. Explain to him or her that a fast rate of growth indicates how healthy the plants are.

Provide a data sheet on which the student will record daily measurements. Demonstrate how to use a ruler to measure the growth of the plants. Tell the student to report on changes in growth.

Intermediate and Secondary Levels.   After school photographs have been received, ask the student to bring in one of the 5″ × 7″ copies. The student can make a frame for the picture as a gift to his or her family. Provide the student with a ruler, and ask the student to trace the photograph and to measure the traced outline.

Provide the student with matting material (cardboard and colored construction paper) and with wood to make a frame. Demonstrate how to use the ruler to measure the mat and frame, and monitor and provide assistance, as needed, as he or she makes the finished frame. Do a number of arts and crafts and construction projects that require measurement.

Family Interventions

Primary Level.   Explain to the parents that there are many ordinary events around the house that require the use of a ruler, such as identifying where to hang a picture, measuring shelf paper to line the kitchen cabinets, and measuring the amount of progress made on a scarf that is being knitted. Encourage them to involve their child whenever they use a ruler and to begin to ask the child to do some simple measurements.

Intermediate and Secondary Levels.   Parents should be encouraged to give their youngster increasing responsibility for carrying out household chores that involve the use of a ruler, such as measuring the area on the surface of his or her bedroom nightstand to determine the size scarf to purchase as a cover for it and measuring the size of a wall area to determine where to hang a favorite poster.

 ## Specific Objective E

The student uses measuring cups and spoons in cooking and other functional activities.

Teacher Interventions

Infant and Toddler/Preschool. Prepare to make microwave bran muffins with the student. Obtain all materials needed, including the measuring cup and spoon, mixing bowl, and muffin tin. Tell the student that you are going to make bran muffins in the microwave.

Ask the student to watch as you pour the milk into the measuring cup and to especially notice when you stop pouring. Tell the student that you stopped pouring the milk when you reached the ½ mark on the measuring cup. Tell the student to watch you as you continue to add the other ingredients.

When you finish mixing the other ingredients, tell the student you are going to pour the muffin mix into the muffin tin. Then bake the muffins and, when the muffins are baked and have cooled, serve them for a snack. Repeat this activity for other food preparation tasks for which a measuring cup and spoons are needed. At this level, simply provide the experience of seeing these utensils being used.

Primary Level. Before starting an arts and crafts lesson, show the student a balloon that has been covered with papier-mâché. Tell the student that he or she will be using papier-mâché to make his or her own special balloon but that he or she needs to make special paste for the papier-mâché.

Tell the student that making the paste, like many things we prepare, requires that we use the exact amount of all its ingredients. Tell the student that you are going to show him or her how to use a spoon called a "measuring spoon" that helps people make exact measurements.

Tell the student to watch as you prepare the papier-mâché paste. Provide the student with the measurements for each item needed. This information should be written and shown to the student. After the student has made the papier-mâché paste, tell him or her to cover newspaper strips with the paste and to put them on preinflated balloons.

Intermediate and Secondary Levels. As you demonstrate how to measure the detergent needed to wash clothes, remind the student that you have already shown him or her how to sort clothes and he or she already knows how to identify quarters needed for operating a coin-operated washing machine. Provide the student with a simplified pictorial and enlarged copy of the directions for measuring detergent.

Ask the student to review the directions and pour the detergent into the measuring cup. Ask the student to look at the picture of the measuring cup that was provided and to examine the cup of detergent he or she has poured. Ask him or her to tell you if the two match.

If you discover that the measuring cup and the pictorial representation do not match, use another measuring cup as an actual model for the student to replicate.

Family Interventions

Infant and Toddler/Preschool. Encourage the parents to conduct a variety of measuring activities using a measuring cup and measuring spoons. Explain that, at this level, the purpose is simply to expose their child to the use of these utensils as an integral part of food preparation and other activities.

Primary Level. Parents can involve their child as a helper in using both a measuring cup and measuring spoons. Urge them to point out the markings on these utensils and to demonstrate how they first look at the recipe or the directions and then use the numbers and abbreviations to identify where to stop adding material to a measuring cup and to select the right measuring spoon to use.

Intermediate and Secondary Levels. Encourage the parents, at these levels, to give the youngster increasing responsibility for completing food preparation and other tasks involving the use of measuring spoons and a measuring cup. At these levels, parents should be encouraged to give the youngster recipes that he or she is to prepare as independently as possible. Tell them to make the youngster's food an important part of a family celebration or special activity such as a picnic.

 ## Specific Objective F

The student uses a scale to measure his or her weight and a food scale to measure in food preparation activities.

Teacher Interventions

Primary Level. Set up the learning area to resemble a grocery store. Bring in real (not plastic) fruit, cloth shopping bags, and a produce scale. Role-play going food shopping to buy fruit and vegetables. Ask the student to help you pick out fruit. Say, "I think I will buy some apples and bananas. Before I buy them I must find out how much they weigh, since I have only a limited amount of money to spend and can only afford 1 pound of each."

Then ask the student to help you weigh the apples by putting them on the scale. (Give the student less than a pound.) Comment on the fact that there is not a pound of apples on the scale by pointing to the dial and the number 1. Then say, "I need just a few more apples to make a pound; please add a few more apples to the scale." Thank the student for helping you.

Next, say, "There is now 1 pound of apples on the scale," while simultaneously pointing to the dial and the number 1.

Intermediate Level. Bring in a supermarket scale, real fruit and vegetables, a shopping bag, and a carry-all shopping cart. Tell the student that he or she is going to practice using scales that are used in supermarkets. Ask the student to name some things that are weighed at the grocery store. If he or she does not name fruit and vegetables, give clues to assist him or her. If the student does name apples and oranges, say, "You are right, and they are called fruit."

Tell the student that in order to estimate how much the fruit might cost, you will weigh the fruit. Explain that the more the fruit weighs, the more it will cost. (At this point, give the student some mental operations to do or have him or her use a calculator to arrive at the cost of different amounts, by pound units, of specific fruit.)

Explain that each large dark number represents 1 pound. Point to the number 1 and tell the student that if the pointer is there (pointing to the number 1), you will know that the fruit weighs 1 pound. Do the same for the other numbers on the scale. Ask him or her to place the fruit on the scale and tell you how much the fruit weighs.

For some students you may wish to introduce the concept of ounces, while for others you may wait to introduce ounces at the next level.

Secondary Level. Bring digital, numerical, and talking bathroom scales, if available, into the classroom. Tell the student that to get certain jobs you must be a particular weight. For example, to be a racehorse jockey you must not weigh over 110 pounds. Tell the student that, while weight is not as important for other jobs, most employment applications and other forms (such as insurance and driver's license applications) will ask for a person's weight. Therefore, he or she must weigh him- or herself at different times in life.

At this point, demonstrate how to use each of the scales. (Note: A person's weight is a very personal thing, so be especially sensitive to a student who is sensitive about his or her weight and modify the activity as necessary.)

Family Interventions

Primary Level. Encourage the parents to take their child with them on food shopping trips. Ask them to demonstrate how they estimate the cost of fruit and vegetables by weighing them on a produce scale (see Figure 3.6).

Intermediate and Secondary Levels. Ask the parents to tell their youngster that knowing how to weigh things is also important when preparing food. Encourage them to demonstrate how to use a scale for weighing recipe ingredients. Ask the parents to say such things as "Today we are going

FIGURE 3.6.   Supermarket scale.

to make [food name] and to do so we must use ___ ounces of ___, so let's look at the scale and read the measurements on it."

Ask the parents to then read the ingredients and weights needed for making the recipe, and to ask the youngster to weigh them on the food scale (see Figure 3.7).

   ## Specific Objective G

The student uses a yardstick and a measuring tape to measure length, width, depth, and height.

Teacher Interventions

Primary Level.   Show the student how to use a tape measure to measure him- or herself to determine clothing sizes. (Note: This may be a very personal

FIGURE 3.7. Kitchen food scales.

area and should be approached with caution. The safe thing may be to limit the activity to the head [hats and caps], collar, and sleeve [shirts] length measurements for male students and floor-to-knee measurements [skirt length and hem measurements] for female students.)

Intermediate Level. Demonstrate how to use a yardstick and measuring tape to measure the classroom floor in a role-play in which you pretend that wall-to-wall carpeting will be purchased. Ask the student to do a similar measurement for a different classroom that is a different size.

Also, measure the classroom bulletin board to determine how many sheets of construction paper will be needed to provide a colorful background. Ask the student to assist you in measuring this large area with a yardstick.

Secondary Level. Explain to the student that sometimes it is important to know the length and the width of something. Explain to the student that how "wide" something is refers to its width. Explain to the student that you may want to get some new furniture in the classroom, but you must first measure the width of the desks to make sure they can fit through the door. Demonstrate this activity by taking a yardstick or measuring tape and placing it on one corner of the desk and bringing it across the front of the desk to the other side.

Ask the student to assist you by first writing down the measurement and later doing the measurement with you writing down the result. Then tell the student that you must measure the width of the doorway. Ask the student if he or she knows how to measure the width of the doorway.

If the student correctly answers this question, tell the student to measure the doorway. If the student answers the question incorrectly, demonstrate the correct way to measure the doorway.

Then ask the student to measure the doorway. Write on the board the measurement for the doorway and one of the desks. Show the student how to determine whether the new desks can be larger than the old ones and, if so, how much larger.

Family Interventions

Primary Level. Encourage the parents to include their child in any measuring activities that take place in the home that involve the use of yardsticks or measuring tape, for example, measuring windows for purchasing drapes, curtains, curtain rods, and other hardware or measuring an area in a room to determine the size furniture that will fit there. Ask the parents to limit the child's role to that of an observer.

Intermediate and Secondary Levels. Ask the parents to require the youngster to be an active participant in collecting household measurements. For example, if the family is in need of new plastic runners for the hallway to protect the carpet, tell the parents to demonstrate taking measurements.

Encourage the parents to provide the youngster with a yardstick or measuring tape and paper and pencil and tell him or her to use the measuring tape to measure the length and then the width of the hallway. Tell the parents to be sure that the youngster writes down these measurements.

Specific Objective H

The student measures objects and recipe items using whole numbers, fractions ($\frac{1}{2}$, $\frac{1}{3}$, and $\frac{1}{4}$), and mixed numbers.

Teacher Interventions

Infant and Toddler/Preschool and Primary Levels. See Goal II, Specific Objective D, Teacher Interventions.

Secondary Level. See Goal II, Specific Objective D, Teacher Interventions. Include activities that require the student to read and carry out recipes with mixed fractions.

Specific Objective I

The student estimates size, distance, and quantity.

Teacher Interventions

Primary Level. Have the student stand in the front of the room with you, and have another student stand at the back of the classroom with a fellow teacher, an aide, or a volunteer. Ask the student to judge the distance between him- or herself and the other student. Compare the student's estimate to the actual distance by using a yardstick to get the correct measurement.

Repeat for various distances in the school building and the school grounds, such as the distance between the play field and the exit door and the distance between the classroom and the cafeteria. Praise the student for improving his or her estimates.

Intermediate Level. During a holiday season, for example, the day before Thanksgiving, place a large jar in the room full of jelly beans or marbles, and ask the student to guess how many pieces of candy or how many marbles are in the jar. Tell the student that another word for guess is *estimate.*

Explain that sometimes when you are not sure exactly how much there is of something, you can guess or make an estimate. Explain that it is a very difficult task to estimate the number of ___s in the jar, but that there will be occasions in his or her life when there will be a real need to estimate, for example, the amount or quantity of an item that one is able to purchase with a given amount of money.

Show the student advertisements from newspapers of items that he or she might wish to purchase in quantity. Give the student a hypothetical amount of money, and ask him or her to estimate how many of the item he or she can buy.

Secondary Level. Ask the student to tell you what size coat, jacket, or sweater he or she wears. Role-play being at an end-of-the-year sale where much of the clothing is out of place on the racks or size labels are missing.

Then show the student these articles of clothing in several different sizes, and ask him or her to pick out a size that he or she thinks would fit. (In the beginning have one item that is his or her size, with the other items being markedly different, and gradually increase the size similarities so that the estimation is more difficult.) Follow up by taking the student to a nearby department store to find his or her size of clothing of various types.

Family Interventions

Primary Level. Ask the parents to take the child for trips in the family automobile into the community. Tell them to explain how to use the odometer to measure distance traveled. Tell them to measure some distances and then to play the "Guess the Distance" game, in which the child attempts to guess the distance between his or her home and key sites in the community, for example, the school, the police station, the firehouse, and a house of worship.

Intermediate and Secondary Levels. Ask the parents to involve the youngster in making decisions about the size of a clothing item that the family would like to purchase as a gift for a relative or friend: for example, "It is Aunt Rose's birthday next week. She loves pretty dresses. I wonder what size dress we should buy?"

Also encourage the parents to involve the youngster as an active participant in making quantity decisions about the amount of food to be purchased and prepared for a house party or for a meal when guests are invited.

GOAL IV.

The student will acquire those functional time measurement skills that facilitate time management.

SPECIFIC OBJECTIVES

The student:

- ❐ A. Identifies and names specific times of day (morning, afternoon, and night) and matches the time of day with appropriate activities.

- ❐ B. Identifies and names the days of the week.

- ❐ C. Identifies and names the months of the year.

- ❐ D. Identifies and names the current day and date.

- ❐ E. Identifies and names the current season and the other seasons in sequence.

- ❐ F. Identifies his or her birthday and birth date.

❐ G. Identifies and names the major holidays.

❐ H. Identifies and names clocks and watches.

❐ I. Identifies and names the time by hour and half-hour on different types of clocks and watches (digital, wrist, numeral, etc.).

❐ J. Is punctual to school, leisure-time, and other appointments and scheduled activities.

 ## Specific Objective A

The student identifies and names specific times of day (morning, afternoon, and night) and matches the time of day with appropriate activities.

Teacher Interventions

Infant and Toddler/Preschool and Primary Levels. Have the student watch as you develop a chart that is divided into sections representing specific times of day. On each section, place pictures or drawings representing activities that occur at specific times of day (e.g., eating a snack, music time, recess time, and going home).

New sections for the chart should be added just prior to the time for the new activity. Once the chart has been established, show the student the chart just before the new activity is to begin, and point to the section of the chart that represents the specific time and activity. Tell the student it is time to ___.

Intermediate Level. Provide the student with several magazines and newspapers. Sit next to him or her and ask him or her to look through the magazines for pictures of activities that might be done in the morning, afternoon, and night. Discuss the activities depicted in the pictures and when they are appropriately done, if applicable.

Provide the student with three large note cards. The cards should have "morning," "afternoon," and "night" written on them. Tell the student to cut out pictures with activities for each of the cards. When the student has finished, review and discuss each of the pictures. Ask the student what is shown in each picture and why he or she has identified that picture as a morning, afternoon, or night activity.

Secondary Level. Every morning, before the school day starts, write the student's morning, afternoon, and projected nighttime activities on the board. Provide the student with a day planning book and pictures of representative activities for him or her to paste in the planning book for each of the periods of the day.

Family Interventions

Infant and Toddler/Preschool and Primary Levels. Encourage the parents to develop a chart that is divided into sections representing specific times of day and to place pictures or drawings representing family-oriented and personal activities that occur at specific times of day (e.g., morning—breakfast; afternoon—lunch; night—bed and story time) on each section of the chart.

Tell the parents to review the chart periodically with their child and to also point out the environmental signs that indicate that it is morning—the early, pale sunlight and the waking of people in the home for school and work; afternoon—the strong rays of the sun and the lunchtime meal; and night—the darkness and the closing down of the house just before everyone's bedtime.

Intermediate and Secondary Levels. Encourage the parents to provide their youngster with a day planner. (The activities in the day planner should indicate what the child will do for the day. The day planner can be developed according to the youngster's reading level.)

If the youngster is a nonreader, tell the parents to engage him or her in cutting out magazine pictures representing the typical events of his or her day. (The parents can place Velcro tabs on the backs of the pictures and in the day planner.)

Tell the parents to ask the youngster to place each picture on the appropriate day of the week, according to the time of day (morning, afternoon, or night).

If the youngster is able to read, tell the parents to assist their youngster in making one-word labels representing each activity. After the labels are made, remind the parents to check whether the youngster understands what the label represents. Tell the parents to show the youngster the labels and to ask him or her to tell them what each label means.

If the youngster has difficulty with some of the labels, encourage the parents to add small pictures to those labels. When the parents and youngster have completed all the labels and pictures, tell the parents to begin using the day planner by asking him or her, every morning at breakfast, what he or she plans to do that day. (See Figure 3.8.)

FIGURE 3.8. Day planner.

 ## Specific Objective B

The student identifies and names the days of the week.

Teacher Interventions

Infant and Toddler/Preschool. During the morning opening exercises, schedule a time to review the calendar. After a regular good-morning song, join the student in singing the "Days of the Week" song. Each time a day of the week is sung, point to it on the calendar. After you finish singing this song, say, "Tell me what today is." If the student answers correctly, praise him or her, and discuss the day's schedule. If there is no response, provide the answer, for example, "Today is Friday. On Fridays we go swimming at the YMCA. It is the last school day of our week. We will meet on Monday after our weekend."

Primary Level. The calendar activity described for the infant and toddler/preschool level should be continued at the primary level. At this level the student should be required to first sing the "Days of the Week" song by him- or herself and then tell you what day it is. In addition, the student will be expected to remove the day-of-the-week language strip from the chalkboard and place it in the proper place on the wall calendar. Then say the date and write it on the calendar. (See Figure 3.9.)

FIGURE 3.9. Classroom calendar.

Intermediate and Secondary Levels. Give each student his or her own calendar. Every morning before beginning class activities, tell the student to look at the calendar and to say what day it is. After the student says the day of the week, ask him or her to discuss the day's plans. Encourage the student to link the day of the week to specific activities.

Relate this activity with the planning journal activity found under Goal IV, Specific Objective A. At these levels include conversations about the previous day's events and plans for the next day or for a day sometime in the future.

Family Interventions

Infant and Toddler/Preschool and Primary Levels. Ask the parents to purchase a large kitchen wall calendar with large blocks for the days of the week and to obtain pictures of the month that might be highly motivating to young children, like a "Sesame Street" character (e.g., Big Bird or Ernie), dogs, or cats. (Something with bright colors would be highly appealing.) Tell the parents that this activity will assist their child in becoming aware of the days of the week and eventually help him or her name them.

During breakfast, the parents can draw the child's attention to the calendar. They can say something like "Look at Big Bird. He says today will be a good day. Let's see what day it is." Demonstrate to the parents how to point to the place on the calendar and simultaneously say the day of the week.

Remind the parents to mark the calendar with a bright red Magic Marker. Encourage them to mark the day with a star or any shape they prefer. Tell the parents to next say the day and ask the child to point to it on the calendar.

Intermediate and Secondary Levels. Parents can ask their youngster what day it is every morning before he or she leaves for school or for a work assignment. If possible, tell them to ask the youngster in the evening about yesterday's activities and anticipated events for the next day and to include in the conversation a reference to the day under discussion.

 ## Specific Objective C

The student identifies and names the months of the year.

Teacher Interventions

Infant and Toddler/Preschool. Continue with the calendar opening activity described in Specific Objective A, but now add the name of the month after identifying the day of the week. Say, "The day of the week is Thursday, and the month is October." Tell the student to watch as you place the name-of-the-month language strip in the proper place on the calendar. Then repeat the day of the week and the month, and ask the student to identify the month.

Primary Level. Review with the student the months of the year by saying them yourself first and then asking him or her to join you in reciting the "Months of the Year" poem. Say, "Thirty days have September, April, June, and November; all the rest have thirty-one, except for February, which has twenty-eight and sometimes twenty-nine."

After reviewing this poem, tell the student you are going to play a game called "I Am a Month." (This game consists of a person saying descriptions of a month until the student names the specific month referred to. For example, say, "I am the month that is often very cold; many people, but not everyone, celebrate Christmas during this month. Tell me what month I am.")

Provide the student with at least three clues before providing him or her with the correct answer, if he or she fails to identify the month.

Intermediate Level. Continue the calendar activity for this level as described under Specific Objective A. Tell the student to identify the month on the wall calendar. If the student identifies it correctly, tell him or her to point to the name of the month on his or her personal calendar.

Secondary Level. At this level the student is expected to identify the names of the months as they relate to activities and events in his or her life. To assist the student in this, make a 12-inch wheel out of tagboard. Divide the wheel into 12 parts, and write the name of a month on top of each part. Make a 6-inch wheel, and divide it into 12 parts.

Write the name of a significant event, holiday, or birthday in each part of the small wheel. Place the smaller wheel over the larger wheel and attach it with a brass paper fastener. (See Figure 3.10.) Tell the student to turn the small wheel until the event he or she has selected lines up with the correct month. (There should be one event for each month so that the student can practice finding the name of each month.)

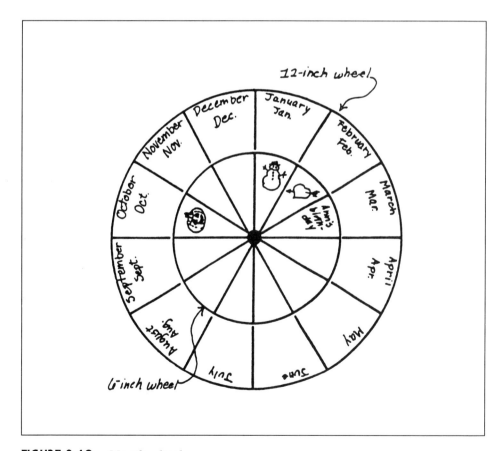

FIGURE 3.10. Month wheel.

Family Interventions

Infant and Toddler/Preschool. Parents can continue with the calendar activity described under Specific Objective A by adding the name of the month after identifying the day of the week. After identifying the day of the week, encourage the parents to say, "The day of the week is Wednesday, and the month is March."

Tell the parents to ask the child to watch them as they mark the day of the week on the calendar and underline the name of the month.

Primary Level. Encourage the parents to periodically ask their child what day of the week it is. Tell the parents to assist the child in pointing to and marking the day on a wall calendar. After the day has been correctly identified, remind the parents to ask the child the name of the month. Tell the parents to give the child the same clues given for the months as suggested in the Teacher Interventions.

Intermediate and Secondary Levels. Encourage the parents to assist the youngster in naming the month and identifying the day of the week by establishing a day planner. (In the day planner, the months are to be circled and the days are to be marked as they occur.) Encourage the parents to periodically ask the child what month and day it is.

Tell the parents to ask the youngster to identify special occasions in that month. Remind the parents to point out the day of a special occasion or event on the day planner: for example, "During the month of February, we celebrate Valentine's Day, and President's Day, and my father's birthday."

 ## Specific Objective D

The student identifies and names the current day and date.

Teacher Interventions

Infant and Toddler/Preschool. As you continue the calendar activities listed under Specific Objective B, include opportunities for the student to see and hear the current date as part of your morning opening exercises. After the student has watched and listened to you name the day of the week, tell him or her the date.

Place a small representative symbol of the month in each square of the calendar. This symbol should have the date for that particular day printed on it. For example, for March the symbol might be little sham-rocks, and when you place the shamrock symbol on the calendar, say, "Today is Wednesday, and it is March 17th. Today is going to be a spe-cial day for us, because we are having a St. Patrick's Day party."

This procedure should be followed every day of the month, even when there is no special event, for example, "Today is Monday, and it is Sep-tember 23rd. Today we are going to work on ___."

Primary Level.   Continue working with the student on the calendar activities that were begun under Specific Objective B. When doing the calendar work, ask the student to name both the day and the date. If you are using the representative pictures with the dates written on them, refer the student to the day before. Say, "Yesterday was March 17th, and it was Wednes-day. Tell me what date it is today."

If the student says, "Today is March 18th," give him or her the pic-ture with that date written on it, and tell him or her to place it on the cal-endar where it belongs. When you first begin this task, point to the loca-tion on the calendar where the symbol should be placed as a prompt.

Intermediate and Secondary Levels.   After each student has marked his or her cal-endar with the correct month, day, and date, on the last day of the pre-vious month, ask the student to say the new month, day, and date each morning of the new month and to circle the date if he or she correctly identifies it. If the student does not identify the correct date, direct him or her to the previous day's date.

Ask the student to find "yesterday" on the calendar and to name the date as well. When the student answers, say, "If yesterday was the 19th, what date is it today?" After the correct answer is given, tell him or her to place a circle around the date on the calendar.

Family Interventions

Infant and Toddler/Preschool and Primary Levels.   Encourage the parents to schedule a morning exercise similar to the opening classroom exercise as described in the Teacher Interventions for these two levels. Review the exercise periodically with the parents so that they sequence it correctly and provide appropriate prompts and rewards.

Intermediate and Secondary Levels.   The activities for this level should be a continu-ation of those started in Specific Objectives B and C. Tell the parents to assign the youngster the household task of marking the calendar with the correct month, day of the week, and date. (The youngster's calendar should have the dates already printed on them, with the previous dates already having been circled by the youngster.) If the youngster does not identify the correct date, remind the parents to direct him or her to the previous day's date.

Specific Objective E

The student identifies and names the current season and the other seasons in sequence.

Teacher Interventions

Infant and Toddler/Preschool. Develop a picture book (including, if possible, pictures and photographs) of the seasons with the student. This picture book should contain various scenes representative of each of the seasons. (Note: If the student lives in a climate where there is little variation in the seasons, use stereotypic pictures or photographs.)

When there are clear signs of the seasons, as early as possible into the season, take the student for a walk in the community, and comment on some of these signs. For example, for winter you might note the frost on the windows, the visible puffs of air on exhalation, snow on the ground, the cold weather, the trees barren of leaves, people wearing cold-weather clothing, and the absence of flowers.

Take a camera with you to take photographs for the class bulletin board. When you return to the classroom, tell the student that there are four seasons during the year and that now the season is winter. Review what was seen on the walk, and tell the student that you are going to help him or her find some pictures that look like the things you saw. When you paste a picture in the notebook, label it with the name of the season. This notebook will become the student's pictorial file of the seasons.

Primary Level. Develop a pictorial season book with the primary-level student in a manner similar to the one for the infant and toddler/preschool level. At this level, the student can take more of an active role in locating the pictures, cutting them out, and labeling the pictures. Before beginning to cut out the pictures, you may want the student to draw a picture that reminds him or her of winter.

Then tell him or her to place that picture in the notebook as the cover page of the section for winter. Explain that people sometimes like to put their own decorations on some of their possessions, especially items they have made themselves. At this level, begin working on the sequence of the seasons by saying such things as "Now it is spring. That means summer comes next."

Intermediate and Secondary Levels. Ask the student to describe the seasons and to name them in order, starting with the present season. Write down or record and then transcribe his or her comments, type them, and include them in his or her picture book.

As various activities occur during the school year that are season-related, tell the student to locate a magazine picture that represents this activity or, better yet, ask him or her to take a photograph of his or her classmates who are engaging in the activity and then place it in his or her season notebook.

Family Interventions

Infant and Toddler/Preschool and Primary Levels. Encourage the parents to take their child for nature walks during each season and collect any objects that are characteristic of the particular season. For example, for fall encourage the parents to collect the fallen, multicolored leaves (and preserve them between sheets of iron-heated waxed paper); for winter they might make a snowball; for spring they might pick some spring flowers (where legal); and for summer they might purchase fruits (like watermelons) that are available and inexpensive only during the summer months.

Intermediate and Secondary Levels. Parents can join their youngster in watching television and videotapes in which the youngster is expected to name the season depicted (in dramatic programs and news events) that are characteristic of a particular season. (Note: Seasonal sports are especially valuable for this activity. What a wonderful thing to say during the waning winter months, "It is almost spring; I can't wait for the baseball season to begin!")

During the winter they might watch together winter sports such as ice skating, ice hockey, and skiing, and during the summer they might watch water sports. If possible, encourage the parents to participate in seasonal sports with the youngster.

 ## Specific Objective F

The student identifies his or her birthday and birth date.

Teacher Interventions

Infant and Toddler/Preschool. Beginning a couple of days before the student's birthday, during calendar time, tell the student that in ___ days it will be his or her birthday. Tell the student that on March 17th it will be his or her birthday. Tell the student the current date as you point to the calendar, and then count off the number of days left before his or her birthday.

Tell the student you are going to write his or her birth date on the chalkboard. As you write this information, say, "This says March 17th, and March 17th is your birth date. This means you were born on that date and it is a date that you will celebrate throughout your life." Tell the student that on his or her birthday his or her classmates will sing "Happy Birthday" to him or her.

Continue this activity every day until his or her birthday. After the student's birthday, discuss the details of the birthday celebration. (See Family Interventions.)

Primary Level.   See the activities for Goal I, Specific Objective J. Introduce the relationship existing between the student's age, the current calendar year, and the year of his or her birth.

Intermediate and Secondary Levels.   See the activities for Goal I, Specific Objective J. At these levels emphasize the relationship existing between the student's age, the current calendar year, and the year of his or her birth. Do so until the student is able to respond correctly to the questions, "What is your birth date?" or "When were you born?" or "What is the date of your birth?"

Family Interventions

Infant and Toddler/Preschool.   Ask the parents to share the activities of the child's birthday celebration with you so that you can discuss it with the student during class time.

Primary Level.   See the activities for Goal I, Specific Objective J.

Intermediate and Secondary Level.   See the activities for Goal I, Specific Objective J.

 ## Specific Objective G
The student identifies and names the major holidays.

Teacher Interventions

Infant and Toddler/Preschool and Primary Levels.   Add a holiday section to the notebook designed under Specific Objective E. Develop the holiday pictures the same way as you did the seasonal pictures. (Note: You need to talk to the parents prior to starting this activity to obtain information about holidays that may be part of the student's cultural background with which you are not familiar and that you need to learn about, or to determine if there are any holidays typically celebrated in schools that are not celebrated by the family or that the family wishes the student not to participate in, e.g., Christmas, Halloween, or Easter.)

Intermediate and Secondary Levels. At these levels work with the student on naming the major holidays celebrated in the major culture as well as those that are part of his or her cultural group and the cultural groups of classmates. Tape the student's discussion of holiday customs and practices in general as well as those specific to his or her family.

Family Interventions

Infant and Toddler/Preschool and Primary Levels. Encourage the parents to discuss the family's unique way of celebrating holidays of the general culture (if they are celebrated) and holidays that they celebrate as part of their own cultural background. Tell them to make certain the celebrations are discussed prior to, during, and after the celebrations.

Intermediate and Secondary Levels. Encourage the parents to require their youngster to take increasing responsibility for planning the family's holiday celebrations. Remind them that the youngster should be involved in the planning stage, in the actual celebration, and in wrap-up sessions.

 ## Specific Objective H

The student identifies and names clocks and watches.

Teacher Interventions

Infant and Toddler/Preschool. While sitting on the floor, place a large clock in front of you and the student. Tell the student that the object in front of him or her is called a clock and that you are going to teach him or her a poem about a mouse and a clock. Recite the nursery rhyme "Hickory, Dickory, Dock." Every time you mention the clock, point to it. If possible, use a xylophone or wind chimes to simulate the sound of chimes when you speak of the clock "striking one."

Primary Level. Give each of the student's classmates a different type of clock (see Figure 3.11). Explain that clocks help us to know what time it is and therefore help us to get to school, work, and leisure activities on time. Tell the student he or she is going to play a game called "Knock, Knock, Who Has a Clock?"

Show the student several different prototype clocks (digital, Roman numeral, Arabic numeral, and some with missing numerals or slashes instead of numerals). Tell him or her you have given clocks like those you just showed him or her to some of his or her classmates, and you want to see how many clocks he or she can find, by knocking on a classmate's desk to see whether that classmate has a clock. As the student proceeds, say, "Knock, Knock, Who Has a Clock?"

Follow the student around the room, and, as he or she finds each clock, verbally reinforce him or her. Reiterate that even though each clock looks different, they are all clocks.

Intermediate Level. Explain to the student that just as there are different types of clocks, there are different types of watches. Bring as many different clocks and watches as you can find to the classroom or learning area.

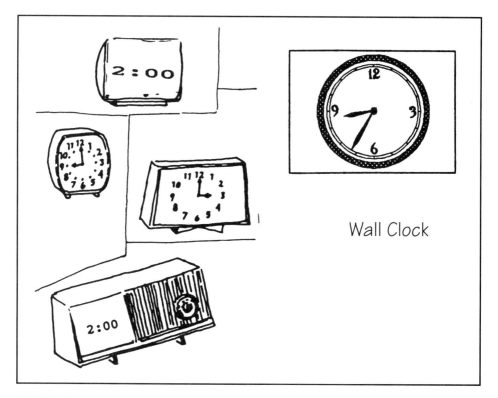

FIGURE 3.11. Types of clocks.

Explain to the student that sometimes watches and clocks are difficult to identify because they may look very different from each other. Show him or her the clocks and watches that you bring in.

Review the distinguishing features of each clock and/or watch. Tell him or her that you have some magazines that you want him or her to look through to find as many watches and clocks that he or she can. After the student locates the watches and clocks, tell him or her to cut them out.

After cutting out the timepieces, tell the student to place them into two separate piles—one pile for the watches and one pile for the clocks. If the student correctly identifies the watches, lend him or her one (of his or her choice) to wear for the rest of the day. (Note: Explain to the student prior to giving him or her the watch that he or she must return the watch before leaving for the day.)

Secondary Level. Take the student for walks through the school, a department store, or other buildings where clocks are located. Point out one of the clocks, and ask the student to find as many other clocks as he or she can while walking through the building. Say, "This is a clock, and, as we walk around, I want you to show me where there are other clocks." Each time the student correctly identifies a clock, praise him or her.

When you return to the classroom, ask the student to describe the clocks he or she saw. Tell him or her to list such things as how many he or she saw, the different colors of the clocks, and the types of clocks (digital, wall, Roman numeral, large, or small). Follow up with a trip to a specialty store that sells and repairs clocks and/or watches.

Family Interventions

Infant and Toddler/Preschool. Ask the parents to obtain a book of nursery rhymes that contains, with appropriate and colorful illustrations, the nursery rhyme "Hickory, Dickory, Dock." Tell them to read this story to their child at bedtime. Tell the parents to point out to the child the two characters of the poem, to especially point to the clock, and, as they say the part of the rhyme about the clock striking 12, to point to the hands on the clock. Encourage them to read the rhyme every night for a week.

After the parents have read the rhyme for two nights, tell them to ask the child questions (e.g., "Where did the mouse run?" and "What time was it on the clock?"). Explain to the parents that for very young children an answer is not expected and that they should answer the question for the child, if necessary.

Primary Level. Parents can point out the various clocks in the house. Remind the parents to point out these clocks to the child at an appropriate time, that is, to point out the clock in the room in which they are doing a specific activity. Remind the parents to tell the child during breakfast that they do not want to be late for work and do not want him or her to be late for school.

Tell them to ask the child at this point to locate the kitchen clock. Remind them to then read the time and say whether they need to hurry or whether they have plenty of time.

Parents can do this same activity in other rooms of the house besides the kitchen. For example, when it is time for bed, they should ask the child to locate the living room clock (or clock-radio or bedroom alarm clock) and show the child their wristwatches.

Intermediate and Secondary Levels. Encourage the parents to take the youngster with them when doing errands in the community. Tell the parents to ask the youngster to locate clocks when they are in a department store or in other buildings where clocks are likely to be located.

If possible, encourage them to visit a jewelry store or a jewelry counter in a department store as well as a specialty shop that sells and repairs clocks. Remind them to involve their youngster in any household purchases of clocks and to give him or her a watch for his or her birthday or other special occasion.

 ## Specific Objective I

The student identifies and names the time by hour and half-hour on different types of clocks and watches (digital, wrist, numeral, etc.).

Teacher Interventions

Infant and Toddler/Preschool. Place a toy clock with movable hands in the classroom or learning area. Give the student opportunities to develop his or her own discovery activities with the clock. The student should be allowed to play with the clock any time while he or she is in the housekeeping work area of the classroom and/or learning area.

When you are directing play in this area, ask the student to show you the clock and also to move the hands to the correct time at a given hour. Say, "[Student's name], find the clock. Now that you've found the clock, let's move the hands to the correct time." At this time, show the student that the time on the toy clock is the same as the time on the classroom clock and your wristwatch.

Primary Level. Place several different clocks in different parts of the room. On the hour, ask the student to look at one of the clocks, and tell him or her the time. Then tell him or her to look at all the other clocks (which you have synchronized) and repeat the time by the hour. Once he or she is able to tell you the time correctly, ask him or her to move the hands of a teacher-made or commercially produced instructional clock to match the time shown on the real clocks.

If the student is experiencing difficulty, use the instructional clock with movable hands to demonstrate how to read the time by the hour. After the student has mastered this skill, proceed to the next level by asking him or her to tell time by the half-hour.

Intermediate and Secondary Levels.   At the beginning of the morning or afternoon session, tell the student that he or she may do a preferred activity at a specific time (e.g., practice the new dance the class has just learned at 2:30). Tell the student to check the classroom clock and/or his or her wristwatch to let you know when that time comes.

Strongly emphasize that, if he or she does not let you know at that specified time, he or she may not be able to do the activity. If the student has difficulty in telling the time, practice telling time by the hour and half-hour.

When you begin this activity, the student may need a prompt to realize that it is time for the activity. A good idea would be to set a kitchen timer to go off when it is time for the activity. Then say to the student, "Do you know what time it is?" Inform the student that he or she should then look at the clock and tell you whether it is time for the activity. After repeating this strategy several times, try to fade out the prompt.

Family Interventions

Infant and Toddler/Preschool.   Suggest that the parents make time an integral part of the life of the household, especially as it affects their child, for example, they should point out the time to the child by saying such things as "Look at the clock. It is night and it says 8 o'clock. That means it's time for bed!" Encourage the parents to repeat this procedure for all the major activities and events of the day and evening.

Primary Level.   While they are in the kitchen with their child during breakfast, first at the hour and then at the half-hour, tell the parents to say to their child that they do not want to be late for work and do not want him or her to be late for school, and then to ask the child to locate the clock in the kitchen and tell them the time. Remind them to do this at other times of the day for specified reasons, for example, "Please, [child's name], check the time on the stove clock for me; I think the casserole is about done."

Intermediate and Secondary Levels.   Parents can note when the youngster's favorite television program comes on and remind the youngster that it is his or her responsibility to check the time to know when to turn on his or her (or the family's) favorite show. Encourage the parents to give the youngster increasing responsibility for guiding his or her life in terms of time.

Tell them to remind the youngster to do things on time and to avoid being late only after there have been a few incidents of lateness. Tell them to share with him or her how they use time to guide and monitor their own lives, especially in terms of work-related responsibilities.

 ## Specific Objective J

The student is punctual to school, leisure-time, and other appointments and scheduled activities.

Teacher Interventions

Primary Level. Prepare a daily schedule of activities for the student. Write them down on individualized activity cards (see Figure 3.12). The activities on the cards should also have pictures with them. This is done so that the student does not have to be able to read words to know his or her schedule.

The cards can be held in a carpenter's apron that can be mounted on a bulletin board at the student's eye level. Remind the student that it is his or her responsibility to be on time or ready for each of the day's activities.

The activities that take place outside of the classroom should have a clock on them indicating the time for the activity. After the student completes each activity, remind him or her to place the activity card in the left pocket of the apron. This activity should assist the student in learning routines and knowing that there is a time and place for all activities.

Intermediate and Secondary Levels. Explain to the student how important it is to be on time for work and other activities. Provide the student with a time card, stamp pad, and time stamper. Tell the student that, as soon as he or she comes to the classroom in the morning, he or she must stop at the work table and stamp his or her time card. Tell the student that, before he or she takes a break, he or she must stamp the time on the card and that upon his or her return, the card must be stamped with that time.

At the end of the day, sit down with the student and check his or her time card. If the student has been on time for all events, give him or her one free-time minute for each activity he or she was on time for. If he or she checked in late during any of the activities, dock one free-time minute for each lateness.

FIGURE 3.12.   Activity cards.

Family Interventions

Primary Level.   Ask the parents to assist you in preparing the child to be punctual when keeping appointments. Ask the parents to inform you when the child has an appointment, for example, with a physician. Then discuss this appointment with the child during calendar time. Also ask the parents to obtain an appointment card from the doctor's office.

Instruct the parents to show the card to their child and to tell him or her the date and time of the doctor's appointment. Remind the parents to mark the appointment on the family's wall calendar and to discuss this appointment with the child every time the calendar notations are reviewed.

When the appointment day arrives, remind the parents to discuss the time of the appointment with the child and to explain that they must leave home early enough so that they will not be late for the appointment. When they arrive at the doctor's office, the parents should react with satisfaction to the fact that they have arrived on time for the appointment.

Intermediate and Secondary Levels.   Encourage the parents to take the youngster to several leisure activities. For example, tell the parents to plan a trip to the movies. Tell the parents to involve the youngster in finding out the starting times of movies by looking in the newspaper (or telephoning the theater).

After the parents and youngster find the starting time, tell the parents to explain that they must leave home at a designated time in order to reach the cinema in time for the movie because they want to see the movie from its beginning.

Once they arrive on time at the theater, remind the parents to announce with satisfaction that they made it on time. Explain to the parents that this activity can be done for any other leisure activity or event that they have planned. Some suggestions would be sporting events, school plays, or cultural exhibitions.

Sample Lesson Plan

Topic Area: Functional Mathematics

Designed by: Terence Post

Time Recommended: 45 minutes

Student Involved: Tyrone (Intermediate Special Class)

Background Information:

The student is now able to satisfactorily meet the specific objectives involving functional money transactions (Goal II) and is beginning to develop a basic understanding that there is a need to measure things in one's life. Tyrone is able to identify and differentiate between a ruler, a yardstick, and a measuring tape and is able to state their purposes. As of yet, he has developed little skill in using a ruler to make simple measurements. For example, he does not always place the left side of the ruler at the starting point of the thing being measured and, at times, will attempt to use the ruler when it is in an upside-down position.

General Goal *(Functional Mathematics III):*

The student will acquire functional measurement skills that facilitate independence in various measurement activities.

Specific Objective *(Functional Mathematics III-D):*

The student uses a ruler to measure the dimensions of objects and things.

Lesson Objective:

When asked to measure several objects and things in the classroom, the student will use a ruler (1 foot with ⅛- and ¼-inch markings) to correctly measure them, will record the measurements obtained without error, and will make appropriate decisions based on the measurements.

Materials and Equipment:

- Two rulers, pencils, notepad, and teacher-made worksheet
- Desk blotter
- Empty fish tank
- Five potted plants (all in identical rectangular pots)

Motivating Activity:

Tell the student about the problems you experienced making a shopping decision. The scenario to be shared with the student concerns a shopping trip taken to purchase a birthday gift for your cousin, Vernon: "I passed a store window and saw a beautiful dress shirt that I thought Vernon would love to have. When I went to buy it, the salesperson asked me what size neck and what length sleeve my cousin Vernon had. I didn't know the answer, so I couldn't buy the shirt. I left the store and walked through the mall until I saw a pair of jeans that I thought Vernon might like. The salesperson asked me what the size of his inseam was. I didn't know that measurement either. So I left that store and ended up buying Vernon a bottle of cologne. I don't even know if he would like cologne as a gift. I guess measurements are important!"

Instructional Procedures:

Initiation—Give the student a ruler (1 foot) with ⅛- and ¼-inch markings, and pass out a worksheet that asks him to measure various lines that have been drawn on the paper. Ask Tyrone to measure each of the lines and to make a note of each one's size in his notepad. Demonstrate the use of the ruler, and provide assistance, as needed, until Tyrone is using the ruler correctly and recording the measurements without error.

Guided Practice—Inform the student that the blotter on your desk is in terrible shape and that you want to order a replacement. Tell Tyrone to measure the blotter because you need its measurements to order a new one. Supervise and provide assistance as needed. Then ask Tyrone to measure the new fish tank that just arrived because you wish to order fish for it but need to know the size of the tank to figure out the number of fish you can stock the tank with. Again, provide guidance, if needed.

Independent Practice—Give the student the task of measuring the flowerpots and the windowsill to determine how many plants will fit on the windowsill. Ask Tyrone to record the measurement of the windowsill and the pots in his notepad and to write the number of plants he thinks can be placed on the sill.

Closure—Share a candy bar that you have carefully measured so that both you and Tyrone are "treated" equally. Give Tyrone the home assignment of measuring a picture frame in his bedroom so that he would know the size of another picture he might purchase if he wished to have a same-sized pair of pictures. (Note: Check with his parents first to determine whether the assignment is feasible.)

Assessment Strategy:

Check to determine whether Tyrone measured the blotter, fish tank, plants, and windowsill correctly; recorded the measurements without error; and made the right decision on the number of plants that could be placed on the windowsill.

Follow-Up Activity or Objective:

If the student achieves the lesson objective, proceed to a lesson on using a tape measure, for example, to measure his neck size and sleeve size to purchase a formal shirt and his head size to purchase a hat or baseball cap.

Observations and Their Instructional Insights:

Suggested Readings

Baker, A., & Baker, J. (1990). *Mathematics in process.* Portsmouth, NH: Heinemann.

Bartel, N. R. (1990). Problems in mathematics achievement. In D. D. Hammill & N. R. Bartel (Eds.), *Teaching students with learning and behavior problems* (5th ed., pp. 289–293). Boston: Allyn & Bacon.

Bley, N. S., & Thornton, C. A. (1989). *Teaching mathematics to the learning disabled* (2nd ed.). Austin, TX: PRO-ED.

Browder, D. M., & Snell, M. E. (1987). Functional academics. In M. E. Snell (Ed.), *Systematic instruction of persons with severe handicaps* (3rd ed., pp. 436–468). Columbus, OH: Merrill.

Cawley, J. F. (Ed.). (1984). *Developmental teaching of mathematics for the learning disabled.* Austin, TX: PRO-ED.

Cawley, J. F., Fitzmaurice-Hayes, A., & Shaw, R. (1988). *Mathematics for the mildly handicapped: A guide for curriculum and instruction.* Boston: Allyn & Bacon.

Cawley, J. F., & Parmar, R. S. (1992). Arithmetic programming for students with disabilities: An alternative. *Remedial and Special Education, 13,* 6–18.

Certo, N., Haring, N., & York, R. (Eds.). *Public school integration of severely handicapped students: Rational issues and progressive alternatives.* Baltimore: Paul H. Brookes.

Clark, G. M., & Kolstoe, O. P. (1990). *Career development and transitional education for adolescents with disabilities.* Boston: Allyn & Bacon.

Davis, R. W., & Hajicek, J. O. (1985). Effects of self-instructional training and strategy training on a mathematics task with severely behaviorally disordered students. *Behavioral Disorders, 10,* 275–282.

Drew, C. J., Logan, D. R., & Hardman, M. (1992). *Mental retardation: A life cycle approach* (5th ed.). New York: Macmillan.

Ellis, E. S., Lenz, B. K., & Sabornie, E. J. (1987). Generalization and adaptation of learning strategies to natural environments. Part I: Critical agents. *Remedial and Special Education, 8* (1), 6–20.

Ellis, E. S., Lenz, B. K., & Sabornie, E. J. (1987). Generalization and adaptation of learning strategies to natural environments. Part II: Research into practice. *Remedial and Special Education, 8* (2), 6–23.

Engelmann, S., & Carnine, D. (1981). *Corrective mathematics.* Chicago: Science Research Associates.

Engelmann, S., Carnine, D., & Steely, D. G. (1991). Making connections in mathematics. *Journal of Learning Disabilities, 24,* 292–303.

Enright, B. (1983). *Enright Diagnostic Inventory of Basic Arithmetic Skills.* North Billerica, MA: Curriculum Associates.

Enright, B., & Beattie, J. (1989). Problem solving step by step in math. *Teaching Exceptional Children, 22,* 58–59.

Evans, D., & Carnine, D. (1990). Manipulatives: The effective way. *Direct Instruction News, 10,* 48–55.

Ferguson, D. L., & Baumgart, D. (1991). Partial participation revisited. *Journal of the Association for Persons with Severe Handicaps, 16,* 218–227.

Ford, A., & Miranda, P. (1984). Community instruction: A natural cues and corrections decision model. *Journal of the Association for Persons with Severe Handicaps, 9,* 79–88.

Guess, D., Horner, R. D., Utley, B., Holvoet, J., Maxon, D., Tucker, D., & Warren, S. (1978). A functional curriculum sequencing model for teaching the severely handicapped. *AAESPH Review, 3,* 202–215.

Haring, T. G., Kennedy, C. H., Adams, M. I., & Pitts-Conway, V. (1987). Teaching generalization of purchasing skills across community settings to children with autism. *Journal of the Association for Persons with Severe Handicaps, 20,* 89–96.

Horner, R. H., Albin, R. W., & Ralph, G. (1986). Generalization with precision: The role of negative teaching examples in the generalized grocery item selection. *Journal of the Association for Persons with Severe Handicaps, 11,* 300–308.

Hunt, N., & Marshall, K. (1994). *Exceptional children and youth.* Boston: Houghton Mifflin.

Johnston, M. B., & Whitman, T. (1987). Enhancing math computation through variations in training format and instructional content. *Cognitive Therapy and Research, 11,* 381–397.

Lipstreu, B. L., & Johnson, M. K. (1988). Teaching time using the whole clock method. *Teaching Exceptional Children, 20,* 10–12.

Lloyd, J. W., & Keller, C. E. (1989). Effective mathematics instruction: Development, instruction, and programs. *Focus on Exceptional Children, 21,* 1–10.

Ludlow, B. L., Turnbull, A. P., & Luckasson, R. (Eds.). (1988). *Transitions to adult life for people with mental retardation: Principles and practices.* Baltimore: Paul H. Brookes.

Mercer, C. D., & Mercer, A. R. (1993). Teaching math skills. In *Teaching students with learning problems* (4th ed., pp. 273–342). New York: Merrill/Macmillan.

Mithaug, D. E., Martin, J. E., & Agran, M. (1987). Adaptability instruction: The goal of transitional programming. *Exceptional Children, 53,* 500–505.

National Council of Supervisors of Mathematics. (1988). *Twelve components of essential mathematics.* Minneapolis, MN: Author.

Nelson, J. R., Smith, D. J., Dodd, J. M., & Gilbert, C. (1991). The time estimation skills of students with emotional handicaps: A comparison. *Behavioral Disorders, 16,* 116–119.

Nietupski, J. A., Clancey, C., & Christiansen, P. (1984). Acquisition, maintenance, and generalization of vending machine purchasing skills in moderately handicapped students. *Education and Treatment of the Mentally Retarded, 22,* 91–96.

Polloway, E. A., Patton, J. R., Payne, J. S., & Payne, R. A. (1989). *Strategies for teaching learners with special needs* (4th ed.). New York: Merrill/Macmillan.

Rainforth, B., York, I., & MacDonald, C. (1992). *Collaborative teams for students with severe disabilities: Integrating therapy and educational services.* Baltimore: Paul H. Brookes.

Reisman, F., & Kauffman, S. (1980). *Teaching mathematics to children with special needs.* Columbus, OH: Merrill.

Sandknop, P. A., Schuster, J. W., Wolery, M., & Cross, D. P. (1992). The use of an adaptive device to teach students with moderate mental retardation to select lower priced grocery items. *Education and Training in Mental Retardation, 27,* 219–229.

Schwartz, S. E. (1977). *Real life math program.* Chicago: Hubbard.

Silbert, J., Carnine, D., & Stein, M. (1990). *Direct instruction mathematics* (2nd ed.). New York: Merrill/Macmillan.

Snell, M. E. (1988). Curriculum and methodology for individuals with severe disabilities. *Education and Training in Mental Retardation, 23,* 302–314.

Whitin, D., Mills, H., & O'Keefe, T. (1990). *Living and learning mathematics.* Portsmouth, NH: Heinemann.

Wilcox, B., & Bellamy, G. T. (Eds.). (1982). *Design of high school programs for severely handicapped students.* Baltimore: Paul H. Brookes.

Wood, S., Burke, L., Kunzelmann, H., & Koenig, C. (1978). Functional criteria in basic math skill proficiency. *Journal of Special Education Technology, 2* (2), 29–36.

Selected Materials/Resources

Bender, M., & Valletutti, P. J. (1981). *Teaching functional academics: A curriculum guide for adolescents and adults with learning problems.* Baltimore: University Park Press.

Brolin, D. E. (1991). *Life-Centered Career Education: A competency based approach* (3rd ed.). Reston, VA: Council for Exceptional Children.

Coble, C. R., Hounshell, P. B., & Adams, A. H. (1977). *Mainstreaming science and mathematics: Special ideas and activities for the whole class.* Santa Monica, CA: Goodyear.

Dever, R. B. (1988). *A taxonomy of community living skills.* Washington, DC: American Association on Mental Retardation.

Dorfman, J. (1975). *Consumer Survival Kit.* New York: Praeger.

Doyle, E. (1980). *Skills for Daily Living Series.* Baltimore: Media Materials.

Engelmann, S., & Carnine, D. W. (1975). *DISTAR Arithmetic* (2nd ed.). Chicago: Science Research Associates.

Enright, B. E. (1989). *Basic mathematics: Detecting and correcting special needs.* Des Moines, IA: Longwood.

Falvey, M. (1989). *Community-based curriculum: Instructional strategies for students with severe handicaps.* Baltimore: Paul H. Brookes.

Ferguson, D. L., & Wilcox, B. (1987). *The elementary/secondary system: Supportive education for students with severe handicaps. Module 1: The activity-based IEP.* Eugene: Specialized Training Program, University of Oregon.

Friebel, A. C., & Gingrich, C. K. (1972). *Math Applications Kit.* Chicago: Science Research Associates.

Glascoe, L. G., Miller, L. S., & Kokaska, C. J. (1991). *Life-Centered Career Education: Activity book two.* Reston, VA: Council for Exceptional Children.

Hannon, K. E., & Thompson, M. A. (1992). *Life skills workshop: An active program for real-life problem solving.* East Moline, IL: Linguisystems.

Huffman, S. (1979). *Get what you pay for: PAL Life Competency Program.* Middletown, CT: Xerox Education.

James, E., & Barkin, C. (1977). *Managing your money.* Chicago: Children's Press.

Jones, W. (1980). *Using Measurement Series.* Baltimore: Media Materials.

Jones, W., & Hanson, R. (1980). *Consumer Mathematics Series.* Baltimore: Media Materials.

Kahn, C. H., & Hanna, J. B. (1979). *Money makes sense.* Palo Alto, CA: Fearon.

McGraw, D., & Turnbow, G. N. (1991). *On my own in the community.* East Moline, IL: Linguisystems.

McGreevey, C., & Kelinson, R. M. (1988). *Blooming math.* East Moline, IL: Linguisystems.

Miller, L. S., Glascoe, L. G., & Kokaska, C. J. (1989). *Life-Centered Career Education: Activity book one.* Reston, VA: Council for Exceptional Children.

Nurss, J. R., & McGauvran, M. E. (1987). *Handbook of skill development activities for young children.* New York: Harcourt Brace Jovanovich.

Peterson, D. L. (1973). *Functional mathematics for the mentally retarded.* Columbus, OH: Merrill.

Rosenberg, R. R., & Risser, J. (1979). *Consumer math and you.* New York: McGraw-Hill.

Schminke, C. W., & Dumas, E. (1981). *Math activities for child involvement* (3rd ed.). Boston: Allyn & Bacon.

Schwartz, S. E. (1977). *Real-life math program.* Chicago: Hubbard.

Shultheis, P., Paine, R., Morgan-Brown, A., Smith, S., & Hanson, R. (1980). *Household mathematics.* Baltimore: Media Materials.

Shultheis, P., Paine, R., Morgan-Brown, A., Smith, S., & Hanson, R. (1980). *Mathematics for banking.* Baltimore: Media Materials.

Shultheis, P., Paine, R., Morgan-Brown, A., Smith, S., & Hanson, R. (1980). *Shopping mathematics.* Baltimore: Media Materials.

Sternberg, L. (1977). *Essential math and language skills.* Northbrook, IL: Hubbard.

Thompson. L. L. (1978). *Consumer mathematics.* Encino, CA: Glencoe.

Wehman, P., Renzaglia, A., & Bates, P. (1985). *Functional living skills for moderately and severely handicapped individuals.* Austin, TX: PRO-ED.

Wilcox, B., & Bellamy, G. T. (1987). *A comprehensive guide to the Activities Catalog: An alternative curriculum for youth and adults with severe disabilities.* Baltimore: Paul H. Brookes.

Zachman, L., Barrett, M., Huisingh, R., Orman, J., & Blagden, C. (1992). *Tasks of problem solving: A real life approach to thinking and reasoning. Adolescent.* East Moline, IL: Linguisystems.